First World War
and Army of Occupation
War Diary
France, Belgium and Germany

1 DIVISION
Divisional Troops
1 Battalion Machine Gun Corps
1 March 1918 - 31 July 1919

WO95/1256/1

The Naval & Military Press Ltd
www.nmarchive.com
Published in association with The National Archives

Published by

The Naval & Military Press Ltd

Unit 10 Ridgewood Industrial Park,

Uckfield, East Sussex,

TN22 5QE England

Tel: +44 (0) 1825 749494

www.naval-military-press.com

www.nmarchive.com

This diary has been reprinted in facsimile from the original. Any imperfections are inevitably reproduced and the quality may fall short of modern type and cartographic standards.

© **Crown Copyright**
Images reproduced by permission of The National Archives, London, England, 2015.

Contents

Document type	Place/Title	Date From	Date To
Heading	B.E.F. France & Flanders 1 Division. Troops. 1 Bn Machine Gun Corps. 1918 Mar To 1919 July. 216 Machine Gun Coy. 1917 Mar To 1918 Feb. 1/S (Pioneer) Bn Welsh Rgt. 1916 June To 1919 Aug.		
Heading	B.E.F. France & Flanders 1 Division. Troops 1 Bn Machine Gun Corps 1918 Mar To 1919 July., 216 Machine Gun Coy. 1917 Mar To 1918 Feb. 1/6 (Pioneer) Bn Welsh Rgt 1916 June To 1919 Aug.		
Heading	WO95/1256/1 Mar 1918-July 1919		
Heading	1st Division War Diary 1st M.G. Bn. March to December From 1st March To 30th June 1918		
War Diary	Canal Bank Sh. 28 NW C 25 DM	01/03/1918	03/03/1918
War Diary	Agadir Camp Sheet 28 N.W. B 30 Carlo	04/03/1918	15/03/1918
War Diary	Armada Camp Sh 28 B 30 C	16/03/1918	23/03/1918
War Diary	Turco Farm Huts-Sh 28 C 14 D 2.4	24/03/1918	31/03/1918
Map	Ref Bethune (Combined) Sheet		
Operation(al) Order(s)	1st Battalion. Machine Gun Corps. Operation Order No. 27	03/06/1918	03/06/1918
Miscellaneous	1st Battalion, Machine Gun Corps		
Operation(al) Order(s)	1st. Battn. Machine Gun Corps Order No. 1.	04/03/1918	04/03/1918
Miscellaneous	Copy Of a latter written by Officer Commanding 1st Inf. Bde. to Captain A.S. Vernon. 6/3/18		
Operation(al) Order(s)	1st. Battalion Machine Gun Corps Order No. 2	09/03/1918	09/03/1918
Operation(al) Order(s)	1st Battalion, Machine Gun Corps Order No. 3	09/03/1918	09/03/1918
War Diary	Amendment To 1st Battalion Machine Gun Corps Order No. 2	13/03/1918	13/03/1918
Operation(al) Order(s)	1st Battalion Machine Gun Corps Order No. 3		
Operation(al) Order(s)	Amendment To 1st Battalion Machine Gun Corps Order No. 3.	16/03/1918	16/03/1918
Miscellaneous	1st Battalion Machine Gun Corps No. 4	22/03/1918	22/03/1918
Operation(al) Order(s)	Special Order	23/03/1918	23/03/1918
Operation(al) Order(s)	1st. Battalion, M.G. Corps. Order No.5	28/03/1918	28/03/1918
Operation(al) Order(s)	1st Battn. Machine Gun Corps. Order No.6.		
War Diary	Turco Huts C 14 d 4.5 sh 28 NW	01/04/1918	08/04/1918
War Diary	Le Quesnoy Sh 36 B 1/40000 E 8.f	09/04/1918	10/04/1918
War Diary	Fouquieres E 22a	11/04/1918	14/04/1918
War Diary	Cosnay D 24 d 9.1.	18/04/1918	23/04/1918
War Diary	Barlin K 32 B 5.6	24/04/1918	30/04/1918
Operation(al) Order(s)	1st Battalion, Machine Gun Corps. Operation Order No. 7.	05/04/1918	05/04/1918
Operation(al) Order(s)	1st Battalion, Machine Gun Corps. Operation Order No. 8	05/04/1918	05/04/1918
Miscellaneous	1st Battalion, Machine Gun Corps. Administrative Instns.	05/04/1918	05/04/1918
Operation(al) Order(s)	1st Battalion, Machine Gun Corps. Operation Order No. 9.	07/04/1918	07/04/1918
Miscellaneous	By Lieut Col Kidder D.S.O. Commanding 1st Batt		
Miscellaneous	Warning Order		
Operation(al) Order(s)	1st Battalion Machine Gun Corps Order No-10	14/04/1918	14/04/1918
Operation(al) Order(s)	1st Battalion Machine Gun Corps Order No 11	15/04/1918	15/04/1918

Operation(al) Order(s)	1st Battn M.G.C. Operation Order 12 Ref Bethune Combined Sheet	20/04/1918	20/04/1918
Operation(al) Order(s)	1st Battn. M.G. Corps. Order No. 13	21/04/1918	21/04/1918
Operation(al) Order(s)	1st Battalion M.G. Corps. Amendment/No 1 To Operation Order No.14.	22/04/1918	22/04/1918
Operation(al) Order(s)	1st Battn. Machine Gun Corps. Order No. 14	21/04/1918	21/04/1918
Operation(al) Order(s)	1st Battalion Machine Gun Corps Operation Order No.15.	23/04/1918	23/04/1918
Operation(al) Order(s)	1st Battalion, Machine Gun Corps Operation Order No. 16.	23/04/1918	23/04/1918
Operation(al) Order(s)	1st Battalion, Machine Gun Corps. Operation Order No. 17	24/04/1918	24/04/1918
Operation(al) Order(s) Miscellaneous	1st. Battn. Machine Gun Corps. Operation Order No. 18 Action of "C" Company, 1st Battalion, Machine Gun Corps, when attached to 166th Brigade 55th Division, on April 9th and days following.	28/04/1918	28/04/1918
Miscellaneous	Report of O.C. "B" Company, 1st Battalion, Machine Gun Corps of operations from the 16th to 13th April, 1918.		
Miscellaneous			
Miscellaneous	Report of O.C. Company Festubert and LE Plantin Positions, Of Second attack on Festubert and Givenchy. April 18th, 1918		
Operation(al) Order(s)	Report of O.C."A" Company, 1st Battalion, Machine Gun Corps of operations from the 18th to the 24th April 1918.	24/04/1918	24/04/1918
War Diary	Barlin K32 F	01/05/1918	31/05/1918
Operation(al) Order(s)	1st Battalion P.G. Corps Order No 19. Ref Map Gorre 1/20,000.	01/05/1918	01/05/1918
Operation(al) Order(s)	1st Battalion, Machine Gun Corps. Order No. 19. Reference Map Gorre 1/20.000	01/05/1918	01/05/1918
Operation(al) Order(s)	1st Battalion, Machine Gun Corps. Operation Order No. 20. Reference Map Gorre 1/20000		
Operation(al) Order(s)	1st Battalion, Machine Gun Corps Order No. 20. Is Hereby Cancelled.	08/08/1918	08/08/1918
Operation(al) Order(s)	1st Battalion, Machine Gun Corps. Order No. 21.	15/05/1918	15/05/1918
Operation(al) Order(s)	1st Battalion, Machine Gun Corps. Order No. 22	17/05/1918	17/05/1918
Operation(al) Order(s)	Amendment No. 1 To 1st Battalion, Machine Gun Corps Operation Order No. 23. Reference para. 3	17/05/1918	17/05/1918
Operation(al) Order(s)	1st Battalion, Machine Gun Corps. Order No. 23.	17/05/1918	17/05/1918
Operation(al) Order(s)	1st Battalion, Machine Gun Corps. Order No. 21.	25/05/1918	25/05/1918
Operation(al) Order(s)	Addendum No.1. to 1st Battalion Machine Gun Corps Order No. 25.	28/05/1918	28/05/1918
Operation(al) Order(s) Miscellaneous	1st Battalion. Machine Gun Corps. Order No. 25. Amendment No. 1 To D1st Battalion, Machine Gun Corps Defence Screen	27/05/1918	27/05/1918
Miscellaneous	Reference 1st Battn. M.G.C. No. 1255 dated 23/5/1918		
Miscellaneous Miscellaneous	1st Battalion, Machine Gun Corps Defence Scheme.		
Miscellaneous	Appendix No. 8 to Machine Gun Defence Scheme, 1st Battalion, M.G.C.		
Miscellaneous	Appendix IV. To 1st Battalion, Machine Gun Corps, Defence Scheme		
Operation(al) Order(s)	1st Battalion, Machine Gun Corps. Order No. 26.	31/05/1918	31/05/1918
War Diary	Barlin K 3.2 F Sh 44	01/06/1918	30/06/1918

Operation(al) Order(s)	1st Battalion, Machine Gun Corps. Operation Order No. 28		
Operation(al) Order(s)	1st Battalion, Machine Gun Corps. Operation Order No. 29	21/06/1918	21/06/1918
Miscellaneous	Appendix. "A"		
Map	Reference map Sheet 36 C.N.W. And Adjoining Sheets.		
Map			
Heading	1st Division War Diary 1st M.G. Bn. March To December From 1st July To 31st December 1918		
War Diary	Barlin K 32 F Sh. 44 F	01/07/1918	31/07/1918
Operation(al) Order(s)	1st Battalion, Machine Gun Corps. Order No. 30.	01/07/1918	01/07/1918
Operation(al) Order(s)	1st Battalion, Machine Gun Corps. Order No. 31.	05/07/1918	05/07/1918
Operation(al) Order(s)	1st Battalion, Machine Gun Corps. Order No. 32.	09/07/1918	09/07/1918
Operation(al) Order(s)	1st Battalion, Machine Gun Corps. Order No. 33	15/07/1918	15/07/1918
Operation(al) Order(s)	1st Battalion, Machine Gun Corps. Order No. 34	16/07/1918	16/07/1918
Operation(al) Order(s)	1st Battalion, Machine Gun Corps. Order No. 35.	22/07/1918	22/07/1918
Operation(al) Order(s)	1st Battalion, Machine Gun Corps Order No. 36.	24/07/1918	24/07/1918
Operation(al) Order(s)	1st Battalion, Machine Gun Corps. Order No. 37.	31/07/1918	31/07/1918
War Diary	Barlin K 32 F Sh 44 F	11/08/1918	22/08/1918
War Diary	EPS	23/08/1918	31/08/1918
Operation(al) Order(s)	1st Battalion, Machine Gun Corps. Order No. 38.	04/08/1918	04/08/1918
War Diary	Maissemy	26/09/1918	30/09/1918
Operation(al) Order(s)	1st Battalion, Machine Gun Corps. Order No. 37		
Operation(al) Order(s)	1st Battalion, Machine Gun Corps Order No. 30	13/08/1918	13/08/1918
Operation(al) Order(s)	1st Battalion, Machine Gun Corps. Order No. 40	18/08/1918	18/08/1918
Operation(al) Order(s)	1st Battalion, Machine Gun Corps Order No. 41	20/08/1918	20/08/1918
Operation(al) Order(s)	1st Battalion, Machine Gun Corps. Order No. 42.	21/08/1918	21/08/1918
Operation(al) Order(s)	1st Battalion M.G.C. Order No. 43	31/08/1918	31/08/1918
War Diary	Arras	01/09/1918	01/09/1918
War Diary	Wancourt	02/09/1918	02/09/1918
War Diary	Fosse Farm N 12 a-o-6	03/09/1918	08/09/1918
War Diary	Y Huts Etrun	09/09/1918	10/09/1918
War Diary	Morcourt Area	11/09/1918	12/09/1918
War Diary	Meraucourt	13/09/1918	13/09/1918
War Diary	Caulaincourt	14/09/1918	19/09/1918
War Diary	Maissemy	20/09/1918	23/09/1918
War Diary	Rzoess?	24/09/1918	25/09/1918
Operation(al) Order(s)	1st Battalion M.G.C. Order No. 43. Ref. Map. Lens 1/100.000	31/09/1918	31/08/1918
Miscellaneous	1st Battalion, Machine Gun Corps. Order No. 44. Reference Map Sheet, 41.B.		
Operation(al) Order(s)	Amendment No. 1 To 1st Battalion, British M.G.O. Order No. 44. Reference Map Sheet 41.B. 1/40,000	07/09/1918	07/09/1918
Operation(al) Order(s)	1st Battalion, Machine Gun Corps Order No. 45. Reference Map Sheet Lens 11, 1/100,000.	08/09/1918	08/09/1918
Operation(al) Order(s)	1st Battalion, Machine Gun Corps. Order No. 46. Reference Maps Lens 11, and Amiens 17, 1/100,000	10/09/1918	10/09/1918
Operation(al) Order(s)	1st Battalion, Machine Gun Corps. Order No. 47.	12/09/1918	12/09/1918
Operation(al) Order(s)	1st Battalion, Machine Gun Corps. Order No. 48	12/09/1918	12/09/1918
Operation(al) Order(s)	1st Battalion, Machine Gun Corps Order No 49	17/09/1918	17/09/1918
Miscellaneous	Copies issued to:-		
Operation(al) Order(s)	Addendum No. 1. To 1st Battalion, Machine Gun Corps Order 49	17/09/1918	17/09/1918
Operation(al) Order(s)	1st Battalion, Machine Gun Corps. Order No. 50	23/09/1918	23/09/1918
Operation(al) Order(s)	1st Battalion, Machine Gun Corps. Order No. 51	26/09/1918	26/09/1918
Miscellaneous	Copies issued to:-		

Type	Description	Date From	Date To
Operation(al) Order(s)	1st Battalion Machine Gun Corps. Order No. 52	28/09/1918	28/09/1918
Miscellaneous	Copies issued to:-		
Map	Maps		
Miscellaneous	Message Form		
Miscellaneous	Appendix To War Diary September 1st Battalion, Machine Gun Corps.	30/09/1918	30/09/1918
Miscellaneous	Report Of action 18th to 20th September 1918		
Miscellaneous	C Company	30/09/1918	30/09/1918
Miscellaneous	D Company.		
Map	Maps		
Map	Gricourt West		
War Diary	Mi5c 3.3	01/10/1918	03/10/1918
War Diary	Maissemy	04/10/1918	10/10/1918
War Diary	La Baraque	11/10/1918	15/10/1918
War Diary	Bohain	16/10/1918	17/10/1918
War Diary	Vaux Andigny	18/10/1918	18/10/1918
War Diary	Lavallee Mulatre	19/10/1918	31/10/1918
Miscellaneous	Summary Of Operations Form 17th To 27th October 1918		
Miscellaneous	Summary Of Operations From 17th To 20th October 1918		
Miscellaneous	Summary Of Operations From 17th To 19th October 1918		
Miscellaneous	Summary Of Operations From 17th To 23rd October 1918		
Operation(al) Order(s)	1st Battalion, Machine Gun Corps. Order No. 53	13/10/1918	13/10/1918
Operation(al) Order(s)	Table "A" To Accompany 1st Battalion, Machine Gun Corps Order 53		
Operation(al) Order(s)	Table "B" To Accompany 1st Battalion, Machine Gun Corps Order No. 53		
Operation(al) Order(s)	1st Battalion, Machine Gun Corps, Order No. 54	15/10/1918	15/10/1918
Operation(al) Order(s)	1st Battalion, Machine Gun Corps. Order No 55	20/10/1918	20/10/1918
Operation(al) Order(s)	1st Battalion, Machine Gun Corps. Order No. 57	22/10/1919	22/10/1919
Miscellaneous	Map (To Accompany 1st M.G. Battn Order No. 57)		
Operation(al) Order(s)	1st Battalion M.G.C. Order No. 58		
Miscellaneous	Serial No Unit		
Operation(al) Order(s)	1st Battalion, Machine Gun Corps. Order No. 59	29/10/1918	29/10/1918
Map	6th Div		
Map	Wassigny		
Map	To Superimpose on Sheet 62B NE 57B S.E.		
War Diary	Lavalle Mulatre	01/11/1918	04/11/1918
War Diary	A Vallee Mulatre	05/11/1918	05/11/1918
War Diary	Fresnay	06/11/1918	06/11/1918
War Diary	Levergies	07/11/1918	08/11/1918
War Diary	Molain	09/11/1918	13/11/1918
War Diary	Prisches	14/11/1918	14/11/1918
War Diary	Les Fontaines	15/11/1918	17/11/1918
War Diary	Renlis	18/11/1918	18/11/1918
War Diary	Boussu Lez Walcourt	19/11/1918	22/11/1918
War Diary	Ives-Gomezee	23/11/1918	23/11/1918
War Diary	Flavion	24/11/1918	30/11/1918
Operation(al) Order(s)	1st Battalion, Machine Gun Corps.	01/11/1918	01/11/1918
Operation(al) Order(s)	1st Battalion, Machine Gun Corps. Order No. 60	02/11/1918	02/11/1918
Operation(al) Order(s)	Table To Accompany 1st Battalion, Machine Gun Corps Order No. 60		

Miscellaneous	Narrative of Action of Machine Guns of 1st Division during the forcing of the passage of the Sambre-Oise Canal, on 4/11/18		
Operation(al) Order(s)	1st Battalion, Machine Gun Corps. Order No. 61	05/11/1918	05/11/1918
Operation(al) Order(s)	1st Battalion, Machine Gun Corps. Order No. 62	06/11/1918	06/11/1918
Operation(al) Order(s)	1st Battalion, Machine Gun Corps. Order No. 63.	08/11/1918	08/11/1918
Operation(al) Order(s)	1st Battalion. Machine Gun Corps. Order No. 64	13/11/1918	13/11/1918
Operation(al) Order(s)	1st Battalion, Machine Gun Corps. Order No 65	14/11/1918	14/11/1918
Operation(al) Order(s)	1st Battalion, Machine Gun Corps. Order No. 66.	18/11/1918	18/11/1918
Operation(al) Order(s)	1st Battalion, Machine Gun Corps. Order No. 67	19/11/1918	19/11/1918
Operation(al) Order(s)	1st Battalion, Machine Gun Corps. Order No. 68	22/11/1918	22/11/1918
Operation(al) Order(s)	1st Battalion, Machine Gun Corps. Order No. 69	23/11/1918	23/11/1918
War Diary	Falaen	01/12/1918	01/12/1918
War Diary	Mesnil St Blaise	02/12/1918	02/12/1918
War Diary	Houyet	03/12/1918	08/12/1918
War Diary	Haid	09/12/1918	09/12/1918
War Diary	Fronville	10/12/1918	10/12/1918
War Diary	Soy	11/12/1918	13/12/1918
War Diary	La Fossee and acter-le-baty	14/12/1918	14/12/1918
War Diary	Regne	15/12/1918	15/12/1918
War Diary	Bouvigny	16/12/1918	16/12/1918
War Diary	Germany Aldringen	16/12/1918	16/12/1918
War Diary	Schonberg	18/12/1918	18/12/1918
War Diary	Kronenberg	19/12/1918	20/12/1918
War Diary	Blankenheimerdorf	21/12/1918	21/12/1918
War Diary	Iversheim	22/12/1918	22/12/1918
War Diary	Flamersheim	23/12/1918	23/12/1918
War Diary	Flerzheim and Luftelberg	24/12/1918	24/12/1918
War Diary	Flerzheim	25/12/1918	31/12/1918
Operation(al) Order(s)	1st Battalion, Machine Gun Corps. Order No 70	30/11/1918	30/11/1918
Operation(al) Order(s)	1st Battalion, Machine Gun Corps. Order No. 71	01/12/1918	01/12/1918
Miscellaneous	Group Organization Chart		
Operation(al) Order(s)	1st Battalion Machine Gun Corps. Order No. 72	02/12/1918	02/12/1918
Operation(al) Order(s)	1st Battalion, Machine Gun Corps. Order No. 73	08/12/1918	08/12/1918
Operation(al) Order(s)	1st Battalion Machine Gun Corps. Order No. 74	09/12/1918	09/12/1918
Operation(al) Order(s)	1st Battalion Machine Gun Corps. Order No. 75.	10/12/1918	10/12/1918
Operation(al) Order(s)	1st Battalion Machine Gun Corps & Order No. 76	13/12/1918	13/12/1918
Operation(al) Order(s)	1st Battalion Machine Gun Corps. Order No. 72	16/12/1918	16/12/1918
Miscellaneous	Apschrift Kriegsministerium		
Operation(al) Order(s)	St Battalion Machine Gun Corps. Order No. 80.	17/12/1918	17/12/1918
Miscellaneous	Gun Chart		
Operation(al) Order(s)	1st Battalion, Machine Gun Corps. Order No. 81	18/12/1918	18/12/1918
Operation(al) Order(s)	1st Battalion Machine Gun Corps. Order No. 77	14/12/1918	14/12/1918
Miscellaneous	General ?		
Operation(al) Order(s)	1st Battalion Machine Gun Corps. Order No. 78	15/12/1918	15/12/1918
Operation(al) Order(s)	1st Battalion Machine Gun Corps Order No. 82	20/12/1918	20/12/1918
Operation(al) Order(s)	1st Battalion Machine Gun Corps. Order No. 83.	21/12/1918	21/12/1918
Operation(al) Order(s)	1st Battalion Machine Gun Corps. Order No. 84.	22/12/1918	22/12/1918
Operation(al) Order(s)	1st Battalion Machine Gun Corps. Order No. 85	23/12/1918	23/12/1918
Heading	1919 Western Division Late 1st Division 1st Bn Mach. Gun Corps Jan-jly 1919		
War Diary	Flerzheim Germany 1/100.000	01/01/1919	31/01/1919
Miscellaneous	Training Programme for week ending 8th February 1919		
Miscellaneous	Educational Training. Evening Classes		
War Diary	Flerzheim	01/02/1919	15/02/1919

War Diary	Lerzheim	16/02/1919	28/02/1919
Miscellaneous	Training Programme for week ending 8th February 1919.		
Miscellaneous	Training Programme for week ending, 15th. February 1919.		
War Diary	Training Programme for week ending 22nd February 1919		
Miscellaneous	Training Programme for week ending 1st March 1919.		
War Diary	Flerzheim	01/03/1919	31/03/1919
Miscellaneous	1st. Battalion, Machine Gun Corps. Training Programme for week ending 24th. March 1919		
Miscellaneous	1st. Battalion, Machine Gun Corps. Training Programme for week ending 15th March, 1919.		
Miscellaneous	Recreational Training Programme Of Sports for Week ending 15th March, 1919		
Miscellaneous	1st. Battalion, Machine Gun Corps. Training Programme for week ending 8th. March 1919		
Miscellaneous	1st Battalion Machine Gun Corps.		
War Diary	Flerzheim	01/04/1919	30/04/1919
Miscellaneous	1st Battalion Machine Gun Corps.		
War Diary	Flerzheim	01/05/1919	31/05/1919
Miscellaneous	1st Battalion Machine Gun Corps.		
Miscellaneous	1st. Battalion Machine Gun Corps. Course For Draft Of The Cheshire Regiment-Week Ending 31st. May 1919.-Second Week.		
Miscellaneous	Course For N M Draft-Week Ending 24th May 1919		
War Diary	Flerzheim	01/06/1919	30/06/1919
Miscellaneous	1st. Battalion Machine Gun Corps.		
War Diary	Flerzheim	01/07/1919	31/07/1919
War Diary	Flerzheim	04/07/1919	31/07/1919
War Diary	Flerzheim	24/07/1919	31/07/1919
Miscellaneous	War Diary July 1919. Names of Officers Reinforcing Battalion in July 1919.		

B.E.F. FRANCE & FLANDERS
1 DIVISION. TROOPS.
1 BN MACHINE GUN CORPS.
1918 MAR TO 1919 JULY.
216 MACHINE GUN COY.
1917 MAR TO 1918 FEB.
1/6(PIONEER)BN WELSH RGT.
1916 JUNE TO 1919 AUG.

B.E.F. FRANCE & FLANDERS
1 DIVISION.   TROOPS
1 BN MACHINE GUN CORPS
1918 MAR TO 1919 JULY.
216 MACHINE GUN COY.
1917 MAR TO 1918 FEB.
1/6 (PIONEER) BN WELSH RGT
1916 JUNE TO 1919 AUG.

1256

WO 95/1256/1

Mar 1918 – July 1919

1st Division

War Diaries

1st M. G. BN. March To December

From 1st March. To 30th June. 1918

WAR DIARY or INTELLIGENCE SUMMARY

Army Form C. 2118.

1 Bn. M.G. Corps

Place	Date	Hour	Summary of Events and Information	Remarks and references to Appendices
CANAL BANK S.18 N.W. C.25.d.1.7	1/3/18		HQ of 1st Bn M.G. Corps formed on 1st Feb 1918 and located at CAMP B.M. Sheet 28NW C.25.d.1.7 Lt. Col. H.F. BIDDER D.S.O. commanding. Major J.G. FREER M.C. 2nd in Cmd.	
			Lt. (Hon. Capt.) Adjutant. Lt. (HEWINS) Quartermaster. Lt. P.R.D. GRATTAN Transport Officer. Seniority 1st Div. 860/2(a) Lodging letter R. Sect. of II.	
			Cpys. A.B.C.D. were ordered to form in the order of 1st 2nd 3rd 4th Division as ordered on Cpys. were to given on the support system. Battalion covered indirect fire carried out by arrangement with the supporting [...]	
"	2/3/18		Indirect fire carried out by arrangement with the infantry.	
"	3/3/18		Indirect fire carried out as ordered in MORAY HOUSE Report. 1st Bde co-operating with indirect fire. Reading cards washed V.A.1.A.8.7 run done last nite. Firing was seen. Infantry rated firing on supporting. Monkobone supplies during the day. Transport all companies and artillery. B.2.d. Central. (H.28. NW.) C.1 REIGERSBURG CAMP H.29.a.6.3. (H.28 NW)	
AGADIR CAMP 28 NW B.30.b.4.0	4/3/18		Batta H.Q. moved to AGADIR CAMP. B Cy inspected by Cy Commander. Appendix A1	
"	5/3/18		General Lewis rifle drill inspection. Operation orders as to relief issued. C. Coy relieved A. Coy in the line. The battn moved to REIGERSBERG CAMP H.29.a.28.4 6a.6.3. 4 indicate [...]	
"	6/3/18		D. Coy relieved B. Coy in the line. Support scheme practice.	
"	7/3/18		Telephone received activity. Enemy artillery activity. Support received the Fort VERNON completing 1st Div. Brigade.	
"	8/3/18		Infantry in [...] enemy artillery [...] supported by our own C.C. [...]	
"	9/3/18		C.O.E.A. received orders to report to officer [...] to the firing line of 33rd Division by 4 Coys to Officers [...]	

WAR DIARY
or
INTELLIGENCE SUMMARY.
(Erase heading not required.)

Army Form C. 2118.

Place	Date	Hour	Summary of Events and Information	Remarks and references to Appendices
ABADIR CAMP Sheet 28 B.26 c.6.3	10/3/18		Situation normal. Every Lewis Gun & Vickers Gun on left. Coy. relief by a Coy of Lancers. Lewis Guns went up on lift Bn. D.C.L.I. Reliefs on off at 8 p.m.	
"	11/3/18		One of our Aeroplanes fell in our lines at 2 a.m. The Buffs & the 13th Bedfns Regt. took up a position on the line including our front to the YPRES-STADEN Railway "C" Company who were in Reserve moved up on Right. We had 2 Coys in front line and 1 Coy. in Support with Coy. H.Q. at ELVERDINGHE.	
"	12/3/18		Situation normal. Enemy got Trench Mortars on our Ranges & fired several Rounds to to a.m. Retaliation from Heavy Artillery for light damage done to trenches by ?	
"	13/3/18		Enemy very quiet. Returned fire from Trench Mortars F.A.G. firing one round at 2 a.m.	
"	14/3/18		Artillery very quiet. No movement by enemy M.G.	
"	14/3/18		Enemy very quiet during the day. SOS signal sent up about 11.40 p.m. by our posts on the TAUBE RIDGE to line 17.7.79 remained about 15 min. but whether an S.R. strike and the reason Whit.	
"	15/3/18		Situation normal. During the day about 4 p.m. we relieved the ? by Battalion ? 13 ? relieved to ARMADA CAMP. SL 28 B.12.6.9.	
ARMADA CAMP SL 28 B.27. a.1.3	16/3/18		Situation normal. Company on working parties on back areas e.g. to 10 K.M. 1 E.A. Proffered from C. mine at DELTA Hoot 18 & Hoot 2 V.D.C.51. from 8 am - 5 pm. till 11.3.	
"	17/3/18		D. Coy attempted B. Coy on the forward form? B. Coy was transferred. CAMP SL B.7.B.c.1. A.10.9.4.2. Minutes moved away the day no men. Enemy rocket one of our form.	
"	18/3/18		Situation normal. Entered here Enjoyed out, moved in way or with 28th Sh. Crafty. Company Relieving Scene taking will very ?	
"	19/3/18		Situation normal. This area where second our form 8th Coy sent out 8 snipers by a Corpl.	

WAR DIARY
or
INTELLIGENCE SUMMARY.
(Erase heading not required.)

Army Form C. 2118.

Instructions regarding War Diaries and Intelligence Summaries are contained in F. S. Regs., Part II. and the Staff Manual respectively. Title pages will be prepared in manuscript.

Place	Date	Hour	Summary of Events and Information	Remarks and references to Appendices
ARMADA CAMP B.30.c.n.2 Sh.28.B	20/3/18		Situation normal. Considerable artillery activity. Capt. HANCOCK M.C. wounded by shell fire. Capt. ANSON posted to D Coy. Lieut. BURNEY to C Coy. Lieut. GEE	
			carried out by arrangement with Infantry.	
"	21/3/18		Situation normal. Warlike exercise of relieving a shell-hole Post carried out. App. A/2 Enemy shell intermittently during the day. Harassing fire carried out in the App. B/2 morning with Rifle Grenades. One of A Coy. Sean Borsthrowers thrown in front the app. c/2 gun pit damaged.	
"	22/3/18		Situation normal. Refe. Grenade activity. Enemy found my party on patrol on left near T.M. activity upon T41.3.5 Sh.29.A & T.11.c.3 St. 28.B. Our own Lewis Gun app. d/2 app.e/2 fire on 5 Ft. Post above the I.[?] Coy.	
"	23/3/18		Situation normal. Some Gas shelling on support system. B Coy returned C Coy in support and C Coy returned D Coy in support. Latter Coy having run Letters St. app.f/2 TURCO FARM HUTS Sh. 28 C.14.g. C.O. goes on leave.	
TURCO FARM HUTS B.28.a B.28.g C.14	24/3/18		Situation normal. Harassing fire carried out by arrangement with the Infantry Batt. H.Q. moved to TURCO FARM HUTS Sh. 28 C.14.g.	
"	25/3/18		Situation normal. 2/Lieut. Lecomepet wounded. Have shipped 1/4 2/ of A Coy wound to TURKESTAN Cros.	
"	26/3/18		Situation normal. During day. Harassing fire carried out by men[?] at S.O.S. on R. Batt. front at 11.1pm. Signal given to Infantry to Infantry attack.	
"	27/3/18		Our Artillery fire S.O.S. opened at 4 a.m. Enemy shows signs of Ridge activity reported but learned not of his new[?] line west of day.	
"	28/3/18		Situation abnormal. Enemy artillery fire were active. Harassing fire carried out 29/3. app.[?]	
"	29/3/18		Situation normal. 2/Lieut. M.W. BELL joins during day. C Company relieved B Company in Support System and B Company in support.	
"			Following guns shot up at TURCO FARM HUTS B.28 C.14 B.14 Guns at ZMAROS B.153 T.7.0.0 U.14 T.40.90 BEAR B.3.10.00 and two old Lewinsel	

WAR DIARY or INTELLIGENCE SUMMARY

Army Form C. 2118.

Place	Date	Hour	Summary of Events and Information	Remarks and references to Appendices
TURCO FARM HUTS - A.28. c.4.d.1.4.	30/3/18		Situation normal. Enemy fire ceased out his engagement with infantry. Stationary gun put in at EAGLE Ch. B.3 T.6.0.0. U. 28. d. 05.85	
"	31/3/18		Situation normal. Artillery T.M.B. & T.M.E. active. Indents for canvas and hosepipe sent in. Work on organisation.	
			Strength at beginning of month	
			Officers 49 O.R. 889	
			" 46 " 887	
			end	
			Casualties :— Officers 1 wounded O.R. 1 killed	
			" 2 ill sick 13 ill sick	
			Drafts :— 12 O.R.	

SECRET.   Copy No. 19

1ST BATTALION, MACHINE GUN CORPS.
OPERATION ORDER NO.27.

Reference BETHUNE combined Sheet.

1. "D" Company will relieve "C" Company in the CAUDRIN Section on the morning of the 5th instant.

2. All details of relief will be arranged between Officers Commanding Companies concerned direct.

3. On completion of relief "C" Company will proceed to billets in BARLIN.

4. Companies will move by rail. Details of trains will be issued later.

5. Completion of relief will be reported to Battalion H.Q. by the code word "JORDAN" and to 3rd Infantry Brigade direct.

6. On completion of relief Group Commander, Left Group will be Major J.S.Snowball.

7. Acknowledge.

                                        Captain and Adjutant,
                                        1st Battalion, Machine
                                              Gun Corps.

Issued at 3.30.p.m. 3/3/18.

Copies issued to:-   (1) O.C."A" Company.
                      (2) O.C."B" Company.
                      (3) O.C."C" Company.
                      (4) O.C."D" Company.
                      (5) Commanding Officer.
                      (6) Transport Officer.
                      (7) Quartermaster.
                      (8) Signalling Officer.
                      (9) Medical Officer.
                      (10) 55th Battn.M.G.C.
                      (11) 1st Infantry Brigade.
                      (12) 2nd Infantry Brigade.
                      (13) 3rd Infantry Brigade.
                      (14) 1st Division "G".
                      (15) 1st Division "Q".
                      (16) War Diary.
                      (17) War Diary.
                      (18) File.
                      (19) File.

SECRET   Copy No. 19

ADDENDUM NO.1 TO
1ST BATTALION, MACHINE GUN CORPS,
ORDER NO.87

1. Reference para.1 add, "Reliefs to be complete by 12 noon."

Capt.& Adjutant,
1st Battalion, Machine
Gun Corps.

Issued at 6 p.m. 5/3/18

Copies issued to all recipients of 1st Battalion M.G.C. Order No.87.

31.	1st Batth. B.W.Corps.	SOKO.
32.	"A" Company, do.	SOKO.
33.	"B" Company, do.	SOKO.
34.	"C" Company, do.	SOKO (Soan)
35.	"D" Company, do.	SOKO (Soan)
36.	28th Brigade, R.F.A.	LUVI.
37.	113th Batty. do.	LUJI.
38.	114th Batty. do.	LUZI.
39.	115th Batty. do.	LUNI.
40.	40th Batty. do.	LUKI.
41.	K/1 T.M. Batty.	DIVE.
52.	59th Brigade, R.F.A.	LURA.
53.	6th Batty. R.F.A.	LUPA.
54.	51st Batty. do.	LUQA.
55.	54th Batty. do.	LUDA.
56.	80th Batty. do.	LUBO.
57.	I/1 T.M. Batty.	DIJE.
38.	1st D.A.C.	FIRA.
39.	23rd Field Coy., R.E.	KIGA.
40.	25th Field Coy., R.E.	KILA.
41.	409th Field Coy. R.E.	SIVI.
42.	1/6th Welsh Regt. (Pioneers)	NOBO.
43.	No. 1 Field Ambulance.	LAKA.
44.	No. 2. do. do.	LAKA.
45.	141st do. do.	MAQA.
46.	Divisional Train.	NOBO.
47.	204th Employment Coy.	PAKA.

SECRET

Appendix A1

Copy No......

1st. BATTN. MACHINE GUN CORPS ORDER No. 1.

1. Battalion reliefs when in the present Divisional Sector will be arranged on the following scheme :-

   FORWARD ZONE.

       1 M.G.Coy. in the Front System.
       1 M.G.Coy. plus the guns of Coy. in CANAL BANK. in Support System with 4 guns in the Front System.

       1 M.G.Coy. less 2 guns in CANAL BANK.
       1 M.G.Coy. in REIGERSBERG M.G. Camp.

2. The period of reliefs will be 6 days.

3. The following reliefs will take place on the night of the 5/6th March 1918 :-
   C.Coy. will relieve A.Coy. in the Front System.
   B.Coy. and 2 guns of D.Coy. will take over the new positions in the Support System, and will relieve the guns of D.Coy. now in position in the Support and Forward System.
   D.Coy. less 2 guns will remain in CANAL BANK.
   A.Coy. will, on completion of relief, return to REIGERSBERG CAMP.

4. All details of relief will be arranged direct between Officers Commanding Coys. concerned. The guns taking up new positions must be in position by 7.0p.m. on the 5th. March 1918.

5. O.C. Companies will report completion of reliefs on the taking up of new positions to Brigades concerned and to Battalion H.Q.

6. Acknowledge.

(signed) A. Shanks.
Capt. & Adjt.
1st Battn M.G. Corps.

4th. March 1918.

Copies to :-
  Div. H.Q.
  "A" Coy.
  "B" "
  "C" "
  "D" "
  1st. Brigade.
  2nd. -do-
  3rd. -do-
  War Diary.
  Qr. Master.
  Transport Officer.
  File.

A 2

Copy of a letter written by Officer Commanding 1st Inf.Bde.
to Captain A.S.Vernon, 6/3/18.

"The 1st Brigade now loses the former No.1 Machine Gun Company in consequence of the new re-organisation.

During the long period in which all of you have served with the 1st Brigade you have had the confidence of all ranks and it is with feelings of regret that I see you withdrawn from my command.

At the same time the improved organisation will give you even greater opportunities of supporting your old comrades, and it is with pleasure that we all realise you will still fight side by side with the Brigade.

I wish you all the best of good luck and good fortune.

(Signed)   Charles Grant,
Brigadier General,
Commanding, 1st Infantry Brigade.

SECRET&

Copy No.

1st. Battalion Machine Gun Corps Order No.2.

Reference Map Sheet B.2. 1/10.000.

1. The 1st. Battalion M.G.C. will relieve 10 Guns of the 35th. Battalion, M.G.C. on the night 10/11th. March 1918

2. "A" Company. 1st Battalion M.G.C, Will relieve the following gun positions.

WATERHOUSE	(V.13b. 2.8.)	1gun.
SENEGAL FARM	(V.7.c. 9.2.)	1gun.
TAUBE FARM.	(V.7.c. 7.92.)	1gun.
OLGA HOUSES	(U.18.b.55.15)	2guns.

    The above positions are held by "A" Company, 35th. Battalion M.G.C,

ROSE HOUSE	(U.24.d.95.20.)	1 gun.
ROSE N.W.	(U.24.d.6.7.)	1 gun.
LOUIE FARM	(U.24.c. 7.9.)	1 gun.
EAGLE TRENCH	(V.28.d. 9.9.)	1 gun.
NAMUR	(V.17.c. 9.2.)	1 gun.

    The above positions are held by "D" Company. 35th. Battalion M.G.C.

3. All details of reliefs will be arranged direct between O.C.CoyS. concerned.

4. "A" Company Headquarters will be established at KEMPTON PARK&

5. These 10 guns be under the orfers of G.O.C.3rd. Inf.Bde.until the 13th. Instant when they will come under the orders of G.O.C. 1st. Inf Bde.

6. The 6 guns of A Company remaining, will be in Divisional Reserve. An inventory of all Trench Stores, documents defence schemes, maps &c taken over will be made, and a copy sent to this Office by 6 p.m. on the 11th instant.

7. Completion of relief will be reported to this Office by code word "CORNHILL". It will also be reported to G.O.C.3rd Infy, Brigade direct.

8. Acknowledge.

A.Shanks,
Lieut.&.Adjutant,
1st Battalion, Machine
Gun Corps.

9th March 1918.

Issued to:-
1. A Company
2. Division
3. Division
4. 1st Bde.
5. 3rd Brigade
6. War Diary
7. War Diary
8. Quartermaster
9. Transport Officer
10. Signalling Officer
11. 35th Bn.M.G.C.
12. File.

SECRET.   Copy No.

1ST BATTALION, MACHINE GUN CORPS ORDER NO.3.

1. On the night of the 11th/12th March the following relief will take place.

	Relieving Company	Company Relieved
16 guns in the Front System of the Forward Zone.	"B"	"C"
4 guns in the Front System of the Forward Zone. 13 guns in the Support System of the Forward Zone	"D"	"B"

2. All details of relief will be arranged direct between O.C.Coys concerned.

3. On relief "C" Company will proceed to billets at REIGERSBERG CAMP. This Company will be in Divisional Reserve and will hold 14 guns in readiness to occupy the right and left supporting batteries.

3. "C" Company will supply one gun complete but without personnel for the use of "D" Company.

4. Completion of relief will be reported to Battalion Headquarters by the code word "CORNWALL"
   "B" Company will also report completion of relief to the 3rd Bde. direct and "D" Company will report completion of relief to the 2nd Brigade direct.

5. The 4 guns of "D" Company in the Front System of the Forward Zone are under the orders of G.O.C. 3rd Brigade.

6. Acknowledge.

                                        A.Shanks,
                                           Lieut.&.Adjt.
                                        1st Battalion, Machine
9/3/18   Gun Corps.

Issued to:-   1. "B" Company   8 Quartermaster
               2. "C" Company   9 Transport Officer
               3. "D" Company   10 Signalling Officer
               4 Division   11 War Diary
               5 Division   12 War Diary
               6 3rd Inf.Bde.
               7 2nd Inf.Bde.

Copy No....   S E C R E T

AMENDMENT TO

1ST BATTALION MACHINE GUN CORPS ORDER NO.2.

Reference para.10 of above order.

These 10 guns will come under the orders of G.O.C.1st Infantry Brigade at 5.0.p.m. to-day, 13/3/18.

A.Shanks,

Lieut.&.Adjt.
1st Battalion, Machine
Gun Corps.

13/3/18.

Issued at 11.30.a.m.

Issued to:-
1. "A" Company
2. Division
3.   -do-
4. 1st Brigade
5. 3rd Brigade
6. War Diary
7. War Diary
8. Quartermaster
9. Transport Officer
10. Signalling Officer
11. ~~35th Bn.M.G.C.~~
12. File

SECRET.   Copy No.

1ST BATTALION MACHINE GUN CORPS ORDER NO.3.

Ref.Sheet 28 N.W. 1/20,000

(1) The following reliefs will be carried out on the night of the 17/18th March 1918.

	Relieving Company	Company Relieved.
16 guns in the Front System of Forward Zone	"D" Company	"B" Company
4 guns Front System of Forward Zone 13 guns in Support System of Forward Zone	"C" Company	"D" Company

(2) All details of reliefs will be arranged direct between O.C.Companies concerned.

(3) On relief "B" Company will proceed to billets in REIGERSBERG CAMP. This Company will be in Divisional Reserve and will hold 14 guns in readiness to occupy the right and left supporting batteries at C,5.d. and C.12.d. respectively.

(4) "B" Company will provide one gun complete without personnel for the use of "C" Company.

(5) Completion of relief will be reported to Battalion Headquarters by the code word "DEVON"
"D" Coy. will report completion to 2nd Inf.Bde and
"C" Coy.   -do-   3rd Inf.Bde.

(6) The 4 guns of "C" Company in the Front System of Forward Zone are under the orders of G.O.C.2nd Inf.Bde.

(7) Acknowledge.

A.Shanks,
Lieut.&.Adjt.
1st Battalion, Machine
Gun Corps

Issued at 2 p.m.

Copies issued to:-
(1) "B" Company   (8) 2nd Inf.Bde.
(2) "C" Company   (9) Transport Officer
(3) "D" Company   (10) Signalling Officer
(4) Division   (11) War Diary
(5)   "   (12)   "
(6) 3rd Inf.Bde   (13) File
(7) Quartermaster

SECRET.  Copy No.....

AMENDMENT TO
1ST BATTALION MACHINE GUN CORPS ORDER NO.3.

Ref.Sheet 28 N.W. 1/20,000.

On the night 17th/18th March the two guns now at BANFF will be withdrawn and will not be relieved.

The two guns of "D" Company now at WINCHESTER and YORK will remain there.

"C" Company will relieve the remaining guns of "D" Company and the two guns of "A" Company now at ROSE and ROSE N.W. giving "C" Company 17 guns in all before.

"A" Company will withdraw their guns from ROSE and ROSE N.W. and will place one gun in SENEGAL in addition to the one there now.

"A" Company will be prepared to place one additional gun at each of the localities LOUIE, EAGLE and BEAR as soon as the accommodation for them is ready.

Acknowledge.

J.Bullpitt,
for Lieut.&.Adjt.
1st Battalion, Machine
Gun Corps

16/3/18

Issued at 3-15 p.m.

Copies issued to all recipients of 1st Battalion Machine Gun Corps Order No.3.

SECRET Copy No.

1ST BATTALION MACHINE GUN CORPS NO.4

nRef.Sheet 28 N.W. 1/20,000

(1) The following reliefs will be carried out on the night of the 23rd/24th March 1918.

	Relieving Company	Company Relieved
16 guns in Front System of Forward Zone	"C" Company	"D" Company
4 guns Front System of Forward Zone		
13 guns in Support System of Forward Zone	"B" Company	"C" Company

(2) All details of reliefs will be arranged direct between O.C.Companies concerned.

(3) Headquarters and details of "B" Company will proceed to TURCO FARM on 23rd instant.

(4) On relief "D" Company will proceed to billets in TURCO FARM at C.15.d. This Company will be in Divisional Reserve and will hold 8 guns in readiness to occupy the right and centre supporting battery positions at C.5.d. and C.12.d. respectively.

(5) "D" Company will provide one gun complete without personnel for the use of "B" Company.

(6) Completion of relief will be reported to Battalion Headquarters by the code word "HUNTING"
"C" Coy will report completion of relief to 2nd Inf.Bde.
"B" Coy   -do-   3rd Inf.Bde.

(7) Battalion Headquarters and all details will proceed to TURCO FARM on 23rd instant and Battalion Headquarters will close at REIGERSBERG CAMP at 3 p.m. opening at TURCO FARM at the same time. Transport and Wagon Lines will remain as before.

(8) Acknowledge.

A.Shanks,
Lieut.&.Adjt.
1st Battalion, Machine
Gun Corps

Issued at 6.15 p.m.

22/3/18 to
(1) "B" Company   (8) 2nd Inf.Bde.
(2) "C" Company   (9) Transport Officer
(3) "D" Company   (10) Signalling Officer
(4) Division   (11) War Diary
(5)   "   (12)   "
(6) 3rd Inf.Bde   (13) File
(7) Quartermaster

M.G.B.151.

To O.C. Company

Special Order.

The Commanding Officer has great pleasure in publishing the following communication which has been received from Divisional Headquarters.
He considers that the action of the guns of "D" Company on this occasion was a good example of a standard expected of the battalion.

                                A. Shanks,
                                  Lieut & Adjt.
23/3/18   1st Battalion, Machine
                                  Gun Corps

Officer Commanding,
   1st Battn. M.G.C.   1st Division No.G.15/3
                                                  22/3/18

(1)   The following extract from a letter from the 2nd Battn K.R.R.Corps in connection with the enemy bombardment at 2.20.a.m. on the morning of the 20th instant is forwarded for information.

(2)   I should like to say that the work of the Machine Gun Corps was splendid. Within a few seconds of the S.O.S. going up the guns at DELTA HOUSE and NORFOLK HOUSE were firing hard on their S.O.S. lines. I dont think any guns could possibly have got into action quicker than they did.

                                          W. Barnes Major,
                                              for Lieut.Col.
                            General Staff 1st Division.

SECRET.   A.10   Copy No. 14

1st. BATTALION, M.G. CORPS.
ORDER NO. 5.

Reference Sheet 28 N.W. 1/20,000.

(1). The following reliefs will be carried out on the night of 29th/30th March 1918.

	Relieving Company	Company Relieved.
16 guns in Front System of Forward Zone.	"B" Coy	"C" Coy

O.C. "B" Coy will relieve only 2 guns at NORFOLK HOUSE the other remaining two guns there, being withdrawn. He will retain 2 guns at BAVAROISE.

	Relieving Company	Company Relieved.
2 guns in Front System of Forward Zone. 13 guns in Support System of Forward Zone.	"D" Coy	"B" Coy

O.C. "D" Coy will also place 2 guns & teams in the positions prepared for them at TMBROS. These 2 guns will come under command of O.C. "A" Coy.

(2) All details of relief will be arranged direct between O.C. Companies concerned.

(3) On relief "C" Coy will proceed to billets at TURCO CAMP and will be in Divisional Reserve. O.C. "C" Coy will hold 8 guns in readiness to occupy the right & centre supporting battery positions at C.12.d.2.3. and C.5.d.5.9. respectively.

(4) "C" Coy will provide one gun complete without personnel for use of D Coy.

(5) Completion of relief will be reported to Battn. H.Q. by the code word "RACING"
O.C. "B" Coy will report completion of relief to 3rd. Inf. Bde.
O.C. "D" Coy   — do —   — do —   2nd Inf. Bde.

(6) Acknowledge.

Issued at 3.30 p.m. 28/3/18

Captain & Adjutant,
1st Battalion Machine
Gun Corps.

Issued to:-

(1) O.C. "A" Coy   (9) 3rd Inf. Bde.
(2) O.C. "B" Coy   (10) Transport Officer
(3) O.C. "C" Coy   (11) Quartermaster
(4) O.C. "D" Coy   (12) Signalling Officer
(5) 1st Division "G"   (13) War Diary
(6) 1st Inf. Bde. "Q" (14) "
(7) 1st Inf. Bde.   (15) File.
(8) 2nd Inf. Bde.

SECRET   Copy No. 14

1st Battn Machine Gun Corps.
ORDER No. 6.

REFERENCE MAP SHEET 28. N.W 1/20,000.

(1) The following reliefs will be carried out on the night of 4th/5th April 1918.

	Relieving Coy.	Coy Relieved
16 guns in Front System of Forward Zone	"C" Coy	"B" Coy

(2) All details of relief will be arranged direct between O.C. Coys. concerned.

(3) On relief "B" Coy will proceed to huts in TURCO CAMP and will be in Divisional Reserve.

(4) O.C "B" Coy will provide one gun complete without personnel for use of "C" Coy.

(5) Completion of relief will be reported to Battn H.Q by the code word "BACON"
O.C "C" Coy. will report completion of relief to 3rd. Infantry Brigade.

(6) Acknowledge.

(signature)
Captain & adjutant,
1st Battalion, Machine
Gun Corps.

Issued at 6.0 p.m 3/4/18.

Issued to:-

(1) O.C "A" Coy   (9) 3rd Inf. Bde
(2) O.C "B" Coy   (10) Transport Officer
(3) O.C "C" Coy   (11) Quartermaster
(4) O.C "D" Coy   (12) Signalling Officer.
(5) 1st Div. "G"   (13) War Diary
(6) 1st Div. "Q"   (14) — " —
(7) 1st Inf. Bde.   (15) File
(8) 2nd Inf. Bde   (16) File.

1 Bn M G Corps
Army Form C. 2118.

WAR DIARY
or
INTELLIGENCE SUMMARY.
(Erase heading not required.)

Instructions regarding War Diaries and Intelligence Summaries are contained in F.S. Regs., Part II. and the Staff Manual respectively. Title pages will be prepared in manuscript.

Place	Date	Hour	Summary of Events and Information	Remarks and references to Appendices
TURCO HUTS C.H.Q.&S Sh 28 NW	1/4/18		Situation normal. Enemy artillery was active during night & F.A. Snipers fired near VACHER FARM & 8.3" from V.26.d.80.10	
"	2/4/18		Situation normal during the day. At 19 P.M. the 1st Glos active rented our support from the POELCAPELLE SPRIET Road. At V.I.S.C. 2.0 Sh. B3" firing and the M.G.s of WATCH, MANTEL much parts of BLACK WATCH much intake to harassment V.8 a area over the S.S. Co-operating. The GLOUCESTERS took over from ourselves.	
"	3/4/18		Situation normal. Much artillery on both during the day. Indirect fire carried out by arrangement with the infantry. Harassing fire orders of from 6pm to midnight	Appendix A
"	4/4/18		Situation normal. Some hostile artillery activity on both and forward area.	
"	5/4/18		Situation normal. Orders red. 40.798 on to relieve Appendix A	
"	6/4/18		Situation normal. A & B Coy refused by the 30th Bn. M.G.C. and B Coy returning to TURCO HUTS. A Coy tented by 3rd Bn. Arrangements made for move under No. SH.0./187	Appendix A
"	7/4/18		Situation normal. C Coy relieved for more service with 13 Y.C. Corps.	Appendix A
"	8/4/18		Batt. moved to take over sector to west of LA BASSEE CANAL Coys moving to their new transport by route march to LE PRESA about F.10.6. D Coy rear sector to mud of FOUQUERIUIL to LE PRESA. They had transport but hire no machine guns Tpt & late march to WARLES-LES-MINES D.9.5.8 Billets were found in the transport and B. C. Coy rear village assigned by brigade.	
LE QUESNOY Sh 36 B Zone E 2.2.	9/4/18		At 4 a.m. military Commander set off from F.H.Q. dashing throughout the day. Third change drew to village concealion about 9 am. F.H.58 men arrived from Right Bn. Coy after being reinforced by Lewis Gun about 10.30 a.m. orders were received from 3rd Bde. that all units stand forward to ready to move forward at instant.	

(A2883) D.D. & L. London, E.C. Sch. 52a Forms/C2118/14
Wt. W80g/M1572 350,000 4/17

Army Form C. 2118.

WAR DIARY
or
INTELLIGENCE SUMMARY.
(Erase heading not required.)

Place	Date	Hour	Summary of Events and Information	Remarks and references to Appendices
LE QUESNOY Sh 36 SE J.10.00 F 9.4.	9/4/18 cont.		Forward movement. All transport except Lewis Gun limbers followed Horse Lines. B & E Coy [?] attacked temporarily to 55th Div (hitting sector) Brigade HQ Coy & one section C Coy 55th Div. Coy disposed between the CANAL and the high ground between TUNNEY and LA BASSÉE. C Coy reported that enemy had attacked N. of LA BASSÉE CANAL in the vicinity of TUNNEY and were known to have reached GEORGE STREET A3.c. Efforts being made to launch LE QUESNOY. Enemy Infantry advanced following the 55th Div down through and taking the village of LE QUESNOY (no gas shell to R. 750.) Information to Coy who were attached to 3rd Inf Bde. C Coy in Reserve Bn B. Gun artillery was very active during the night	Appendix B
"	10/4/18		On return to the situation caused by the [MANY?] Divisions retiring the flanks of the 55th Div were refused. B Coy advanced from BETHUNE to VAUXHALL A.14 a.0.2 from FAUVIL. Enemy Artillery very active. A Coy ordered to move to FOUQUIÈRES E.7. & a.3. CANAL Junction N. of CANAL	
FOUQUIÈRES E 22 a.	11/4/18		Still concentrating on back areas and 7 the Trench activity N. of CANAL. Enemy Artillery active on back areas. A Coy moved to vicinity of HOUCHIN E.15.d.	
"	12/4/18		Night clear day. Situation unaltered. Shelling took area continued. A Coy moved to trenches in vicinity of FOUQUIÈRES, E.14.c. B Plates still sent out and C Capt. CORNWELL Ham C went for duty to 50th Batt. being unaltered. Capt. CAMPBELL M.C. Ham C	
"	13/4/15		Situation unaltered. Fresh shelling in action. Lt F.V.ANDERSON died of wounds Casualties O.R. 10	
"	14/4/15		C Coy 55th returned to Coy in the FESTUBERT LINE. Lieut. David Bracken O in C. Coy moved to HESDIGNEUL. E. 23.d. Major VERNON appointed 2i/c 55th Batt. Lieut FITZWILLIAMS took over O in C. of B. (Headquarters of A Coy transferred) outside shelling active.	
"	15/4/18			
"	16/4/18		April 16th. Coy were active by Bn Coy moved the Bn Coy during the night Coy returned by Bn Coy to SARR in the Line from BREWER CORNER, movement quiet. Coy Operation Order No.10	Appendix C
"	17/4/18		3.15.a.m. Coy moved to BOSNAY D 2 and 9.1. A Coy relieved H Coy NRA Batts. with 16 Batt. Coy moved to the GIVENCHY line. 9 two guns and one officer of B Coy were attached to A Coy for duty (Operation Order No.11	Appendix A
BOSNAY D 2 & 9.1	19/4/18		Information from a prisoner this morning of an impending attack. Allied guns [?] Enemy bombarded [?] lines at 4 a.m. 9 guns shelling from craters J of LA BASSÉE CANAL	Appendix C

WAR DIARY
or
INTELLIGENCE SUMMARY.

(Erase heading not required.)

Army Form C. 2118.

Place	Date	Hour	Summary of Events and Information	Remarks and references to Appendices
GOSNAY D.24.d.9.1	18/4/18		The Infantry attack was launched at 8 a.m. the objective being the LABASSEE CANAL BANK. After some local successes the enemy was repulsed with cat-	
			ROUTE A. X.29. Regt G.9. line. FESTUBERT KEEP X.26.C. afront of GIVENCHY. The attack over ran supports of Coys are attached.	Appendix 3
"	19/4/18		Operations still calmer with fighting in progress. Enemy shelled in forward area inflicting small & rather annoying losses.	
"	20/4/18		An successful counter-attack. The enemy were worked from ROUTE A KEEP and N.E. Keep in N.E. to GIVENCHY L. SPEAD and to gain touch here in the line. Some prisoners. 2nd Limbs. recovered and Pull. E. Coy. Lieut. C. Morris SR Capt. 33rd Bath. forward to billets in HESDIGNEUL. Opn. Order No. 72.	Appendix R.
"	21/4/18		Situation quieter. C. Coy. 55th Bath. returned to the Battr - B Coy 55th Bath came under the orders of the lines Bath. Opr Order No. 73	"
"	22/4/18		Bridge scouts bombarded front from 4 to 6 am. E. Infantry got across A KEEP X.29.a. Operation there was made through ours & own artillery was neither either first and the return is reported as small previously being 12 of the Infantry into front front of the enemy.	"
"	23/4/18		Situation quieter Enemy shrunk by 9 inch 59 Bath. right front out succeeding.	"
BARLIN R.32 L.3.6	24/4/18		Both Battns. relieved to BARLIN A coy relieved by A Coy 59 Bath. 5 B.CH. produced to billets at BARLIN. Capt. CORNWALL RAM.C. Awarded M.C. for good work at LE QUESNOY F.8.L. on the 9th inst	
"	25/4/18		Situation returned at Some Butter Knife Ridge (Capt returned to Battns) and B Coy returned from over of A Coy of B. Bath (Pioner Kent ANZERANS) der by HOHENZOLLERN SECTOR. No were of C. Co. Mordred my trunk spur in by J. and BARLIN Opn. Order No. 74. Situation observed with other territory Opn. Order No. 74 R.13 L.7.9.	
"	26/4/18			
"	27/4/18		Situation normal. Arthur on fire. Long range guns continued to fire on BERLIN & BERLIN BRUAY REBREUVE (Absent on MBr. mounts brickwork observed on warehouse Opn order No 5 72	

Army Form C. 2118.

WAR DIARY
or
INTELLIGENCE SUMMARY.
(Erase heading not required.)

Place	Date	Hour	Summary of Events and Information	Remarks and references to Appendices
BARLIN K32 4.50	28/4/18		Situation normal. Machine gun long range fire covering in fire on BARLIN and BRUAY. Capt. PEARSON (temporarily attached to B Coy) warned to proceed to Carrières + Company on the 31st Bath.	
	29/4/18		Situation normal. Machine Guns B Coy relieved by A Coy + proceeded to billets at BARLIN.	
	30/4/18		Situation normal. Weather fine and sunny.	
			STRENGTH at beginning of month:— Officers 46 O.R. 887	
			" at end " Officers — O.R. —	
			CASUALTIES Officers wounded 5 O.R. 130	
			Officers gassed 3 O.R. 6	
			8 136	
			DRAFTS Officers Nil O.R. 47	

J. Wigan Lt Col
Comdg 11th Bn
[illegible]

SECRET.   Copy No. 15.

1st BATTALION, MACHINE GUN CORPS.

OPERATION ORDER NO. 7.

Ref.Sheet 28 N.W. 1/20,000

(1)   The 1st Division is being relieved by the 30th and 36th Divisions on the nights of the 6th/7th and 7th/8th April 1918.

(2)   On the night of the 6th/7th April the 3rd Infantry Brigade and detachment of 31 machine guns of this battalion will be relieved in the Forward Zone in Right Brigade Sector by the 107th Infantry Brigade, one Battalion of 109th Infantry Brigade and 36th Battalion, M.G.C.

(3)   On relief "D" Company will proceed with Transport complete to SIDEE CAMP where they will come under the orders of the 3rd Infantry Brigade. "B" Company will proceed to DARCO HUTS.

(4)   On the night of 7th/8th April the 1st Infantry Brigade less reserve battalion and detachment of 14 guns of this battalion will be relieved in the Forward Zone Left Brigade Sector by 89th Infantry Brigade, 30th Division and one Company of 30th Battalion, Machine Gun Corps.

(5)   On relief "A" Company complete with Transport will move to Centre Sector West ELVERDINGHE AREA where they will come under the orders of 1st Infantry Brigade.

(6)   Guns and detachments will not be withdrawn from any locality until the Infantry relief at that locality has been completed.

(7)   On the afternoon of the 8th April "C" Company complete with Transport, will proceed to SIDEE CAMP where they come under the orders of the 3rd Infantry Brigade.

(8)   Details as to billets will be arranged between O's C.Coys and the Brigades concerned direct.

(9)   Details of relief will be arranged direct between O's C. Companies concerned.

(10)   Acknowledge.

                                        Captain & Adjutant,
                                        1st Battalion, Machine
Issued at 3-30.p.m. 5/4/18   Gun Corps.

Issued to:-   (1) "A" Company   (7) 1st Bde.   (13) Transport Off.
                (2) "B" Company   (8) 2nd Bde.   (14) Sig. Officer.
                (3) "C" Company   (9) 3rd Bde.   (15) War Diary
                (4) "D" Company   (10) 30th Bn.M.G.C. (16) War Diary
                (5) Division "G"   (11) 36th Bn.M.G.C. (17) SS.
                (6) Division "C"   (12) Quartermaster (18) File

SECRET   Copy No. 13

1ST BATTALION, MACHINE GUN CORPS.

OPERATION ORDER NO. 8.

With reference to 1st Battalion M.G.C. Operation Order No. 7 the following will be the detailed arrangements for the relief.

(1) Gun Limbers and teams of "A" and "B" Companies, 36th Battalion M.G.C. will start from REIGERSBURG Transport Lines at 6 p.m. with a guide provided by the Transport of this Battalion.

(2) "B" and "D" Companies of this Battalion will provide guides to meet the above at KEMPTON PARK at 7 p.m. One guide will be sent from each gun position. Where guns are in pairs one guide will be sent from the pair. The Nos.1 of the 36th Bn.M.G.C. now at the gun positions will accompany these guides.

(3) Limbers must not cross the STEENBECK before 7.30.p.m.

(4) All trench stores, maps, S.O.S. charts, work on hand &c will be handed over. Ten belt boxes will be handed over at each gun position and two petrol tins. Guns, tripods, and remaining belt boxes will be brought out, also all surplus petrol tins.

(5) O's C. "B" and "D" Companies will arrange for their own limbers to come up and take out guns and stores. If train transport of gun teams of "D" Company to SIEGE CAMP is available, this will be notified later. 310 belt boxes will be handed over by 36th Bn.M.G.C. at REIGERSBERG Transport Lines. O.C."D" Company will arrange to collect 180 of these, and O.C."B" Company 180. The belts will probably be unfilled.

(6) "C" Company and Headquarters and details of "D" Company will be clear of their present billets by 4.30.p.m. and will proceed to SIEGE CAMP under arrangements to be made by O.C. Companies after consultation with 3rd Infantry Brigade.

(7) Acknowledge.

                                                Captain & Adjutant,
                                                1st Battalion, Machine
                                                   Gun Corps.

Issued at 2.30.p.m. 5/4/18

Issued to:- (1) "A" Company   (6) Division "G"   (11) Sig. Officer.
            (2) "B" Company   (7) Division "Q"   (12) War Diary
            (3) "C" Company   (8) 36th Bn.M.G.C. (13) War Diary
            (4) "D" Company   (9) Quartermaster   (14) File
            (5) 3rd Brigade   (10) Transport Off. (15) File

SECRET.   1st BATTALION, MACHINE GUN CORPS.   Copy No.

ADMINISTRATIVE INSTNS.

With reference to 1st Battalion M.G.C. Order No. 8,

(1) Reference para, 5, the personnel of "D" Coy. in the line will proceed by train from BROOKLYN Station at 2a.m. on 7-4-18. They will be at the Station ready to entrain at 1-50a.m. and the senior Officer will report to the O i/c Train when all ranks are present. (Guns and equipment will be taken out by limbers under arrangements to be made between O's C. Companies and Transport Officer direct). They will detrain at ELVERDINGHE 1¾ hours later. O.C."D" Coy. will arrange to send guides to guide them to billets.

(2) Reference para. 4, a complete list of ammunition, reserve rations, trench stores etf. handed over and a copy of receipts for same will be sent to Battn. H.Q. by 9a.m. 7-4-18.

(3) Reference para. 6., O.C. "C" and "D" Coys. will each detail one Officer to report to the Area Commandant SEIGE JUNCTION at 10a.m. 6-4-18 who will allot billets and transport lines.

(4) The Transport Officer will detail one water cart to proceed with "C" Company. This will be for the use of both "C" and "D" Coys during the move.

                        (signed) A. Shanks.
                                 Capt. & Adjt.
                            1st Battalion, Machine Gun Corps.

Issued at 11-45p.m 5/4/18.

Issued to:-   (1) B. Coy.   (6) Transport Officer.
             (2) C. Coy.   (7) Quartermaster.
             (3) D. Coy.   (8) 36th Battn. M.G.C.
             (4) 1st Div. Q.   (9) File.
             (5) 3rd Bde.

SECRET.

1st BATTALION, MACHINE GUN CORPS.

OPERATION ORDER No.9.

Reference Sheet 28.N.W. 1/20,000.

(1) "B" Company will entrain tomorrow at PESELHOEK on Serial Train No. 1, leaving at 9a.m. Troops must arrive at Station at 8a.m.

(2) "B" Company will march to the Station independently, leaving TURCO CAMP at 4-30 a,m.

(3) H.Q's Mess Cart and "B" Coy's Kitchen will be at TURCO CAMP at 2-30a.m. and will start for PESELHOEK at 3-30a.m.. These vehicles, together with one water cart, will travel by the Omnibus Serial No. 1 Train leaving PESELHOEK at 9a.m.

(4) The vehicles must be at PESELHOEK Station at 6a.m.

(5) O.C."B" Company will detail an Officer to conduct these vehicles.

(6) Acknowledge.

          (signed) A. Shanks.
              Capt. & Adjt.
           1st Battalion, Machine Gun Corps.

Issued at 6-40p.m.

7th April, 1918.

Issued to :- (1) "B" Coy. (5) War Diary
     (2) Q.M.   (6) do.
     (3) Signal Officer (7) File
     (4) Medical " (8) File.

SECRET
REF. MAP. Sh 36B. 1/10,000

By Lieut. Col. Fedden DSO
Commanding 1st Batt. M.G. Corps.

1. D Coy of the 1st Batt. M.G.C. will relieve the Coy of the 55th Batt. M.G.C. now attached to the 2nd Inf. Bde. on the night of the 9/10th in the line.

2. Arrangements for relief will be made between Coy Commanders, subject subject to the approval of the G.O.C. 2nd Inf. Brigade.

3. H.Q. 2nd Inf. Bde. & the Coy of the 55th Batt. are at ANNEQUIN (F.29.C.3.3.)

8/4/18

H Joyce L.
for Capt & Adjt
1st Batt. M.G.C.

Issued at 8.10 pm
Copy No 1 2nd Inf. Bde.
       2 D Coy 1st Batt. M.G.C.
       3 1st Div. G
       4 1st Div. Q

To OC B Coy
      C Coy   1st Batt. M.G.C

SECRET

<u>Warning Order</u>

1. 32nd Inf. Bde. will be ordered to relieve 33rd Inf. Bde. of 11th Div. in present Left Sector 11th Div. Front, on 10th inst.

2. One detachment of 2.9 M.G.s will be required to relieve the M.G.s of 11th Div. in above Sector. Date of relief probably 11th inst.

3. This detachment will be provided by 14 guns B. Coy. and 14 guns C Coy. of the Batt.

4. Reconnaissances by all concerned will be carried out on the 9th inst.

5. H.Q. 32nd Inf. Bde. is at CHATEAU DES PRES, SAILLY LABOURSE F.27.d.2.8.

6. Detailed instructions will be issued later.

                                               A.E. Hawkes
                                               Capt. & Adjt.
                                               1st Batt. M.G.C

Copies to
<u>G.O.C. 32nd Inf. Bde.</u>

SECRET.   Copy No 17

REF. MAP. GORRE 1/10000.

1ST BATTALION MACHINE GUN CORPS ORDER No 10.

1. The 16 Guns of "C" Coy 55th Battn. M.G.C. now in position will be withdrawn to Coy. Headquarters on the night of the 15/16th inst. These guns will not be relieved but arrangements will be made for taking over the defence of the Bridge by the 3rd Division. The boxes of S.A.A. taken up to the ESSARS LOCALITY will be left there.

2. On the night of the 16/17th inst. the above guns will relieve the guns of "B" Coy. 55th Batt. M.G.C. in the FESTUBERT-LE-PLANTIN line under arrangements to be made by O.C. 55th Battn. M.G.C.

3. On the night of the 16/17th inst. "B" Coy. 1st Batt. M.G.C will relieve 14 Guns of "D" Coy. 55th Battn. in the line from BREWERY CORNER westwards. All the guns of "B" Coy are available for this relief except the 2 guns at VAUXHALL BRIDGE.
    The defence of the Bridge + the LE PREOL LOCALITY will be taken over by Lewis guns of the Tank Corps under arrangements to be issued later.

4. All details of Relief will be arranged between O.C. Corps concerned direct.

5. The 16 Guns of "C" Coy. 55th Battn. M.G.C. and the 14 Guns of "B" Coy. 1st Battn. M.G.C. above mentioned will be under the orders of G.O.C. 3rd Infantry Brigade to whom completion of relief will be reported.

6. Acknowledge.

                                                   [signature]
14/4/18. Issued at 10/45 p.m.   1st Bn M.G.C.

Issued to:-
1-4 A.B.C.D Coys 1st Batt M.G.C.   11. 1st Division "Q"
5. C. Coy. 55th Batt. M.G.C.   12. 2nd Infantry Brigade
6. 55th Batt. M.G.C.   13. 3rd Infantry Brigade
7. 53rd Division   14. Transport Officer
8. 3rd Battn. M.G.C.   15. Signalling
9. 3rd Division "G"   16. S.S.O.
                                           17/18. WAR DIARY
                                           19. File

SECRET.   COPY No 15

REF. MAP.

1ST BATTALION MACHINE GUN CORPS ORDER No 11.

1. On the night of the 17/18th inst. 'A' Coy. plus 2 guns of 'B' Coy. now at VAUXHALL BRIDGE will relieve the 18 guns under 'A' Coy. 55th Batt: M.G.C. at present in position about GIVENCHY.

2. All details of relief will be arranged between O.C. Coys. concerned direct.

3. The 2 guns of 'B' Coy. at VAUXHALL BRIDGE are placed under the orders of O.C. 'A' Coy. from the morning of the 17th inst. and their No 1 will be at his disposal to go into the line on the night 16/17th. The guns will be rationed by 'A' Coy for consumption on 18th inst. onwards.

4. 'B' Coy. will attach an Officer to 'A' Coy. to report to O.C. 'A' Coy. at 4.0 p.m. on 17th inst. at BREWERY GORRE.

5. The above 18 Guns will be under the Command of G.O.C. 1st Infantry Brigade to whom completion of relief will be reported.

6. ACKNOWLEDGE.

Issued at 12.15 p.m.
15/4/18.

                                           Shankright Adjt.
                                           1st Bn M G Corps.

Issued to :-

1-4. A.B.C & D Coys.   11. Transport Officer
5. 1st Infantry Bde.   12. Signalling "
6. 2nd "   "   13. Quartermaster
7. 1st Division 'G'   14/15. War Diary
8. 1st   "   'Q'   16. File.
9. 55th Division
10. S.S.O.

1st. Battn. MGC Operation Order 12

SECRET. Ref BETHUNE combined Sheet   Copy No. 4

1. On the night of 20/21st inst "C" Coy 1st Bn. MGCorps will relieve "B" Coy 55th Bn. MGC.
2. All details of relief will be arranged between OC Coys concerned direct.
3. The four guns of "C" Coy 1st Bn. MGC attached 6th Welsh Regt. will be withdrawn from BEUVRY during the evening of the 20th inst in order to effect this relief.
4. On relief "B" Coy. 55th Bn. will move to billets vacated by C Coy 1st Bn. at HESDIGNEUL reporting arrival to Battn HQ 1st Bn. Tram arrangements have been notified.
5. On completion of relief C Coy 1st Bn. MGCorps will come under the orders of 3rd Inf Bde to whom completion of relief will be reported.
6. Acknowledge.

Issued at 12 noon 20/4/18.

M Sharp Capt. A/Adjt.
1st Bn. MGCorps.

1. C Coy 1st Bn
2. C Coy 55 Bn
3. 1st Div G
4. — G
5. 3rd Inf Bde
6. 2M
7. Sig Offr.
8. 2O
9. 3rd Bn MGC
10. 55 Bn MGC
11. SSO
12. A Coy 1st Bn
13. B Coy 1st Bn
14. War Diary
15. —
16. File
17. —

1ST BATTN. M.G. CORPS.
ORDER NO. 13

Copy No. 10

SECRET.

Ref. Map - BETHUNE combined Sheet

1. "C" Coy 55th Bn. M.G.Corps will move today by lorries to HURIONVILLE and will rejoin 55th Bn M.G.Corps on arrival there.
2. Motor Lorries to convey the Coy. to HURIONVILLE will be at the road junction at E.25.d.4.9. at 2pm today.
3. Acknowledge.

Grant, Capt. & Adjt.
1st Battalion
M.G.Corps.

Issued at 10.50am 21/4/18 to

1. C.Coy 53 Bn
2. 55 Bn M.G.C.
3. 1st Division
4. —
5. S.S.O
6. Transport Off
7. 2 i/c
8. Sig Officer
9. War Diary
10. —
11. File
12. —

SECRET

1st BATTALION M.G. CORPS.
AMENDMENT No. 1 TO OPERATION ORDER NO. 14.

Copy No. 10

Para. 2. for "night 22/23rd April 1918"
read "night 23/24th April 1918"

A. Shanks
Capt & Adjutant
1st Battalion
M.G. Corps.

Issued at 8 pm 23/4/18 to

All recipients of 1st Battalion Machine Gun Corps Order No. 14.

SECRET.

1ST BATTN. MACHINE GUN CORPS.

ORDER NO. 112.

Copy No. 11

BETHUNE Map (combined Sheet)

1. The 166th Infantry Bde is relieving the 3rd Infantry Bde in the line on the night of the 21st/22nd April 1918.

2. "D" Coy 55 Bn M.G.C. will relieve "B" Coy 1st Bn M.G.C. on the night of the 21st/22nd April 1918 and will come under the orders of the 166th Infantry Bde. to whom completion of relief will be reported.

3. On relief of the 3rd Infantry Bde. "B" Coy less two guns and "C" Coy 1st Bn. M.G.C. will come in action on front of 166th Infy Bde.

4. All arrangements for relief will be made between Company Commanders direct.

5. Team transport will probably be provided under arrangements to be notified later.

6. The transport of "D" Coy 55 Bn M.G.C. will move by road to join the transport of 1st Battalion at D 30. central on the 22nd April 1918.

7. On relief "B" Coy. 1st Bn M.G.C. will move to HERDIGNEUL.

8. ACKNOWLEDGE

A. Newton
Capt. & Adjutant,
1st Battalion,
M.G. Corps.

Issued at 5 pm 21/4/18
Copies to:-

1. D Coy 55 Bn. M.G.C.
2. 55th Bn. M.G.C.
3. B Coy 1st Bn. M.G.C.
4. 166th Inf. Bde.
5. 1st Division "G"
6. — " — "Q"
7. Quartermaster
8. Signalling Offr.
9. Transport Officer
10. War Diary
11. —
12. File
13. —
14. — S.S.O.
15. — O.C. "A" Coy 1st Bn
16. — O.C. "C" Coy 1st Bn
17. — O.C. "D" Coy 1st Bn

1st BATTALION MACHINE GUN CORPS

ORDER No. 15

No. 14

Map (reference sheet)
Map

1. ... Bn. ... pos less 2 guns will relieve
   ... Bn. M.G.C. less 2 guns on the line
   ... /24th April 1918.

2. ... M.G.C. will arrive at GORRE
   ... between 8 and 8.30 p.m. "C" Coy 1st Batt
   M.G.C. will find guides at GORRE BREWERY
   for the following at 8.0 p.m.
        FESTUBERT   T.I.
        FEST ...   M.G.V.9.
   and guides to ... Headquarters.

3. Tripods and ... will be
   handed over ... will be
   brought ...

4. On relief ... 1st Bn. M.G.C. will proceed
   to billets ... d by D Coy 55th Bn. M.G.C.
   in LABOURSE by motor lorries. Lorries to
   convey the company will be at F.19.b.
   at 1 a.m. 24th inst.

5. Gun limbers, S.A.A. limbers and Field Kitchens
   ... Coy ... will move to the LABOURSE
   ...

6. ... of relief "B" Coy 55th ... will
   ... orders of G.O.C. 16 Inf Bde
   ... on completion of relief will ...
   Coy, 1st Bn. will report completion ...
   ... 1st Battn. H.Q. by ... the ...
   message "your A.S.112 received"

7. ACKNOWLEDGE

   ...
   ... Battalion Machine
   Gun Corps.

Issued at 8.30 ... to

1. A Coy 1st Bn. M.G.C.   9. 1st Divn. Q
2. B   10. Engr. Offr.
3. C   11. Transport Offr.
4. D   12. I.S.O.
5. E   13. War Diary
6.   14. ...
7. 1st ... Bn.   15. File
8. 1st Divn. G   16. ...

SECRET

1ST BATTALION, MACHINE GUN CORPS

OPERATION ORDER NO. 16.

Copy No. 15

Reference GORRE Map, Sheet 1/20,000

(1)   The 1st Infantry Brigade will be relieved tonight 23/24th April 1918 by 164th Infantry Brigade in the GIVENCHY Section.
On completion of this relief the 18 guns in this section will come under the orders of the relieving Brigade.

(2)   "A" Company, 1st Battalion, Machine Gun Corps plus 2 guns will be relieved by "A" Company, 55th Battalion, Machine Gun Corps plus 2 guns in the GIVENCHY Section on night 24/25th instant.

(3)   All details of relief will be arranged direct between Officers Commanding Companies concerned.

(4)   Tripods and 14 belt boxes per gun will be handed over. All surplus belt boxes will be brought out.

(5)   On completion of relief "A" Company, 1st Battalion, Machine Gun Corps plus 2 guns will proceed to billets to be notified later. Means of Transport will be notified later.

(6)   Acknowledge.

Capt. & Adjt.
1st Battalion, Machine
Gun Corps.

Issued at 9 p.m. 23/4/18.

Copies issued to:-
(1) "A" Coy. 1st Bn. M.G.C.
(2) "B" Coy. 1st Bn. M.G.C.
(3) "C" Coy. 1st Bn. M.G.C.
(4) "D" Coy. 1st Bn. M.G.C.
(5) 55th Battn. M.G.C.
(6) 164th Infantry Brigade
(7) 1st Division "G"
(8) 1st Division "Q"
(9) 1st Infantry Brigade
(10) S.S.O.
(11) Quartermaster
(12) Signalling Officer
(13) Transport Officer
(14) War Diary
(15) War Diary
(16) File
(17) File

SECRET   Copy No. 14

1ST BATTALION, MACHINE GUN CORPS.

OPERATION ORDER NO. 17.

Reference BETHUNE Map, Combined Sheet.

(1)　　The 3rd Infantry Brigade is relieving the 32nd Infantry Brigade in the HOHENZOLLERN Section on the night 24/25th April.
　　　Brigade Headquarters, CHATEAU DES PRES, SAILLY LABOURSE.

(2)　　The 1st Battalion, Machine Gun Corps is relieving 26 machine guns of the 11th Battalion, Machine Gun Corps in the HOHENZOLLERN Section on the night 25/26th April.
　　　Upon completion of relief these guns will come under the orders of the B.G.C. 3rd Infantry Brigade, to whom, as well as to H.Q. 1st Battn. M.G.C. completion of relief will be reported by the code word "TIGER".

(3)　　"C" Company, 1st Battn. M.G.C. will relieve 16 guns of and 2 German Guns of "D" Company, 11th Battn. M.G.C. (Headquarters, ARLEQUIN HOUSE) and "B" Company, 1st Battn. Machine Gun Corps will relieve 10 guns of "A" Company, 11th Battn. M.G.C. (Headquarters, NOYELLES, L.17.b.40.85)

(4)　　All details of relief will be arranged between Company Commanders concerned direct.

(5)　　Lists of Trench Stores and Iron Rations taken over, will be forwarded to Battalion Headquarters.

(6)　　Acknowledge.

　　　　　　　　　　　　　　　　　　　　　Capt. & Adjt.
　　　　　　　　　　　　　　　　　　　　　1st Battalion, Machine
　　　　　　　　　　　　　　　　　　　　　　　Gun Corps.

Issued at 12 noon 24/4/18

Copies issued to:-　(1) "A" Company, 1st Bn. M.G.C.
　　　　　　　　　　(2) "B" Company,　　-do-
　　　　　　　　　　(3) "C" Company,　　-do-
　　　　　　　　　　(4) "D" Company,　　-do-
　　　　　　　　　　(5) 11th Battn. M.G.C.
　　　　　　　　　　(6) 3rd Infantry Brigade
　　　　　　　　　　(7) 1st Division "G"
　　　　　　　　　　(8) 1st Division "Q"
　　　　　　　　　　(9) R.S.O.
　　　　　　　　　　(10) Quartermaster
　　　　　　　　　　(11) Transport Officer
　　　　　　　　　　(12) Signalling Officer
　　　　　　　　　　(13) War Diary
　　　　　　　　　　(14) War Diary
　　　　　　　　　　(15) File
　　　　　　　　　　(16) File

SECRET

1st. BATTN. MACHINE GUN CORPS.
OPERATION ORDER No. 18.

Copy No. 15

Reference BETHUNE map, combined sheet.

1. On the afternoon of 29th/30th inst. "A" Coy. less 6 guns will relieve "B" Coy. less 6 guns in the HOHENZOLLERN section.

2. All details of relief will be arranged by O's C Coys concerned direct.

3. On relief "B" Coy. will proceed to billets in BARLIN.

4. Trams will be provided under arrangements to be notified later.

5. On completion of relief "A" Coy. less 6 guns will come under the orders of G.O.C. 3rd Infy. Bde. to whom completion of relief will be reported. Completion of relief will be reported to Battn. HQ using code message. Your A.S.15 received.

6. Acknowledge.

Brent.
Capt. & Adjt.
1st Battalion, Machine
Gun Corps.

Issued at 10.a.m 28/4/18

Copies issued to:
(1) "A" Coy
(2) "B" Coy
(3) "C" Coy
(4) "D" Coy
(5) 3rd Infy. Bde.
(6) 1st Div. "G"
(7) —"— "Q"
(8) S.S.O.
(9) Q.M.
(10) Sigs. Officer
(11) Transport Offr.
(12) War Diary
(13) —"—
(14) File
(15) —"—

Copy 16 to B Coy Details

Action of "C" Company, 1st Battalion, Machine Gun Corps, when attached to 166th Brigade 55th Division, on April 9th and days following.

April 9th.

The Germans attacked on a wide front and broke through North of FESTUBERT. "C" Company under Captain F.G.GURNEY was ordered to join the 166th Brigade during the morning and proceeded from LE QUESNOY to LE HAMEL arriving there about midday. This Company was loaned to the 55th Division to replace one of their Companies then in process of being relieved. The Brigadier had decided to hold the line of the small canal running in front of LES GLATIGNIES at all costs and also if possible to hold MESPLAUX FARM and LES FACONS, 700 yards in front of this Canal. The farm in 9.c. central was also being held. His right was fairly secure but he had few troops to hold the above sector. His guns were at once disposed as shown on the plan A.

On the following morning (10th April) at 11.15 a.m. a heavy enemy barrage was put down on our localities followed by an attack on MESPLAUX FARM. This was driven back by the R.E. personnel and the guns holding the farm, assisted by the two guns at X.14.d. 5. 9. each of which fired two belts at parties crossing their front. It was determined during the afternoon to move two guns forward to the farm in 9.c. central. where a gap had occurred. They were accordingly moved up at night under 2/Lieut.P.MARKS from MESPLAUX FARM and took up positions in front of that farm.

At 11.30 a.m. the next morning (11th April) the enemy put down a barrage and attacked again. The two forward guns inflicted heavy casualties. One of them was overwhelmed and lost but the other under Sergeant Black, who was wounded managed to withdraw after turning round and firing to the rear to clear a way through the enemy who had got behind it. The men reported that many of the Germans attacking them were drunk.

The attack on MESPLAUX FARM was again renewed at 2 p.m. The Infantry Officers here were all either killed or wounded. 2/Lieut.P.MARKS organised some infantry and rushed a gun up to the neighbourhood of X.14.b. central to fill a gap. Two guns were at the same time thrown forward from the Canal Bank line under 2/Lieut.F.BARKER to come into action at LES FACONS. This Officer with a Corporal reconnoitred through the garden of the farm where there were a few infantry and then signalled to his guns to come up successively. They got into action at 3.30 and 4.p.m. respectively among the buildings (not shown on the map) east of the road at about 15.c.8.8. Here they at once got targets. First a German machine gun firing from a haystack 200 yards off was engaged and silenced. The gun was afterwards brought in with a half expended belt in it. The ammunition boxes were riddled with bullets and the gunner was dead beside it. After that the targets consisted of parties of about twenty of the enemy coming across the open in file at about 600 yards distance making for a wood at about 15.a.0.9. where they were trying to assemble. Each gun fired about 10,000 rounds and certainly inflicted very large casualties from time to time, searching the wood in which the enemy were trying to mass. 2/Lieut.F.BARKER had obtained a Lewis Gun and was up in the loft of a barn, on either side of which were his gun positions. He was able to observe and direct the fire of his guns besides doing some firing himself. The enemy's attempts to attack continued till dark after which he tried a bombing raid, but was in all cases completely repulsed by rifle and machine gun fire. During the night the guns were moved forward to a trench in front of the farm.

On the following day (12th April) the enemy again attempted to advance at this point in small parties of 5 but was again stopped. More infantry had now been brought into the line, and it was decided that 5 guns forward would be sufficient. The dispositions were therefore rearranged as in Map B. three of the guns and one spare gun being kept in reserve. A fine opportunity was obtained of firing on parties of the enemy running out of houses that were being shelled by our artillery.

There were no further attacks, and the Company was relieved on the 14th April.

The total casualties during this period were 1 Officer and 30 Other Ranks. One gun was lost and one destroyed by shellfire.

Report of O.C. "B" Company, 1st Battalion, Machine Gun Corps
of operations from the 16th to 18th April, 1918.

16-4-18. Situation quiet. "B" Company (less two guns at A.14.a.0000) relieved by Lewis Guns of 11th Battalion Tank Corps. On relief "B" Coy. relieved 14 guns of "D" Coy. 55th Battalion M.G.C. in FESTUBERT sector. Gun positions as follows :-

BREWERY GROUP (2nd Lieut. EDGELL)
    1 gun at S.26.a.0.7. (CAILLOUX KEEP.S.)
    1 " " S.20.c.0.1. (" " N.)
    1 " " S.25.a.7.8. (On the flank)
    1 " " S.25.a.6.7.   do.
Section Headquarters S.25.a.7.6.

Two guns at ROUTE A KEEP S.29.b.7.8. under Lieut. Wadley. Section Headquarters, S.29.b.7.8.

Two guns at ROUTE E KEEP S.29.d.9.2. under 2nd Lieut. Booth. Section Headquarters S.29.b.22 7.8.

Six guns in TUNING FORK LINE under 2nd Lieut. Grant,
    1 gun at X.29.c.1.9.
    1 gun at X.29.c.2.8.
    1 gun at X.29.c.1.6.
    1 gun at X.29.c.1.5.
    1 gun at X.29.c.1.3.
    1 gun at X.29.c.1.2.
Section Headquarters at X S.28.d.9.1.

Company Headquarters at GORRE BREWERY, F.3.a.Central, Transport at GOSNAY (Reference Maps GORRE 1/20,000 & BETHUNE combined sheet 1/40,000)

17-4-18. Situation very quiet. Prisoner taken at CAILLOUX KEEP stated that the 4th ERSATZ Division was going to attack within the next 48 hours. The two left guns in TUNING FORK moved to positions in LOISNE KEEP (X.22.b.9. Reference Map GORRE 1/20,000. All guns were warned of the impending attack and careful preparations were made to meet it, all sentries being particularly alert. A large amount of S.A.A. was available at each position.

18-4-18. At 4-15a.m. the enemy opened a steady bombardment of front and back areas with shells and trench mortars of all calibres, a large amount of gas being used. This continued until about 7a.m. when the shelling of the front system became intense but quietened down considerably in the back areas. Casualties as a result of the bombardment were 1 Officer and 4 Other ranks. The action of the guns was as follows:-

CAILLOUX KEEP (4 guns, 2nd Lt. Edgell). The intense bombardment lasted here until 8-45 a.m. the barrage then lifting about 500 yards. At 8-50a.m. the enemy could be seen advancing through the smoke and dust in dense masses. The original attack developed from the direction of the road in X.24.d. The two left flank guns opened rapid fire at a range of 800 yards on the enemy as he emerged from the trees on to the road running S.E. in S.19.d. He did not press an attack on the left flank but continued to cross our front along the road running through 19.d. and 20.c. Here they came within a range of 600 yards of the CAILLOUX KEEP N. gun which opened fire and poured six belts into them in rapid succesion before they were able to deploy. The enemy then opened out and attemped to work round our right flank. The gun at CAILLOUX KEEP S. was now able to get into action at 600 yards range and the attempt definitely stopped. By now ROUTE A KEEP had been lost and the left gun put out of action by shell fire. The enemy was thus enabled to advance more easily and pushed troops through in large numbers on our left flank. Reinforcements had now come up on the N.E. and were pressing the attack with great vigour on our front and right flank thus enveloping the guns on three sides. From now onwards all three guns were continuously in action. Owing to the enormous shell craters their field of fire was considerably masked so the guns had to frequently change their positions to take on the targets as they presented themselves. The gun at CAILLOUX KEEP N changed its position no less than 8 times during the fighting. As the action proceeded the enemy endeavoured to push forward

his light machine guns and considerably harrassed our guns by snipers who crept forward and fired from shellholes picking off six of our Nos. 1 & 2. These were however all successfully engaged and no enemy machine gun was allowed to come into action. About 11 a.m. the attack subsided somewhat but the enemy still tried to push forward by breaking up into small groups, though now with less ardour. About 11-30 a,m. the enemy appeared to realise the futility of his efforts and threw off his equipment and in spite of the efforts of Officers and N.C.O's who could be seen trying to rally them, they began to run in all directions thoroughly demoralised and finally retired in disorder. A few snipers still remained but these were taken on by the infantry, whilst our guns raising their sights to 1000 yards followed the beaten enemy in his retreat and increased the toll of casualties. During the engagement the guns fired 30,000 rounds every shot at a target. In addition everyone, Officers, Batmen, runners and spare numbers, used rifles freely and materially assisted by their fire in stemming the attack. Every assistance was given by the infantry who realising that everything depended upon the machine guns devoted their main energy to keeping them going. Their assistance in filling belts, bringing up ammunition, observing and indicating targets was invaluable. That the enemy suffered a heavy defeat at this point is evidenced by the fact that for 36 hours afterwards he was continually carrying in his wounded and burning and burying his dead. The casualties inflicted by the four guns are computed to easily to have run into four figures.
ROUTE A KEEP. (2 guns. Lieut.R.C.Wadley) and TUNING FORK E KEEP (2 guns 2nd Lieut. J.H.Booth. These two KEEPS were not subjected to very fire until about 8 a.m. when they were exposed to the full force of the enemy barrage. Almost at once the dug-out of the left gun at ROUTE A KEEP was blown in, three of the team and the ammunition being buried. After about one hour of intense shelling the infantry, after suffering heavy casualties, were withdrawn from ROUTE A KEEP to the TUNING FORK swith line. The No. 1 on the right gun was then killed and the gun knocked out. Corpl. Duchars, although wounded, took out the lock and the team and the left gun were withdrawn to the TUNING FORM swithh line. Meantime E KEEP had been heavily barraged. Almost the first shell had blown in the dig-out of Lt. Booth and rendered him unconcious. He was moved to another dug-out which was also blown in and there left for dead. Owing to the intense shellfire the infantry ordered a withdrawal to the TUNING FORK switch line where the guns came under the orders of Lieut. Wadley. The teams were rearranged and when the barrage lifted off E KEEP the infantry and machine guns returned. ROUTE A KEEP was by this time occupied by the enemy. The guns were got into action and excellent targets were obtained on the right and left of A KEEP. As a large amount of ammunition had been blown Pts. Holloway and Wilkinson were sent down for more. It was taken up under a heavy barrage by Corpl. Foster. The guns were effective in stopping the enemy debouching from A KEEP and advancing on the flanks. About 5,000 rounds were fired by these guns.

19-4-18. Situation quiet, very little shelling. 2nd Lt. S.R.Brant buried at GORRE Cemetry 20-4-18. 1st South Wales Borderers made a counter attack with the object of retaking ROUTE A KEEP. The attack was successful and two guns from ROUTE E were put in position there. The guns at LOISNE KEEP also co-operated. No. 16999 Corpl. Foster A volunteered to take the two teams into position. Lieut. R.C.WADLEY was wounded about 9 p.m. whilst visiting his guns at ROUTE A KEEP.
21-4-18. Fairly quiet day. Enemy artillery rather active during evening. We took over two guns of "C" Company in GORRE WOOD. "C" Company relieved our two guns at WINDY CORNER.
22-4-18. Enemy successfully attacked ROUTE A KEEP and remained in possession. Two gun teams either killed or taken prisoner. Enemy attack took place about 4 a,m. At 8 p,m. our guns at GORRE WOOD and two guns from TUNING FORK LINE co-operated in "CHINESE" attack on ROUTE A KEEP. They fired 12,000 round indirect fire on ROUTE A KEEP from the GORRE WOOD positions. The infantry attack at midnight was unsuccessful.
23-4-18. Company relieved in line by "D" Company 55th Battalion M.G.C. On relief Company proceeded to billets in HEBDIGNEUL.

Report of O.C.Company FESTUBERT and LE PLANTIN
positions, of second attack on FESTUBERT and
GIVENCHY, April 18th, 1918.

At 4-15a.m. 18/4/18 the enemy opened a bombardment on the whole front line system. This bombardment was particularly severe and carried out with all calibre guns including some very heavy pieces. It continued for about 2 hours. The machine guns of "C" Company 25th Battalion, M.G.C. attached to the First Division were as shown on the attached map. The general policy of employment which had been impressed on all Officers and men throughout the Company was to "place no faith in loopholes. All concrete pill-boxes were to be used only as shelters from shellfire. Two men were to be ready to instantly leave the pill-box when the shelling would allow, or when enemy were sighted and to mount the gun on a previously prepared spot adjacent to the pill-box where if possible an allround traverse could be obtained and where there was a certain amount of protection from rifle fire. In many instances a shellhole was found to be the most satisfactory and easily adapted for that purpose by the construction of a gun platform inside the hole. In every case where employed the above policy was found to be most satisfactory way of dealing with the situation. The men showed no hesitation in leaving the shelters when the occasion arose to do so.

The morning of the 18th was dull and hazy and visibility was poor. It was noticed, however, that the German steel helmets were very conspicuous appearing almost white. The enemy did not wear cloth helmet covers. It was also noticed that the enemy advanced to the attack wearing full pack which was found to contain liberal rations, including two loaves of bread per man. The German infantry were dressed in new clothes. When first sighted he appeared in orderly formation of blobs of 8 to 12 men which presented admirable targets. The German infantry although repeatedly shot down persisted in their endeavour to advance and in front of FESTUBERT did not desist until fighting had been in progress for over 2½ hours. The pillboxes of reinforced concrete were found to be of great value as shelters, one of them (M.G.V.10) surviving two direct hits from fairly heavy (probably 5.9's) shells.

Action of Guns.

Lewis. 5. Enemy first sighted coming from "O.B.Line" and working southwards towards GIVENCHY. He presented good targets and was soon stopped.
Lewis. 4. Enemy first seen direct front and to left front of gun making for "VILLAGE LINE". Large numbers were seen to fall and survivors to throw down their packs and run back to the "O.B.Line" some running for protection to the ditch near YELLOW ROAD. At about 8 a.m. the enemy were seen in LE PLANTIN on the left of the gun position crossing the FESTUBERT-WINDY CORNER ROAD. The gun was taken on to the road and fired with effect on the enemy who then turned and endeavoured to get back to the "O.B.Line". On his return journey he again came under the fire of this gun.
M.G.V.7. This gun worked in conjunction with Lewis. 6. The enemy were seen to the direct front, some moving southwards, the majority making towards LE PLANTIN. These latter were being fired on when an enemy machine gun opened fire on the team. The enemy gun was observed firing from the "O.B.Line". The gun commander immediately engaged it and after a sharp duel silenced it. During this duel a traversing handle of our gun was shot away. Later this gun came under rifle fire from the direction of M.G.V.7.a. and the enemy were observed on the road behind this position. (Lewis. 4 then moved as above)
M.G.V.7.a. This gun was in position slightly in front of the "VILLAGE LINE". Very few infantry were in the vicinity of the gun. The enemy succeeded in reaching the gun and later investigation showed signs of a sharp hand to hand fight. Two of the team were found dead in the emplacement and a third badly wounded was found a few yards away. A large pile of empty cartridge cases and some German bombs were also found. Our bomb boxes were empty and the gun was missing.
M.G.V.8. The enemy were first seen on the south side of FESTUBERT in the vicinity of BARNTON ROAD advancing S.W. in parties of 8 or 10. They were effectively dealt with. Later enemy was seen in large numbers in the Orchard on the right of the gun (approx.A.2.c.60.40.) where he appeared to be digging in.

Many were seen to go into the house at A.2.c.40.70. An Infantry Officer asked if this gun could assist him in clearing the Orchard and House of the enemy. For this the gun was taken to a position nearer the Orchard from where it fired into the Orchard. Later the infantry cleared up the Orchard and House. Those of the enemy who endeavoured to regain their line were shot down by this gun. Seven prisoners were taken. The gun then returned to its position. Throughout this fight very good targets were presented.

M.G.V.S.2. Early in the morning of the 18th a heavy shell struck this emplacement completely burying the gun. It was, however, soon dug out and was found to be undamaged. It was then taken to V.S. position and fired in conjunction with V.S. on enemy near FESTUBERT.

Post. 2. From this position the enemy were first seen advancing from the "O.B.Line" towards BARNTON ROAD Trench and VILLAGE LINE. It was impossible to engage the enemy from the emplacement and the gun was taken forward about 50 yards into the Churchyard. The enemy were now about 300 to 400 yards from the gun and were advancing in orderly groups. The gun fired with very good effect. Later enemy endeavoured to work his way down BARNTON Trench. This trench had been completely blown away for about 10 yards at A.2.b.10.55. Post 2. with other guns obtained excellent targets here. A number of the enemy had already succeeded in occupying BARNTON Trench and these deployed Northwards jumping into shell-holes which they started to consolidate.

Post.1. Enemy first seen about A.2.a.30.30, and the gun was moved to approx. A.1.b.70.70, where they could be seen jumping into BARNTON Trench moving towards WILLOW Road. They were here fired on at a range of 400 yards. The enemy was very persistent in his endeavour to reach the FESTUBERT Road between BARNTON Road and WILLOW Road, and the gun was in action for over 3½ hours during which time it accounted for large numbers of the enemy.

Post.3. Kept in original position to protect left flank of FESTUBERT. Very few of the enemy were seen here. Later, during the afternoon, the emplacement was knocked in by shell-fire burying the gun and 3 men which, despite repeated efforts, it was impossible to recover. A new gun was procured and placed in position at approx. X.30.d.05.55.

Post. East Keep. The Keep was subjected to a sharp and concentrated bombardment. The machine gun here was not heard firing during the action and it is believed to have been destroyed by shellfire. The complete team are missing. A new gun was procured and placed in position at approx. A.1.b.85.85.

M.G.V.10.a. Enemy first seen near Post. East Keep moving obliquely in file. Plenty of cover for enemy here. He appeared to dig in. Soon after sighting enemy this gun was hit by a shell fragment.

M.G.V.10. Gun in emplacement firing due North. No enemy seen in this direction, and the gun was taken out to V.10.a. and directed on enemy at Post. East Keep. The left flank being protected by Post. 3., V.10. moved to replace V. 10.a.

M.G.V. 9. Enemy first seen making towards BARNTON Trench in short rushes. This gun fired from its loophole on to very good targets. After continuous firing it was found that owing to the cordite fumes filling the emplacement the No. 1 became exhausted and partially gassed. The No. 2 was completely overcome by the fumes and was resuscitated with difficulty. This gun was then sent to V.10.position.

M.G.V.9.a. Enemy first seen around Post. East Keep and moving across front of gun. Progress of enemy soon stopped and he appeared to dig in behind debris.

Serre 1 and 2. Throughout action obtained no view of the enemy.

Report of O.C. "A" Company, 1st Battalion, Machine Gun Corps
of operations from the 18th to the 24th April 1918.

18/4/18. Heavy bombardment was opened against our front at 4.25 a.m. followed shortly after dawn by an enemy attack in force. Heavy fighting continued throughout the day. The attack was repulsed. The two guns under 2/Lieut. MELVILLE in the pill-box at A.9.c.30.91 and A.9.c.26.87. were forced to retire owing to fumes. Sergeant Grant got the guns and team outside the pill-box where they did great execution with both guns and rifles. It can be said that no Germans got past this point. The guns in MOAT FARM under Lieut. ROHDE and Lieut. Merville at A.9.c.22.65 and A.9.c.18.71 did well; again the use of rifles was a feature of the defence. The forward gun under Sergt. Waddie at A.9.c.75.84 was never in touch and the whole team is missing. The gun to the right at A.9.c.85.34. was forced to withdraw with the infantry to GIVENCH KEEP at A.9.c.6.4. and was not in touch with Lieut. Rohde. Further to the South the gun at SIDBURY HILL A.14.b.81.68 had little to do owing to the defence in front, and this was the same with the four guns at PONT FIXE A.14.b.10.24., A.14.b.21.30, A.14.b.42.27 and A.14.b.47.25. The four guns on the South side of the Canal A.15.c.29.62 A.15.c.73.55., A.15.c.78.54. and A.15.c.83.53. had wonderful targets and did splendid work under Lieut. Lowdon. The casualties were 10 wounded; one died of wounds, one Officer slightly wounded who remained at duty. Loss of guns - one gun complete. The same evening the counter attack was made at 7-30p.m. which did not materially alter the position. Reinforcements and Guns with rations arrived at 11-50p.m. per PONT FIXE and by the night of 18th/19th, which was fairly quiet the gun teams and positions were ready for any further work.

19-4-18. Touch was obtained with Corpl. WAUGH in the GIVENCH KEEP but all search failed to find anything of Sergt. WALDIE. It was not considered advisable by Brigade to replace this gun and the front line of defence was left as follows :- Pillbox- MOAT FARM - GIVENCHY KEEP - CANAL LINE. At 3-30p.m. 2nd Lieut. SHEAD was selected to take the four guns from PONT FIXE with the second wave of the Northants. and consolidate the position. These arrangements were perfected and two guns were sent up from Battalion to replace those at PONT FIXE. Casualties, 1 wounded, 5 missing 20-4-18. The barrage started at 4-24 a.m. The guns advanced with the second wave a part of which actually gained the objective before the first wave. Corpl. USHER in charge of the two right flank guns was the first man in the objective after an Officer of the Northants. After gaining the objective the No.1 carrying a tripod became a casualty. Corpl. USHER returned for it leaving his team to consolidate. Being badly sniped at he tied a wire to the tripod and crawled back to his position, pulling the tripod behind him. On arriving at his position he found the had had to take cover; he got them out and the gun into action; further than that he kept Lieut. SHEAD and ourselves at forward H.Q. fully in touch, so that later in the day when the gun and positions had been blown in we were able to replace with guns and S.A.A. etc.. During the advance the gun on the extreme left was blown up so that we only got three guns at the objective. Casualties, 3 killed - one died of wounds, 2 wounded. At 5-25p.m. the O.C. Battalion visited Company Headquarters at GORRE BREWERY, F.3.c.Central. As many reliefs as possible were sent up and 2nd Lieut. BERRA relieved 2nd Lieut. JAMES of "B" Coy. during the night.

21-4-18. Further reports of casualties arrived as follows :- 4 wounded 2 remained at duty. Telephone lines were mended and connected to PONT FIXE. At 12-40 p.m. the latest news reference our front line was mapped and passed on to each Officer. Relief of teams was arranged where possible and the two teams of "B" Coy. under 2nd Lieut. BERRA were relieved by two teams of "C" Coy. at WINDY CORNER. A German gun was mounted and manned here, and another at the pillbox at A.9.c.20.91., also a Lewis Gun was salved and brought into action by Lieut. ROHDE at MOAT FARM.

22-4-18. The position of the them forward guns under 2nd Lieut. SHEAD had to be changed. One was put in at HALF MOON STREET. Another at UPPER CUT, while the third was withdrawn to the end of CALEDONIAN ROAD near GIVENCHY KEEP A.9.c.40.50. The feature of operations to date was the help in regard to carrying parties, filling belts, and protection given by the Infantry Battalions. It is regretted that we had three casualties amongst the carriers of the Northants. allotted to us. The Brigade decided to withdraw the two forward guns at UPPER CUT and HALF MOON STREET and to mount them at a second line East and West of LONE FARM at A.7.d.40.45. and F.12.c.90.45., the change to take place at midnight 22nd/23rd April, 1918. One gun remained at CALEDONIAN ROAD IN charge of Lieut. ROHDE and the two LONE FARM guns came under the command of 2nd Lieut. BERRA at WINDY CORNER.

23-4-18. General situation was good. Warning order for relief arrived. Crosses for the killed were made and sent up.

24-4-18. The Company was relieved by a Company of the 55th Battalion M.G.C. and proceeded to billets at BARLIN. Relief carried out successfully.

SUMMARY OF OPERATIONS.

We went into the line with 16 guns of our own and two of "B" Company. We lost four guns from which were replaced and our casualties were 31 Other Ranks.

WAR DIARY
or
INTELLIGENCE SUMMARY.

(Erase heading not required.)

Army Form C. 2118.

Place	Date	Hour	Summary of Events and Information	Remarks and references to Appendices.
BARLIN K.32.d.	1/5/18		Situation normal. Routine drill. Some rounds of hostile artillery fire brought down.	JK
"	2/5/18		Situation normal. Training drills & HV firing. Situation fair, quiet but for enemy LV fire operating on BARLIN. EA active throughout the day.	JK
"	3/5/18		Situation normal. Carrying out firing training. Good aimed & effective EA work. RA Fire yellow	JK
"	4/5/18		Relief by 4 coys 2nd Bn MGC took place as programmed. Lt McCOMBS OC "A" Coy. 2/Lt McHEWINS OC "B" Coy relieved. "D" Coy relieved "C" Coy at BARLIN	Appendices JK
"	5/5/18		Situation normal. Routine duties. During day B Coy relieved Lts at Villers au Bois and DINCHY A214.	JK
"	6/5/18		Situation normal. Whole battery took over PONTFIXE, A142 and DINCHY A214. ARNEQUIN, PONTFIXE. ARNEQUIN, ARNEQUIN POINTS Nos R212, K15 & N10 E2 carrying our own over 19 SAGGEE CONTROL lower. Wounded damaged with rifle fire over ground to CRASH N.5 Cent.	JK
"	7/5/18		Situation normal. Operating still could aimed firing during daylight hours. SINP SR ELMOR & Cpl HOWE have been posted to "D" Coy and W. HARRISS to "B" Coy. Hostile artillery active on village line.	JK
"	8/5/18		Situation quiet. No enemy attempt to enfilade work on ridges R. A. Coy moved to SAILLY LA BOURSE. Units relieved of by Inf and D Coy moved to Billets at NIEUX 155 Kms as arranged. Opn Order No 20 as to relief by D Coy cancelled.	Appendices JK
"	9/5/18		Situation normal in the line. Further change and re-billeting took place at BART'S BATTERY S.22 c. 8 carried out under of Brgdr Brev Two Guns of A Coy at BART'S BATTERY in section to cover a field by 11th Div.	JK
"	10/5/18		Situation normal. Slight enemy shelling but no casualties. Further firing carried out by regiment. 2/Lt 7m HEYLAND D.S.O. taken over in charge of the Regt Coy at 14=45	JK
"			BARDERLAND took over of the 28th in place of the 3rd Inf Regt from the 8th Batt.	JK
"	11/5/18		Situation completed. Light artillery fire. Some enemy artillery found out by evening found well defensive	JK

WAR DIARY or INTELLIGENCE SUMMARY

Army Form C. 2118.

Place	Date	Hour	Summary of Events and Information	Remarks and references to Appendices
BARLIN	1/5/18		Lt SMYTH Gloucester Regt apptd to M.G.C.	
K.52.d.	14/5/18		Situation normal. Harassing fire burst & set by enemy on our wire & infantry	
"	15/5/18		Situation normal. Hostile retaliatory shells on VERMELLES & CUINCHY after our Stokes shelled HOHENZOLLERN with Thermite bombs	
"	16/5/18		Situation normal. British retaliatory shells on NOEUX LES MINES Etal Major K.9.21	Appendix A.
"	17/5/18		Situation normal. British retaliatory shells on Enemy messengering trench. Weather fine with good visibility	
"	18/5/18		Situation normal. Weather fine with good visibility	
"	19/5/18		Situation normal. Weather fine with good visibility. M.C's awarded to 79th R.C. WADLEY, 3/Lt A.H.EDGELL, G.S.SHEAD, R.S.MELVILLE. D.C.M. awarded to No. 1793 Sgt HAYNES & 22802 Cpl J.USSHER	
"	10/5/18		Situation normal. Alterations carried out in disposition of guns.	Appendix 1 & 2.
"	17/5/18		Situation normal. B Coy relieved by C Coy in CAMBRIN Sector & proceeded to billets in BARLIN. 2/Lt Egerton Colvin M.C.	Appendix 3.
"	18/5/18		Situation normal. Weather fine. Major BURNEY OC. C Coy awarded the M.C. en revolving very active harassing fire in neighbourhood of AUCHY	
"	19/5/18		Situation normal. Major FITZWILLIAMS OC A Coy & Capt W.O. MAUDSLEY 7 days special leave to U.K. Capt OXFORD MC RAMC attached to Bath in place of Capt CAMPBELL MC RAMC	
"	20/5/18		Situation normal. Hostile TM's on Infantry. MG's fairly active. Distant fires carried out in ambush positions South side of infantry	
"	21/5/18		Situation normal. Hostile artillery active. Gas shelling from K12c. Gfo to A74d 2r10 on division Street. Harassing fire carried out by machine guns & with Yapp Weather fine.	
"	22/5/18		Situation normal. Heavy hostile shelling N of CANAL. Harassing fire carried out. Weather fine.	
"	23/5/18		Situation normal. Harassing fire carried out. Weather fine. 1st Batt. M.G.C Defence Appendix B	Appendix B
"	24/5/18		Situation normal. Scheme issued with amendments. 2/Lt in support if need carried out by 2nd NRRC on arrival front and support lines A.2.8 col	

WAR DIARY or INTELLIGENCE SUMMARY

Army Form C. 2118.

(Erase heading not required.)

Instructions regarding War Diaries and Intelligence Summaries are contained in F.S. Regs., Part II. and the Staff Manual respectively. Title pages will be prepared in manuscript.

Place	Date	Hour	Summary of Events and Information	Remarks and references to Appendices
BERLIN K.32.E	24/5/18		At 12.30 am. Four prisoners of 209 R.I.R. 107 Div and 1 L.M.G. taken, a number of enemy seen with picks and shovels thrown in by wide barrage. Our Casualties 3 officers and 17 O.R. wounded. Weather cold and rainy. Ten Forward guns in HOHENZOLLERN SECTOR and 4 reserve guns at SAILLY LABOURSE taken by the A. Coy. relieved by B. Coy. A. Coy. proceeded to billets at BARLIN. (from Order M.G. 4)	J.R. Appendix A
"	25/5/18		Situation normal. Mobile drilling schemes & reconnaissance with infantry. Held Service at 9am by Rev. H.C. DAY. M.C. A.Machielof to Battn:	J.R.
"	26/5/18		Situation normal. Held Service. Honours for carried out the arrangement with infantry. Military M'dal awarded to following men:— 125746 Pte. S. BANKS. C. Coy Authority 11 Corps. R.O. N° 238 25079 " J. HEAPHY " " " 102919 " J. POWER " " Dated 19 May 1918. 62375 " A. CROUCH	J.R.
"	27/5/18		Situation normal. Mobile drilling any enemy planes flying low over HINGES Line. During day E.A. very active. Long hostile enemy patrol held was driven my fire. Carried out the arrangement with Inf. M'dof. C.C.L. FITZWILLIAMS A Coy reported from leave.	J.R.
"	28/5/18		Situation normal. Enemy hostile f lack over Entrenched. Harassing fire carried out by arrangement with Inf. Major J.E. FRERE assumed Command during temporary absence of Col. HEYLAND. D.S.O on leave.	J.R.
"	29/5/18		Situation continued. 18 New guns in D. Coy. in HOHENZOLLERN SECTOR relieved by A. Coy. John & Guns. D. Coy. proceeded to billets at BARLIN. Harassing fire carried Appendix A out by arrangement with Inf.	J.R. Appendix A
"	30/5/18		Situation normal. Hostile artillery mile active in back areas. Harassing fire carried out by arrangement with Inf.	J.R.
"	31/5/18		Situation normal. Indirect fire carried out by our reserve guns.	J.R.

NOTE MILITARY MEDAL awarded to following NCO's & men: M. N°28238 Sergt MORRISON.M. N°20372 Sergt GRANT. V.J. N°28894 Pte. PALETHORPE. J N°32160 Pte. SHARP. A.V. N°44761 Pte. CAMPBELL. R N°28769. Pte. McKECHNIE. A N°60275 Sgt. POLEMAN I. N°10699 Cpl. FOSTER. A N°16907. Sergt. DUNN. R N°66984. Cpl. ALDERSLADE. H. N°28203 B. BAKER. R.J. N°12039 Pte. BRIDLE.W.E. N°9878 Pte. OWEN. E.

Army Form C. 2118.

WAR DIARY
or
INTELLIGENCE SUMMARY.
(Erase heading not required.)

Instructions regarding War Diaries and Intelligence Summaries are contained in F. S. Regs., Part II. and the Staff Manual respectively. Title pages will be prepared in manuscript.

MACHINE GUN CORPS.
No. 126

Place	Date	Hour	Summary of Events and Information			Remarks and references to Appendices
BARLIN K32L			Strength of Batt. 1st May 1918	Officers 42	O.R. 787	
			Do 31st May "	46	880	
			Casualties for month of May	—	14	
			Drafts " " "	6	131	
			Officers taken on strength :— Lt.Col. H.M.HEYLAND. D.S.O.			J.R.
			Capt. C.Y. FORD. M.C. R.A.M.C.			
			2/Lt A.E. ELVIDGE			
			2/Lt W HARRISS			
			2/Lt W.D. SOUTER. D.C.M.			
			2/Lt J. REAST.			
			Officers struck off strength :— Lt.Col. BIDDER. D.S.O.			J.R.
			2/Lt J. REAST.			

SECRET

1st. BATTALION. M.G. CORPS.

ORDER NO. 19

Copy No. 16

Ref. Map. GORRE. 1/20,000.

(1) The 1st Infantry Brigade is relieving the 2nd Infantry Bde. in the CAMBRIN Section on the night of 2nd/3rd of May 1918. On completion of this relief the guns of "D" Coy. 1st Battn. M.G.Corps will come under the orders of G.O.C. 1st Inf. Bde.

(2) "B" Coy. will relieve "D" Coy in the CAMBRIN Section on the 4th May 1918.

(3) All details of relief will be arranged by O's C. Coy. concerned direct.

(4) On relief "D" Coy will proceed to billets in BARLIN.

(5) Trams or lorries will be provided under arrangements to be notified later.

(6) On completion of relief "B" Coy. will come under orders of 1st Inf. Bde. to whom completion of relief will be reported. Completion of relief will be reported to Battn. H.Q. by code message "A.5.5.X received".

(7) Acknowledge.

Shanks
Capt & Adjt.
1st Battalion Machine Gun Corps.

Issued at 4 p.m, 1/5/18

Copies issued to:-

(1) "A" Company
(2) "B" Company
(3) "C" Company
(4) "D" Company
(5) Transport Officer
(6) Quartermaster
(7) Signalling Officer
(8) Medical Officer
(9) 1st Inf. Bde. "G"
(10) 1st Division "G"
(11) " " "Q"
(12) 55 Bn. M.G.C.
(13) S.S.O.
(14) War Diary
(15) "
(16) File
(17)

SECRET.   Copy No. 14

1st BATTALION, MACHINE GUN CORPS.
ORDER NO. 19.

Reference Map GORRE 1/20,000.

1. The 1st Infantry Brigade is relieving the 2nd Infantry Brigade in the CAMBRIN Section on the night of 2nd/3rd May, 1918. On completion of this relief the guns of "D" Company, 1st Battn. M.G.Corps will come under the orders of G.O.C. 1st Inf. Bde.

2. "B" Coy. will relieve "D" Coy. in the CAMBRIN Section on the 4th May, 1918.

3. All details of relief will be arranged by O's C.Companies concerned direct.

4. On relief "D" Coy. will proceed to billets in BARLIN.

5. Trains or lorries will be provided under arrangements to to notified later.

6. On completion of relief "B" Coy will come under the orders of 1st Inf. Bde to whom completion of relief will be reported. Completion of relief will be reported to Battn. H.Q. by Code Message "A.S.5.X. received".

7. ACKNOWLEDGE.

                            (signed) A.SHANKS. Capt. & Adjutant.
                                    1st Battalion, Machine Gun Corps.

Issued at 4p.m. 1/5/18

Copies issued to:-

1. "A" Coy.   9. 1st Inf. Bde.
2. "B" Coy.   10. 1st Division, "G"
3. "C" Coy.   11. 1st Division "Q"
4. "D" Coy.   12. 55th Battn. M.G.C.
5. Transport Offr.   13. S.S.O.
6. Signalling "   14. War Diary.
7. Quartermaster.   15.   do.
8. Medical Offr.   16. File.
                          17.   do.

SECRET. Copy No. 14

1st BATTALION, MACHINE GUN CORPS.

OPERATION ORDER NO. 20.

Reference map GORRE 1/20,000.

(1) "D" Company, plus two guns will relieve "C" Company plus two guns, in the HOHENZOLLERN Section on the 9th inst.

(2) All details of relief will be arranged by O's C. Companies concerned direct.

(3) O.C. "C" Company will hand over two guns complete with belt boxes to O.C. "D" Company without personnel.

(4) On relief "C" Company will proceed to billets in BARLIN.

(5) Trains or lorries will be provided under arrangements to be notified later.

(6) On completion of relief "D" Company will come under the orders of 3rd Infantry Brigade to whom completion of relief will be reported.
Completion of relief will be reported to Battalion Headquarters by the Code message "Your A.S.10.X. received".

(7) ACKNOWLEDGE.

M. Shanks
Capt. & Adjt.
1st Battalion, Machine Gun Corps.

Issued at
6-30p.m.
7-5-18 to,

(1) "A" Coy.	(9) 1st Division "G"
(2) "B" Coy.	(10) 1st Division "Q"
(3) "C" Coy.	(11) 3rd Infantry Bde.
(4) "D" Coy.	(12) S.S.O.
(5) Quartermaster.	(13) War Diary.
(6) Transport Offr.	(14) War Diary.
(7) Sigs. Officer.	(15) File.
(8) Medical "	(16) File.

1st BATTALION, MACHINE GUN CORPS ORDER NO. 20,

IS HEREBY CANCELLED.

1st BATTALION
MACHINE GUN CORPS.
No. 766
Date.

[signature]

Capt. & Adjutant.
1st Battalion, Machine Gun Corps.

Issued at 12.noon.
6/5/18.

To all recipients of 1st Batt. M.G.Order No. 20.

SECRET   Copy No. 15.

1ST BATTALION, MACHINE GUN CORPS.

ORDER NO.21.

Reference MAP GORRE 1/20,000.

(1) "D" Company plus 2 guns will relieve "C" Company plus 2 guns in the HOHENZOLLERN Sector on the 13th.

(2) All details of relief will be arranged between Officers Commanding Companies direct.

(3) O.C. "C" Company will hand over two guns complete with equipment to O.C. "D" Company.

(4) On relief "C" Company will proceed to billets in NOEUX.

(5) On completion of relief "D" Company will come under the orders of the 2nd Infantry Brigade. "C" Company will be in Divisional Reserve with the 3rd Infantry Brigade.

(6) Completion of relief will be reported to Battalion Headquarters by the message "your A.S.10.X" received and to Brigade Headquarters concerned direct.

(7) On completion of relief "D" Company Transport will join the Battalion Transport at BARLIN. Transport Officer will arrange with O.C. "C" Company to send "C" Company Transport to NOEUX and for fighting limbers for relief.

(8) Acknowledge.

                                        Captain and Adjutant,
                                        1st Battalion, Machine
                                        Gun Corps.

Issued at 9.a.m. 13/5/18

Copies issued to:-
    (1) "A" Company.
    (2) "B" Company.
    (3) "C" Company.
    (4) "D" Company.
    (5) C.O.
    (6) T.O.
    (7) Q.M.
    (8) Sig.Officer.
    (9) M.O.
   (10) 2nd Infantry Bde.
   (11) 3rd Infantry Bde.
   (12) 1st Division "G"
   (13) 1st Division "Q"
   (14) War Diary
   (15) War Diary
   (13) War Diary
   (17) File
   (18) File

SECRET.

1st BATTALION, MACHINE GUN CORPS.
ORDER NO. 22.

1. Reference 1st Division No. G.351/1 dated 15/5/18, Machine Gun Organisation.

2. The following alterations in the disposition of Machine Gun Companies will take place on the 18th inst.

3. **LEFT BRIGADE.**

    Group Commander. Major J.S. SNOWBALL, H.Q., ANNEQUIN FOSSE.

    (a) Forward Guns. 9 Guns of "B" Coy. in and East of the VILLAGE LINE and POMT FIXE, as in attached map.
    Headquarters of O.C. at Headquarters of Infantry Battalion in the line in CAMBRIN.N.SUB-SECTION.

    (b) Rear Guns. 7 Guns of "B" Coy. in CAMBRIN Locality as in attached map.
    Headquarters of O.C. at Headquarters of Support Infantry Battalion in CAMBRIN.

4. **RIGHT BRIGADE.**

    Group Commander. Major T.G.ANSON. H.Q., SAILLY LABOURSE.

    (a) Forward Guns. 10 Guns of "A" Coy. East of the VILLAGE LINE, as in attached map.
    Headquarters of O.C. at Infantry Coy. Headquarters in RAILWAY KEEP.

    (b) Rear Guns. 14 Guns of "D" Coy. at BARTS, VERMELLES, FACTORY, BULLY & VALLEY Posts, as in attached map.
    Headquarters of O.C. at Infantry Support Battalion Headquarters, in ANNEQUIN FOSSE.

    (c) ANNEQUIN DEFENCES. 4 Guns of "D" Coy. as in attached map.
    Headquarters of O.C. at ANNEQUIN FOSSE.

5. All details of the necessary reliefs to effect these dispositions will be arranged by O's.C. "A" & "D" Coys. direct.

6. All Runners, Orderlies, etc., will be thoroughly instructed and tested in the new dispositions. Group Commanders will ensure the efficacy of their communications.

7. Command will pass to Group Commander Right Brigade on completion of relief, which will be reported to Battalion Headquarters and to Headquarters Right Brigade, using the Code Message "Your A.S.22 received"

8. ACKNOWLEDGE.

Captain & Adjutant.
1st Battalion, Machine Gun Corps.

Issued at 10.0a.m. 17/5/18.

Copies issued to :-

Copy to C.O.
Sig O.
CMGO

1. "A" Coy.,
2. "B" Coy.,
3. "C" Coy.,
4. "D" Coy.,
5. 1st Div. "G"
6. 1st Inf. Bde.
7. 2nd Inf. Bde.
8. 3rd Inf. Bde.
9. 11th Battn. M.G.C.
10. 55th " "
11. War Diary.
12. War Diary.
13. File.
14. File.

AMENDMENT No. 1 to 1st BATTALION, MACHINE GUN CORPS
OPERATION ORDER No. 23.

Reference para. 3.

For "BOEUX-LES-MINES" read "BARLIN".

                       Capt. & Adjutant.
                1st Battalion, Machine Gun Corps.

Issued at 10.30p.m. 17/5/18.
    to
      All recipients of Order No. 23.

SECRET.

1st BATTALION, MACHINE GUN CORPS.
ORDER NO. 23.

Copy No. 16

Reference Map GORRE 1/20,000.

1. "C" Company will relieve "B" Company in the CAMBRIN Section on the 18th instant.

2. All details of relief will be arranged direct between Officers Commanding Companies concerned.

3. On relief "B" Company will proceed to billets in HOEUX-LES-MINES.

4. On completion of relief "C" Company will come under the orders of the 1st Infantry Brigade and MAJOR F.G.GURNEY will be group Commander for CAMBRIN Group.

5. Completion of relief will be reported to Battalion H.Q. by the Code Message "Your A.S.26.X. received" and to 1st Infantry Brigade direct.

6. On completion of relief "C" Company Transport will join the Battalion Transport at BARLIN. Transport Officer will arrange to send "B" Company Transport to HOEUX-LES-MINES and to send limbers for relief.

8. Acknowledge

Captain and Adjutant,
1st Battalion, Machine
Gun Corps.

Issued at 1 p.m. 17/5/18

Copies issued to:-
(1) "A" Company
(2) "B" Company
(3) "C" Company
(4) "D" Company
(5) Commanding Officer
(6) Transport Officer
(7) Quartermaster
(8) Signalling Officer
(9) Medical Officer
(10) 1st Infantry Brigade
(11) 2nd Infantry Brigade
(12) 3rd Infantry Brigade
(13) 1st Division "G"
(14) 1st Division "Q"
(15) 55th Battn.M.G.C.
(16) War Diary
(17) War Diary
(18) File

SECRET.   Copy No. 17

1st BATTALION, MACHINE GUN CORPS.

ORDER No. 84.

Reference Map CORPS 1/20,000.

                                    forward

1. "B" Company will relieve the 10 guns of "A" Company in the Right Brigade Group on the 24th inst.

2. Details of relief will be arranged between the O's C. Companies direct.

3. On completion of relief these guns of "B" Coy will come under the orders of the Group Commander, Right Brigade Group.

4. On relief "A" Company will proceed to billets in DARLIN.

5. Completion of relief will be reported to Battalion Headquarters by the code word "BING" and to the 2nd Infantry Brigade direct.

6. Companies will move by rail. Details of trains will be issued later.

7. ACKNOWLEDGE.

                                                for Capt. & Adjutant.
                                     1st Battalion, Machine Gun Corps.

Issued at 2.0 p.m. 25/5/18

Copies issued to :-

(1)	"A" Coy., 1st Bn., M.G.C.	(10)	1st Infantry Brigade.
(2)	"B" Coy., do.	(11)	2nd Infantry Brigade.
(3)	"C" Coy., do.	(12)	3rd Infantry Brigade.
(4)	"D" Coy., do.	(13)	1st Division, "G"
(5)	Commanding Officer.	(14)	1st Division, "Q"
(6)	Transport Officer.	(15)	55th Battn. M.G.C.
(7)	Quartermaster.	(16)	War Diary.
(8)	Signalling Officer.	(17)	War Diary. ✓
(9)	Medical Officer.	(18)	File.

1st
BATTALION
MACHINE GUN CORPS.

No ....
Date ....

SECRET.

ADDENDUM No.1 to 1st BATTALION MACHINE GUN CORPS ORDER No. 25.

1. On completion of relief Group Commander Right Brigade, Group will be Major C.C.L. FITZWILLIAMS.

                                                Capt. & Adjutant.

28th May, 1918.   1st Battalion, M. G. Corps.

Issued to all recipients of 1st Bn. M.G. Corps Order No. 25.

SECRET.   COPY NO. 15

1st BATTALION, MACHINE GUN CORPS.

ORDER NO. 25.

1. "A" Company, plus 2 guns, will relieve "D" Company plus 2 guns in the HOHENZOLLERN Section on the 29th inst.

2. All details of relief will be arranged between Officers Commanding Companies concerned.

3. O.C. "D" Company will hand over 2 guns complete to O.C. "A" Coy.

4. On completion of relief the guns of "A" Company will come under the orders of the Group Commander, Right Brigade Group.

5. On completion of relief "D" Company will proceed to billets in BARLIN.

6. Companies will move by rail. Details of trains will be issued later.

7. Completion of relief will be reported to Battalion Headquarters by the Code word "BANG, and to 1st Brigade direct.

8. ACKNOWLEDGE.

                                              Captain & Adjutant.
                                         1st Battalion, Machine Gun Corps.

Issued at 10.0. p.m., 27/5/18.

Issued to:-

(1) "A" Coy., 1st Bn., M.G.C.
(2) "B" Coy.,   do.
(3) "C" Coy.,   do.
(4) "D" Coy.,   do.
(5) Commanding Officer.
(6) Transport Officer.
(7) Quartermaster.
(8) Signalling Officer.
(9) Medical Officer.
(10) 1st Infantry Brigade.
(11) 2nd Infantry Brigade.
(12) 3rd Infantry Brigade.
(13) 1st Division "G".
(14) 1st Division "Q".
(15) War Diary.
(16) War Diary.
(17) File.
(18) File.

SECRET.

AMENDMENT No. 1 to 1st BATTALION, MACHINE GUN CORPS
DEFENCE SCHEME.

1. Reference 1st Battalion M.G.C., No.1255, d/d 23/5/18.

2. Para. 4. For "A.14.d.5.1." read "A.21.c.1.7."

3. Para. 5. For "A.20.c.4.7." read "A.19.d.55.25."

Captain & Adjutant.
1st Battalion, Machine Gun Corps.

25th May, 1918.

To all recipients of 1st Battn. M.G.Corps Defence
Scheme dated as above.

1st BATTALION MACHINE GUN CORPS.
No. 1327

~~To 1st Division "G"~~
~~O.M.G.O.~~

1ST BATTALION MACHINE GUN CORPS.
No. 1255
Date...........

Reference 1st Battn. M.G.C. No.1255 dated 23/5/1918

DISPOSITIONS.   Para. B 3 (1) 4th line

               For Valley Battery 2 guns
                  A.25.d.23.33.
                   read
               Valley Battery
    1 gun   A.25.d. 55.15.
    1 gun   A.25.d. 80.20.

To all recipients of 1st Battalion, M.G.Corps Defence Scheme.

                               Capt and Adjutant
                         1st Battalion, Machine Gun Corps.

27/5/1918.

1ST BATTALION, MACHINE GUN CORPS
DEFENCE SCHEME.

CAMBRIN and HOHENZOLLERN Sections.

A. TACTICAL ORGANISATION

(1) The Defensive Organisation of the machine guns on the Divisional Front is arranged so as to protect as far as possible the main line of resistance and such portions of ground forward of it as give observations over our rear lines.

(2) On the left the guns have not been pushed as far forward as the Main Line of Resistance, as there this is here well within Trench Mortar range, and the chances of guns surviving a heavy bombardment would be very small. The guns are, therefore, arranged to sweep the ridge and prevent any advance over it.

(3) The rear machine gun defences consist mainly of the CAMBRIN Locality Defences and a series of "batteries" or guns tactically grouped to cover the wide slopes up to the VILLAGE LINE and the ridges in front.
ANNEQUIN FOSSE also becomes a small defended locality with machine guns disposed so as to form a defensive flank should occasion arise.
In the same way the two left rear guns of CAMBRIN locality have further positions with a view to defence against an enemy advance along the North of the LA BASSEE Canal.

(4) There are further prepared machine gun positions in the SAILLY-TUNING FORK Line which would be manned by reserve guns in case of a successful enemy attack on the forward system. The positions are supplied with ammunition and in many cases are furnished with splinter-proof shelters and deep dug-outs.

(5) Reserve guns are billeted in BARLIN with Battalion Headquarters, but when operations are expected they are tactically billeted in NOEUX-LES-MINES with the Brigade with which they would be normally employed.

B. DISPOSITIONS.

(1) All guns in the line are grouped into Forward and Rear Guns and are disposed manned as under.

(2) Forward Guns Right Brigade.

```
R.57        )
R.57.a.     )              G. 4.c.15.90.
Central Keep   A )
Central Keep   B )         G. 3.d.60.15.
Tunnel Guns    A           A.27.d.20.40.
Tunnel Guns    B           A.27.d.37.25.
Railway Alley              A.27.c.20.55.
Railway Alley              G. 3.a.77.52.
Railway Alley              G. 3.a.87.50.
Railway Gun                G. 3.d.23.80.
```

(2)

(II) **LEFT BRIGADE.**

E.30.a.	A.15.d.20.50.
V.50.	A.21.c.15.85.
V.49.	A.20.d.92.15.
V.43.	A.23.b.58.50.
V.47.	A.23.b.30.10.
V.55	A.20.b.85.75.
V.53.	A.20.b.85.75.
P.F.5.	A.14.d.35.58.
P.E.1.	A.14.d.54.91.

3. **REAR GUNS (1) RIGHT BRIGADE.**

Factory Battery, A.	A.26.d.40.50.
" " B.	A.23.d.42.32.
Factory Post, 2 guns,	G.2.b.20.90.
Valley Battery, 2 guns,	A.25.d.23.35.
Bully Battery, 4 guns,	G.1.d.08.94.
Vermelles Battery, 2 guns,	G.8.b.40.80.
Barts Battery, 2 guns,	G.9.c.55.90.

(II) **LEFT BRIGADE.**

C.3.	A.20.a. 3. 8.
C.2.	A.20.a.30.75.
N.M.G.18.	A.20.a. 3. 2.
M.M.G.10.	A.20.c.58.30.
M.M.G.13.	A.20.c.38.35.
M.M.G.14.	A.20.c.38.40.
C.1.	A.25.b.85.10.

4. In addition are the ANNEQUIN Locality Guns disposed as under.

Quinn Battery, 2 guns	L. 3.a.15.77.
Annie Battery,	F.29.c.92.23.
Annequin Battery	F.29.d. 7. 7.

C. **CONTROL:**

1. The Machine Gun Battalion is responsible for the tactical organisation of the guns, and works from Battalion Headquarters through a Senior Machine Gun Officer attached to each Brigade as Machine Gun Group Commander.

2. The Machine Gun Group Commander carries out the wishes of Brigade Commanders in conformity with the Divisional Scheme. He has in his group an O.C.Forward and an O.C.Rear guns, who live at or near convenient Infantry Command posts. These officers are responsible for maintaining liaison with Infantry Battalion Commanders, and carrying out their wishes as far as possible in accordance with the Group Commanders orders.

3. Group Headquarters are disposed as follows:-

Right Brigade Group	F.27.d. 1. 0.
Left Brigade Group	F.29.c.90.00.

(3)

4.   Officers Commanding Forward Guns have their Headquarters as follows:-

    Right Brigade Group   G.3.c.75.20.
    Left Brigade Group   A.14.d.5. 1.

5.   Officers Commanding Rear Guns have their Headquarters as follows:-

    Right Brigade Group   F.29.c.90.00.
    Left Brigade Group   A.20.c. 4. 7.
    Annequin Defences   F.29.c.90.00.

Acknowledge.

[signature]
Captain and Adjutant,
1st Battalion, Machine
Gun Corps.

23/5/18.

Issued to:-

(1) "A" Company,   (9) 3rd Inf.Bde.
(2) "B" Company,   (10) 11th Bn.M.G.C.
(3) "C" Company,   (11) 55th Bn.M.G.C.
(4) "D" Company,   (12) War Diary,
(5) 1st Division G.   (13) War Diary
(6) 1st Div.Artly.   (14) File.
(7) 1st Inf.Bde.   (15) File
(8) 2nd Inf.Bde.

Copies to:-   Commanding Officer.
               Signalling Officer
               Intelligence Officer
               O.M.G.O.

Issued to :-

1. "A" Coy., 1st Bn., M.G.C.	9. 2nd Infantry Brigade.
2. "B" Coy., do.	10. 3rd Infantry Brigade.
3. "C" Coy., do.	11. 1st D.A.C.
4. "D" Coy., do.	12. S.S.O.
5. Transport Officer.	13. War Diary.
6. Quartermaster.	14. War Diary.
7. 1st Division "Q"	15. File.
8. 1st Infantry Brigade.	16. File.

1ST BATTALION MACHINE GUN CORPS.
No. 1104
Date................

Copy to :- C.O.
Second-in-Command.
Signalling Officer.

"C" Echelon.
  Cookers.
  Company H.Q.Chargers.
  Battalion H.Q.Transport.
  4 G.S.Wagons.

2. On receipt of orders from Battalion Headquarters "A" and "B" Echelons will join their respective Company Headquarters.
  As soon as operations become mobile the principle should be adopted that Fighting Limbers and Section Officers chargers should join Section Headquarters.

4. "C" Echelon with the Q.M.Store will move under orders issued to the Transport Officer, who will keep a mounted orderly at Battalion Headquarters.

5. Transport Officer will ensure that the Company Transport N.C.O's know their way to their Company Headquarters, and reconnoitre the routes thero.

6. All Company Quartermaster Sergeants will remain with the Q.M. Stores and the rationing of Companies will be maintained on the present system. Refilling will be by G.S.Wagons which will deliver to Company Headquarters.

7. S.A.A. Once "B" Echelon has joined the Company Headquarters Companies will be responsible for maintaining their Mobile Reserve of S.A.A. Supply with S.A.A. will be direct from the S.A.A. Section of the D.A.C. The Officers and Warrant Officers in each Company responsible for S.A.A. supply will get into touch with the advanced Section D.A.C. at BALLY BUNION DUMP.

8. Arrangements are being made to take over responsibility for M.G., S.A.A. in the various Brigade dumps. These will be kept filled under Battalion arrangements on demands from Group Commanders. When S.A.A. is required transport will be sent to BALLY BUNION DUMP, where it will be met by the Company Officer or W.O. responsible for S.A.A. supply.

9. Once active operations take place all S.A.A. should be kept mobile as long as possible, and Companies should avoid making dumps unless it is absolutely necessary.

10. Casualties to guns and equipment will be communicated to Battalion Headquarters by the quickest possible means - telephone - visual - or runner. Every effort will be made to replace as early as possible.

11. Casualties to personnel will be notified direct to Battalion Headquarters. During heavy fighting estimated casualties for given periods should be submitted as occasion permits.

12. ACKNOWLEDGE.

         Capt. & Adjutant.
         1st Battalion, Machine Gun Corps.

Appendix No. 11 to Machine Gun Defence Scheme, 1st Battalion, M.G.C.

1st BATTALION, MACHINE GUN CORPS.
ADMINISTRATIVE ARRANGEMENTS.

In the event of active operations taking place the Machine Gun Companies will continue to be administered and supplied by the Battalion.

Transport will be divided into A, B & C Echelons, and will be distributed as under :-

"A" Echelon.	Fighting Limbers.
	Section Officers Chargers.
"B" Echelon.	S.A.A. Limbers.
	Company H.Q. Limbers.
	Cookers.
	Company H.Q. Chargers.
"C" Echelon.	Battalion H.Q. Transport.
	4 G.S. Wagons.

3. On receipt of orders from Battalion Headquarters "A" and "B" Echelons will join their respective Company Headquarters.
   As soon as operations become mobile the principle should be adopted that Fighting Limbers and Section Officers chargers should join Section Headquarters.

4. "C" Echelon with the Q.M. Store will move under orders issued to the Transport Officer, who will keep a mounted orderly at Battalion Headquarters.

5. Transport Officer will ensure that the Company Transport N.C.O's know their way to their Company Headquarters, and reconnoitre the routes there.

6. All Company Quartermaster Sergeants will remain with the Q.M. Stores and the rationing of Companies will be maintained on the present system. Refilling will be by G.S. Wagons which will deliver to Company Headquarters.

7. S.A.A. Once "B" Echelon has joined the Company Headquarters Companies will be responsible for maintaining their Mobile Reserve of S.A.A. Supply with S.A.A. will be direct from the S.A.A. Section of the D.A.C. The Officers and Warrant Officers in each Company responsible for S.A.A. supply will get into touch with the advanced Section D.A.C. at BALLY BUNION DUMP.

8. Arrangements are being made to take over responsibility for M.G., S.A.A. in the various Brigade dumps. These will be kept filled under Battalion arrangements on demands from Group Commanders. When S.A.A. is required transport will be sent to BALLY BUNION DUMP, where it will be met by the Company Officer or W.O. responsible for S.A.A. supply.

9. Once active operations take place all S.A.A. should be kept mobile as long as possible, and Companies should avoid making dumps unless it is absolutely necessary.

10. Casualties to guns and equipment will be communicated to Battalion Headquarters by the quickest possible means - telephone - visual - or runner. Every effort will be made to replace as early as possible.

11. Casualties to personnel will be notified direct to Battalion Headquarters. During heavy fighting estimated casualties for given periods should be submitted as occasion permits.

12. ACKNOWLEDGE.

Capt. & Adjutant.
1st Battalion, Machine Gun Corps.

APPENDIX IV.

To 1st Battalion, Machine Gun Corps, Defence Scheme.

(a) ANTI-AIRCRAFT.

1. The following guns will be employed on Anti-Aircraft work in execution and extension of the Divisional Defence Scheme.

2. RIGHT GROUP.　　　　　　　　Forward Guns.

　　(1) One gun from Central Keep at G.3.d.35.15.

　　　　　　　　　Rear Guns.

　　(1) One gun from BARTS BATTERY　　at G.9.a.3.8.
　　(2) One gun from VERMELLES BATTERY　at G.8.b.0.6.
　　(3) One gun from BULLY BATTERY　　at G.1.d.2.6.
　　(4) One gun from ANNEQUIN　　　　at F.29.d.70.65.
　　(5) One gun from Factory Post at　at G.2.b.25.70.

3. LEFT GROUP.　　　　　　　　Forward Guns.

　　(1) One gun in VILLAGE LINE　　at A.26.b.30.30.
　　(2) One gun in VILLAGE LINE　　at A.20.b.95.75.
　　(3) One gun at POINT FIXE　　　at A.14.d.70.60.

　　　　　　　　　Rear Guns.

　　(1) One gun in CAMBRIN　　　　at A.20.a.55.00.
　　(2) One gun at　　　　　　　　A.25.b.80.05.

4. Companies will ensure that the strictest discipline is exercised at all firing at aircraft and that all N.C.O's and men are thoroughly instructed in the rules laid down on the brown cards.

5. Supplies of S.A.A. up to 5,000 rounds ordinary and 1,000 rounds tracer per A.A. position should be dumped at the position. Tracer S.A.A. will be used economically and belts containing any tracer S.A.A. will be kept in specially marked boxes and will not be used for ground firing.

6. All enemy aircraft sighted will be reported in the daily intelligence report and also the number of rounds fired on any machine engaged.

7. Enemy aeroplanes will only be engaged at night, when there can be not the slightest doubt as to their identity.

(b)

1. The following guns will be employed on anti-tank defence.

2. RIGHT GROUP.

　　(1) Left Gun VERMELLES BATTERY　　G. 8.b.40.00.
　　(2) Left gun BARTS BATTERY　　　　G. 9.a.55.05.
　　(3) Left Gun CENTRAL KEEP　　　　G. 3.d.30.15.

LEFT GROUP.

　　(1) V.47.　　　　　　A.26.b.35.10.
　　(2) V.50.　　　　　　A.21.c.15.65.
　　(3) N.L.G.10.　　　　A.20.c.58.30.
　　(4) N.L.G.13.　　　　A.20.c.68.35.

3. A minimum of 500 rounds of A.P.S.A.A. will be maintained with each anti-tank gun. Belts containing A.P.S.A.A. will be kept in specially marked boxes and will only be used actually against Tanks.

4. All gun teams of anti-tank guns will be carefully instructed in the appearance and marking of our own and enemy tanks. They will also be shown drawings of enemy tanks, giving the most vulnerable points.

5. Only the guns detailed will fire actually on enemy tanks. All others will concentrate on the Infantry following up behind. It must be impressed on them that they can inflict far more damage by this method.

P.T.O.

(b) continued :-

    6.   Gun teams detailed for firing on the tanks should be warned to look out especially for any signs of an enemy tank bringing its weapons into action. They will endeavour to frustrate any such attempts by fire directed on the loopholes and flaps.

(c)

1. Harassing fire will be carried out nightly under arrangements made by the Battalion.

2. It will be executed by batteries placed as under :-

    RIGHT GROUP.

        (1) SUSSEX TRENCH BATTERY, G.3.c.6.6.   4 guns.
        (11) FACTORY POST BATTERY, A.26.d.47.35.   4 guns.

    LEFT GROUP.

        (1) SIMPSONS BATTERY, A.20.c.65.74,   4 guns.

3. A reserve of 15,000 rounds will be maintained for harassing fire at the nearest convenient site for belt filling to each battery.

4. No other guns will be employed for Harassing Fire without special application to Battalion Headquarters. No gun will in any case do harassing fire from its battle position.

5. ACKNOWLEDGE.

20th May, 1918.

                      Captain & Adjutant.
                1st Battalion, Machine Gun Corps.

Issued to :-

"A" Coy. 1st Bn., M.G.C.		Divisional Artillery.
"B" Coy.,	do.	1st Infantry Brigade.
"C" Coy.,	do.	2nd Infantry Brigade.
"D" Coy.,	do.	3rd Infantry Brigade.
1st Division "G"		

Copies to :-   C.O.
                  Intelligence Officer.
                  C.M.G.O.

SECRET.   Copy No. 17

1st BATTALION, MACHINE GUN CORPS.

ORDER No. 23.

1. "D" Company will relieve the 10 forward guns of "B" Company in the HOHENZOLLERN Sector on the 2nd proximo., and also 4 guns in reserve at SAILLY LABOURSE.

2. All details of relief will be arranged between Officers Commanding Companies concerned direct.

3. On completion of relief the guns of "D" Company will come under the orders of the Group Commander, Right Brigade Group.

4. On completion of relief "B" Company will proceed to billets in DAHLIN.

5. Companies will move by rail. Details of trains will be issued later.

6. Completion of relief will be reported to Battalion Headquarters by the Code word "WAIGLE", and to the Brigade in the line direct.

7. "D" Company will hand over two guns complete to "B" Company.

8. ACKNOWLEDGE.

                                            Captain & Adjutant.
                                    1st Battalion, Machine Gun Corps.

Issued at 10.0 p.m. 31/5/18.

Issued to:-

(1) O.C. "A" Coy. 1st Bn., M.G.C.   (11) 1st Infantry Brigade.
(2) O.C. "B" Coy.,   do.   (12) 2nd Infantry Brigade.
(3) O.C. "C" Coy.,   do.   (13) 3rd Infantry Brigade.
(4) O.C. "D" Coy.,   do.   (14) 1st Division "G".
(5) Commanding Officer.   (15) 1st Division "Q".
(6) Transport Officer.   (16) War Diary.
(7) Quartermaster.   (17) War Diary.
(8) Signalling Officer.   (18) File.
(9) Medical Officer.   (19) File.
(10) 11th Battalion, M.G.C.

WAR DIARY
or
INTELLIGENCE SUMMARY
(Erase heading not required.)

Army Form C. 2118.

Instructions regarding War Diaries and Intelligence Summaries are contained in F.S. Regs., Part II. and the Staff Manual respectively. Title pages will be prepared in manuscript.

1ST BATTALION MACHINE GUN CORPS.
No. 2146

Place	Date	Hour	Summary of Events and Information	Remarks and references to Appendices
BARLIN S.13.d Sh 44	1/6/18		Situation normal. Harassing fire carried out by one officer & sub section infantry.	S.R.
	2/6/18		Situation normal. 8h 40 military active & harassing fire carried out by one officer & sub section infantry. Sub section from D Coy. on 456-15 left 2.Lieut H.STOKES returned to duty on arrival from No.6 I.B.D. Lieut F.G. PROCTER to hospital sick. 7.Lieut BRAIN (Canadian Corps Res.M.G.)	S.R.
	3/6/18		Situation normal. Harassing fire, trench shelling on battery positions carried out. M.C.s posted to 1st M.E. BARKER from 7th Bn: and P.MARKS the. Cpl. and D.O.C.M. to No.7378 Cpl. & No.22587 Sjt E BLACK & to No.85660 Pvt D. JONES all of E. Coy.	S.R.
	4/6/18		Situation normal, shelling fire. Cannot pull the strongpoint with 40th in support. No 10H1 in Sqn. F.16. 18780 rounds fired by our Communication Snipers & another. Moving 7002 rounds were fired and 1 mainman by 5" gun 100 P.T.R. 207th P.W. Captured & Moving Snipes 7702 rounds of ammunition in ambulance Map 51.TV 20000. 2/Lieut SNELL & Quart Msgr	S.R.
	5/6/18		Situation normal. A.B. SHARTS, City relieved by A.G. & B battery of HUYFORD BATT.M.GUN. Canadian Brigade on our right. One friendliness relived by one of the Divisions was temporary on our right. One relived by another – B.L. HEYLAND attaching from loan returned to proceed to NOEUN LES MINES for another. Brit: HEDGEL M.C. awarded the M.C. to Capt. DAVSON and HOTHEYZIELAN. Listed asserting the Ratt	S.R.
	6/6/18		Situation normal. But line walking a duty. York shelling fire carried out by enemy from Van shelling. J.D. MELVILLE MC active operations Engineers engaged in lively good burnt out.	S.R.
	7/6/18		Situation normal. Ship mains of activity or a front of sending artillery and some gas shelling. Lieut LA CARLILE transferred to U.K. on duty. Battalion fire carried out by arrangement with Infantry	S.R.
	8/6/18		Enemy artillery incompleta activity in H.V. area reserve lines. Matter full harassing fire with harassing fire carried out.	S.R.
	9/6/18		Situation normal. Front shelling of trench line with heavy minnies fire. Harassing fire carried out by arrangement with Infantry.	S.R.
	10/6/18		Situation normal. Shelling activity below normal. Harassing fire carried out.	S.R.

WAR DIARY or INTELLIGENCE SUMMARY

Army Form C. 2118.

1ST BATTALION MACHINE GUN CORPS
No. 246

Place	Date	Hour	Summary of Events and Information	Remarks and references to Appendices
BERLIN K.3.2.d.4.4.	1/6/18		Slight increase of hostile artillery activity. Harassing fire carried out by amalgamated sub-sections.	o/s
"	2/6/18		Harassing fire carried out by enemy. Enemy artillery active in several sub-sections. Harassing fire carried out.	o/s
"	3/6/18		Situation normal. Enemy artillery fairly active. Weather cloudy with fair visibility. Harassing fire carried out by amalgamated Sub-sections.	o/s
"	4/6/18		Visibility fair. Enemy artillery activity of trouble with M.G's. Harassing fire carried out by C Coy in HOHENZOLLERN Sector & proceeded to billets at BERLIN. B Coy relieved by E Coy. B Coy relieved to billets at BERLIN.	o/s
"	5/6/18		Situation normal with usual artillery activity. Weather fine but windy. Harassing fire carried out.	o/s
"	6/6/18		Situation normal. Enemy M.G's active sweeping the crest on the village line. Weather cloudy. Harassing fire carried out.	o/s
"	7/6/18		Situation normal. Enemy shelled with 4.2's and some sub-sectors of BERLIN. Harassing fire carried out.	o/s
"	8/6/18		Situation normal. Lieut. FRASER and 2/Lt. JOYCE proceeded to U.K. on duty. Harassing fire CAMBRIN Sector relieved some sub-sections during the night on relief.	o/s
"	9/6/18		Situation normal. Hostile artillery normal. Harassing fire carried out.	o/s
"	10/6/18		Situation unchanged. Enemy artillery activity below normal. Harassing fire carried out. A Coy & Batt. Transport inspected by Corps Commander awarded ribbons presented to 4 Officers and 19 O.R.	o/s
"	11/6/18		Situation unchanged. Artillery activity on both sides below normal. Harassing fire carried out.	o/s
"	12/6/18		Situation normal. Hostile artillery below normal. B Coy relieved by A Coy in CAMBRIN Sector. E Coy relieved to billets at BERLIN. Enemy Bomb No. 29.	Appx 29 Appx A
"	13/6/18		Situation normal. Light weather. Hostile artillery activity. Harassing fire carried out. 9 cases of PUO evacuated. Harassing fire carried out.	o/s
"	14/6/18		Situation normal. Artillery activity normal. Harassing fire carried out. Increase in number of cases of PUO.	o/s
"	15/6/18		Situation normal. Hostile Artillery below normal. Harassing fire carried out. Further cases of PUO reported.	o/s

Army Form C. 2118.

WAR DIARY
or
INTELLIGENCE SUMMARY.
(Erase heading not required.)

1ST BATTALION MACHINE GUN CORPS.
No. 2216

Place	Date	Hour	Summary of Events and Information	Remarks and references to Appendices
BARLIN K.37.b.L.t.	26/6/18		Situation normal. Enemy artillery quiet. E.A. was active during day. No harassing fire carried out.	
"	27/6/18		Situation unchanged. Enemy artillery below normal. No harassing fire carried out.	
"	28/6/18		Situation unchanged. Enemy artillery activity below normal. Harassing fire carried out.	
"	29/6/18		Situation normal. Enemy artillery in active. Harassing fire carried out.	
"	30/6/18		Situation normal. No increase in artillery activity. Aerial activity increased on both sides. Total no. of R/O cars 9 Officers and 178 O.R.	

Strength of Battalion June 1st Officers 46 O.R. 880
"   "   "   " 30th   "   47   "   890

Casualties for June 8 Officers 32 O.R.
Drafts " "

Officers taken on the strength are:—

Lieut. M.G. Hart
H.J. Thorpe
2/Lt. E.J. Hislop
T. Friend

SECRET   Copy No. 17

1ST BATTALION, MACHINE GUN CORPS.
OPERATION ORDER NO.28.

Reference BETHUNE combined sheet.

(1) "C" Company plus 2 guns will relieve "A" Company plus 2 guns in the HOHENZOLLERN Section on the 14th instant.

(2) All details of reliefs will be arranged between Officers Commanding Companies concerned direct.

(3) O.C."A" Company will hand over 2 guns complete to O.C."C" Company.

(4) On completion of relief "A" Company will proceed to billets in BARLIN.

(5) Companies will move by trains, details of which will be issued later.

(6) Copies of receipted trench store lists will be forwarded to this Office by 9 a.m. 16/5/18.

(7) Completion of relief will be reported to Battalion H.Q. by the code word "BOIS" and to 3rd Infantry Brigade direct.

(8) On completion of relief Group Commander Right Group will be Major F.G.Gurney, M.C.

(9) Acknowledge.

Captain and Adjutant,
1st Battalion, Machine
Gun Corps.

P.T.C.

Issued at 6 p.m. 13/6/18.

Copies issued to:—
(1) O.C. "A" Company
(2) O.C. "B" Company
(3) O.C. "C" Company
(4) O.C. "D" Company
(5) Commanding Officer
(6) Transport Officer
(7) Quartermaster
(8) Signalling Officer
(9) Medical Officer
(10) 11th Bn.M.G.C.
(11) 1st Infy.Brigade.
(12) 2nd Infy.Brigade.
(13) 3rd Infy.Brigade.
(14) 1st Division "G"
(15) 1st Division "Q"
(16) War Diary
(17) War Diary
(18) File
(19) File

SECRET.   Copy No. 5

1st BATTALION, MACHINE GUN CORPS.

OPERATION ORDER No. 29.

Reference BETHUNE combined sheet.

1. "A" Company, plus 1 gun, will relieve "B" Company plus 1 gun, in the CAMBRIN Section on the 22nd inst.

2. All details of relief will be arranged between Officers Commanding Companies direct.

3. O.C. "B" Company will hand over two guns complete to O.C. "A" Company.

4. On completion of relief "B" Company will proceed to billets in DARLIN.

5. Companies will move by train, details of which will be issued later.

6. Copies of receipted Trench Store Lists will be forwarded to this Office by 9.0 a.m. 24/3/18.

7. Completion of relief will be reported to Battalion Headquarters by the Code words "AVEC PALME", and to 1st Infantry Brigade direct.

8. On completion of relief Group Commander, Left Group, will be Major O.C.L. FITZWILLIAMS.

9. ACKNOWLEDGE.

                                                        Captain & Adjutant.
                                                   1st Battalion, Machine Gun Corps.

21st June, 1918.

Issued at 10.0 a.m. to

(1) O.C. "A" Company.   (11) 1st Infantry Brigade.
(2) O.C. "B" Company,   (12) 2nd Infantry Brigade.
(3) O.C. "C" Company,   (13) 3rd Infantry Brigade.
(4) O.C. "D" Company,   (14) 1st Division "G".
(5) Commanding Officer,   (15) 1st Division "Q".
(6) Transport Officer.   (16) War Diary.
(7) Quartermaster.   (17) War Diary.
(8) Signalling Officer.   (18) File.
(9) Medical Officer.   (19) File.
(10) 55th Battn., M.G.C.

APPENDIX. "A"

1ST BATTALION MACHINE GUN CORPS.
No. 1708
Date

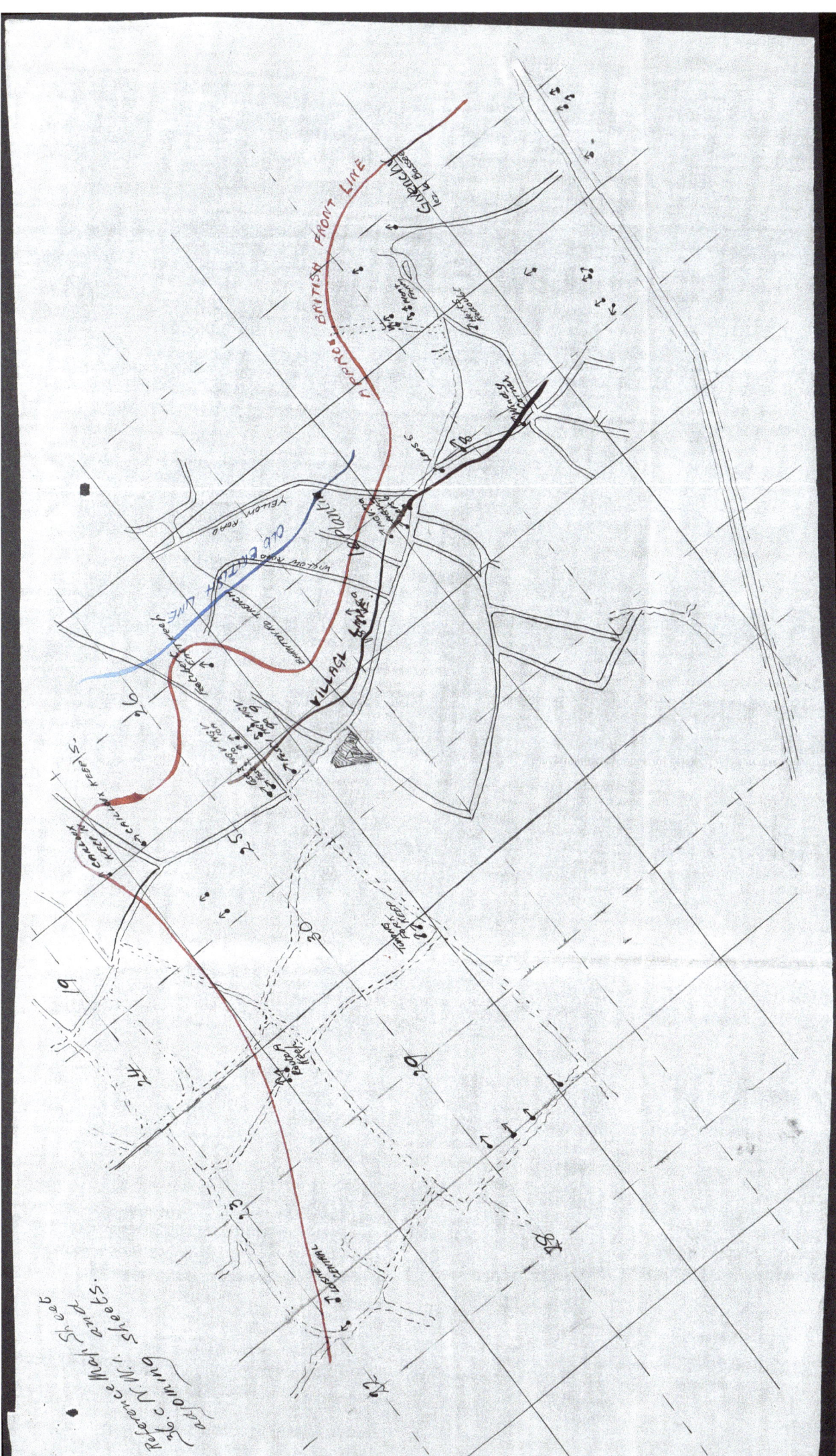

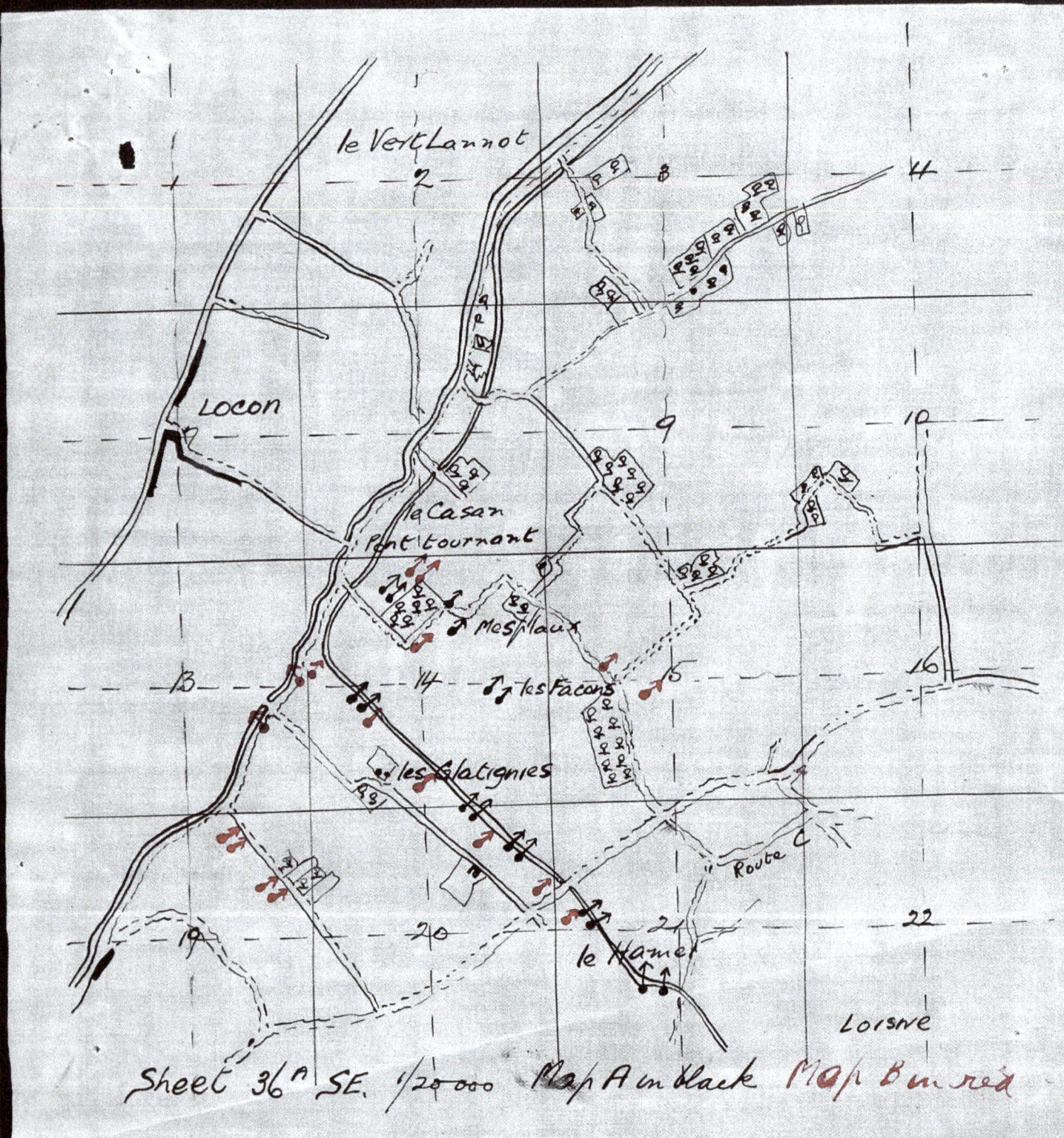

1st Division

War Diaries

1st M.G. BN. March to December

From 1st ~~May~~ ~~July~~ To 31st December 1918

Army Form C. 2118.

WAR DIARY
or
INTELLIGENCE SUMMARY.
(Erase heading not required.)

1ST BATTALION MACHINE GUN CORPS.
No. 34/9/1
Date.............

Instructions regarding War Diaries and Intelligence Summaries are contained in F.S. Regs., Part II. and the Staff Manual respectively. Title pages will be prepared in manuscript.

Place	Date	Hour	Summary of Events and Information	Remarks and references to Appendices
BARLIN K.32.d. S.L. 44.L	1/7/18		Situation normal. Increase in enemy activity on front. Harassing fire carried out. 2/Lt. C.O. DAVIES and Lt. W. McLEAN taken on strength of Batt. and posted to D & C Coys respectively.	JFS
"	2/7/18		Situation unchanged. 9 Malling about normal. Harassing fire carried out.	JFS
"	3/7/18		Situation normal. Harassment Milling. Enemy M.Gs active. Attack on aircraft Coy reinforced by B Coy 4 guns relieved by B Coy 4 guns in the HOHENZOLLERN sector and proceeded to billets in BARLIN. Trench fight & visibility good. No harassing fire carried out.	JFS
"	4/7/18		Situation normal. Hostile artillery more active. Harassing fire carried out. Night work from ammunition.	APPENDIX 'A' JFS
"	5/7/18		Situation normal, but hostile artillery slightly more active. Night's work. Harassing fire carried out by arrangement with the Infantry.	JFS
"	6/7/18		Situation normal. Decrease in hostile artillery activity. Guns Company relief between "C" and "D" Coys in the HOHENZOLLERN Sector. McGranahy fire carried out.	APPENDIX 'A' JFS
"	7/7/18		Situation unchanged. Hostile artillery slightly more normal. Indirect Concentration with rapid fire carried out on Ypres Salient at Sarpe being fired round area to N. and S. of Trenches near EPINOIS trench line 369. T.R. 10. ERSATZ O.W. RICHARDSON'S SPUR 15 N.W. of from front. Light enemy artillery activity. Harassing fire carried out.	JFS
"	8/7/18		Situation normal. Enemy artillery quiet. Harassing fire carried out.	JFS
"	9/7/18		Situation normal. Enemy artillery inactive. A Coy relieved by C Coy in CARTAIN Sector proceeded to billets in BARLIN. No retaliation for our harassing fire. APPENDIX FIRE RIDGE from M.32.	APPENDIX 'A' JFS
"	10/7/18		Situation unchanged. Enemy artillery quiet. No harassing fire carried out.	JFS
"	11/7/18		No change. Harassing fire carried out.	JFS

WAR DIARY or INTELLIGENCE SUMMARY

Army Form C. 2118.

1ST BATTALION MACHINE GUN CORPS.
No. .... Date ....

Place	Date	Hour	Summary of Events and Information	Remarks and references to Appendices
BARLIN K.32.d.4. & 24.4.	13/7/18		Hostile artillery much more active than on previous days. Harassing fire carried out.	J.B.
"	14/7/18		Situation normal. Hostile artillery inactive. Harassing fire carried out.	J.B.
"	15/7/18		Situation unchanged. Enemy artillery quiet. Harassing fire carried out.	J.B.
"	16/7/18		The War-Ga-"D" Coy relieved by "A" Coy 3rd (R.H.B.) Bttn. Guards M.G. Bttn. at BARLIN. "D" Coy proceeded to billets at HOHENZOLLERN Sector.	APPDX "A"
"	17/7/18		Situation normal. T.M activity on our front line at intervals. Gas in artillery. Harassing fire carried out.	J.B.
"	18/7/18		Situation normal. Hostile artillery active. Reserve Bttn. at intervals. "C" Coy relieved by "A" Coy in CAMBRIN Sector and proceeded to billets at BARLIN. Order No. 31.	APPENDIX "A"
"	19/7/18		Situation unchanged. Hostile artillery active at intervals during night. Great activity below.	J.B.
"	20/7/18		Situation normal. Gas in town right under fire during night. 15000 rounds fired in support of raid. An enemy's front trench line. 1000 rounds also fired in wire and 1000 rounds Harassing fire on the LA BASSÉE Rd. Enemy artillery and M.G. fire activity was usual. Raid not strong.	J.B.
"	21/7/18		Ticketyfication were obtained from held.	J.B.
"			Situation normal. Enemy artillery active at intervals. Harassing fire carried out.	J.B.
"	22/7/18		Situation unchanged. Enemy artillery inactive. Raid was carried out by our Infantry at 3.40 am. Int: we intercepted 2 hours wire obtained. Harassing fire was carried out 1900 rounds being fired in support on wire also 5000 on hostile tracks.	J.B. J.B.
"	23/7/18		Situation normal. Enemy artillery active on rear-line. Harassing fire carried out 2000 rounds in wire 10,000 rds. long fired from dusk to dawn. In addition 1400 rds were fired at low-flying E.A.	J.B.
"	24/7/18		Situation normal. Enemy artillery more active whilst dawn relieved in the early morning when enemy put down counter-preparation. Harassing fire carried out 21,000 rounds long fired in wire and 5000 rounds on approaches to AUCHY from HAINES. D Coy in the HOHENZOLLERN Sector & proceeded to billets at BARLIN. Order No. 35.	APPENDIX "A"

WAR DIARY
or
INTELLIGENCE SUMMARY.
(Erase heading not required.)

Army Form C. 2118.

1st BATTALION MACHINE GUN CORPS.

Instructions regarding War Diaries and Intelligence Summaries are contained in F. S. Regs., Part II. and the Staff Manual respectively. Title pages will be prepared in manuscript.

Place	Date	Hour	Summary of Events and Information	Remarks and references to Appendices
BARLIN K.32.d. Sh.44.A	25/7/18		Situation normal. 8000 rounds fired on gaps in wire. Lt Col H M HEYLAND assumed Command of Battalion vice Major FRERE.	off
"	26/7/18		Situation normal. Enemy artillery quiet. 10,000 rounds fired on gaps in wire. approaches from HAINES to AUCHY. A Coy relieved by C Coy on the CAMBRIN Sector and proceeded to billets at BARLIN. Order No 36.	off APPENDIX "A"
"	27/7/18		Situation normal. Enemy artillery showed slight activity. 17,000 rounds fired on gaps in wire.	off
"	28/7/18		Situation normal. Enemy artillery slightly active. 250 Gn trajection successfully discharged on SPOTTED DOG A.29.b. 9pm on wire. Rifts under fire all night.	off
"	29/7/18		Situation normal. Enemy artillery quiet. 31,000 rounds fired on gaps in wire. E.A. dropped 6 bombs on PONT FIXE A.11.d	off
"	30/7/18		Situation normal. Enemy artillery more active than usual on CAMBRIN Sector throughout day. Light rain caused our previous being brought in 86th R.I.R. Enemy attempted to raid in front of relaibation trench own off, by light & S.A. fire.	off
"	31/7/18		Situation normal. Enemy artillery more active. 5000 rounds fired on gaps in wire and 2000 rounds on LABASSEE Rd.	off

	Officers	O.R.
STRENGTH at beginning of month	46	894
" " end "	47	900

CASUALTIES 8 O.R.

SECRET.

Copy No. 15

1ST BATTALION, MACHINE GUN CORPS.
ORDER NO. 30.

Reference BETHUNE combined Sheet, 1/40,000.

(1) "B" Company plus 2 guns will relieve "C" Company plus 2 guns in the HOHENZOLLERN Section on the 3rd instant.

(2) All details of reliefs will be arranged between Officers Commanding Companies concerned direct.

(3) O.C. "C" Company will hand sufficient guns to complete necessary number to O.C. "B" Company.

(4) On completion of relief "C" Company will proceed to billets in BARLIN.

(5) Companies will move by trains, details of which will be issued later.

(6) Copies of receipted trench stores lists will be forwarded to this Office by 9 a.m. 5/7/18.

(7) Completion of relief will be reported to Battalion H.Q. by the code word "WOOD" and to 2nd Infantry Brigade direct.

(8) On completion of relief Group Commander Right Group will be Major J.S. Snowball.

(9) Acknowledge.

Lieut. and A/Adjutant,
1st Battalion, Machine
Gun Corps.

Issued at 7 p.m. 1/7/18.

Copies issued to:-

(1) O.C. "A" Company, 1st Battn. M.G.C.
(2) O.C. "B" Company, -do-
(3) O.C. "C" Company, -do-
(4) O.C. "D" Company, -do-
(5) Commanding Officer. -do-
(6) Transport Officer, -do-
(7) Quartermaster, -do-
(8) Signalling Officer, -do-
(9) Medical Officer, -do-
(10) 11th Battalion, M.G.C.
(11) 1st Infantry Brigade.
(12) 2nd Infantry Brigade.
(13) 3rd Infantry Brigade.
(14) 1st Division "G".
(15) 1st Division "Q".
(16) War Diary.
(17) War Diary.
(18) File.
(19) File.

SECRET   Copy No.

1ST BATTALION, MACHINE GUN CORPS.

ORDER NO.51.

Reference BETHUNE combined Sheet, 1/40,000.

(1) An inter-Company relief will take place between "B" Company and "D" Company in the HOHENZOLLERN Section on the 6th instant.

(2) All details of relief will be arranged between O's C.Companies concerned direct.

(3) Copies of receipted Trench Store Lists will be forwarded to this Office by 9.a.m. 8th instant.

(4) Completion of relief will be reported to Battalion Headquarters by the Code Word, "CRUMP" and to 2nd Infantry Brigade direct.

(5) On completion of relief Group Commander Right Group will be ~~Major Robinson~~ Major J.S.Snowball.

(6) Acknowledge.

                                                    Lieut. and A/Adjutant,
                                                    1st Battalion, Machine
                                                    Gun Corps.

Issued at 2 p.m. 5/7/18.

Copies issued to:-

        (1) "A" Company, 1st Battalion, M.G.C.
        (2) "B" Company,   -do-
        (3) "C" Company,   -do-
        (4) "D" Company,   -do-
        (5) Commanding Officer,   -do-
        (6) Transport Officer,   -do-
        (7) Quartermaster,   -do-
        (8) Signalling Officer,   -do-
        (9) Medical Officer,   -do-
        (10) 11th Battalion, Machine Gun Corps.
        (11) 1st Infantry Brigade.
        (12) 2nd Infantry Brigade
        (13) 3rd Infantry Brigade
        (14) 1st Division "G"
        (15) 1st Division "Q"
        (16) War Diary
        (17) War Diary
        (18) War Diary
        (19) File
        (20) File

SECRET   1ST BATTALION, MACHINE GUN CORPS.   Copy No. 13

ORDER NO.32.

Reference BETHUNE combined sheet, 1/40,000.

(1) "C" Company, plus 2 guns, will relieve "A" Company plus 1 gun, in the CAMBRIN Section on the 10th instant.

(2) All details of relief will be arranged between Officers Commanding Companies concerned direct.

(3) O.C. "A" Company will hand over 3 guns complete to O.C. "C" Company.

(4) On completion of relief "A" Company will proceed to billets in BARLIN.

(5) Companies will move by train, details of which will be issued later.

(6) Copies of receipted Trench Store Lists will be forwarded to this Office by 9.a.m. 12th instant.

(7) Completion of relief will be reported to Battalion H.Q. by the code word "FORDO" and to 1st Infantry Brigade direct.

(8) On completion of relief Group Commander, Left Group, will be Major F.G.Gurney, M.C.

(9) Acknowledge.

Lieut. and A/Adjutant,
1st Battalion, Machine
Gun Corps.

Issued at 2.p.m. 9/7/18.

Distribution overpage.

Copies issued to:-   (1) O.C. "A" Company
                     (2) O.C. "B" Company
                     (3) O.C. "C" Company
                     (4) O.C. "D" Company
                     (5) Battalion H.Q.
                     (6) 55th Battalion, M.G.C.
                     (7) 1st Infantry Brigade.
                     (8) 2nd Infantry Brigade.
                     (9) 3rd Infantry Brigade.
                     (10) 1st Division "G"
                     (11) 1st Division "Q"
                     (12) War Diary.
                     (13) War Diary.
                     (14) File.

SECRET

1ST BATTALION, MACHINE GUN CORPS.
ORDER NO.33

Copy No. /8

Reference BETHUNE combined sheet, 1/40,000.

(1) "A" Coy.3rd (R.H.G) Battn. Guards M.G.Regt. plus 2 guns will relieve "D" Coy.1st Battn.M.G.C.plus 2 guns in the HOHENZOLLERN Section on the 16th instant.

(2) All details of relief will be arranged direct between O.C.Coys.concerned

(3) O.C."D" Coy.will hand over 2 guns complete to O.C."A" Coy.3rd.(R.H.G) Battalion Guards M.G.Regt.

(4) On completion of relief "D" Coy. will proceed to billets in BARLIN.

(5) "A" Coy.3rd (R.H.G) Bn. will move by bus & "D" Coy.1st Battn.will move by train details of which will be issued later.

(6) O.C."D" Coy.will detail one man per gun team to remain with "A" Coy. 3rd (R.H.G) Battn. for 24 hours after completion of relief.

(7) Completion of relief will be reported to Battn.H.Q. by the code word "TOBY" and to 2nd Infantry Brigade direct.

(8) On completion of relief Group Commander Right Group will be Major J.S.Snowball.

(9) Acknowledge.

Issued at 5.p.m. 15/7/18

Captain and Adjutant,
1st Battalion, Machine
Gun Corps.

Distribution overpage.

Copies issued to:-
(1) O.C."A" Company
(2) O.C."B" Company
(3) O.C."C" Company
(4) O.C."D" Company
(5) Battalion H.Q.
(6) "A" Coy.3rd (R.H.G) Battn.Guards M.G.Reg
(7) 3rd(R.H.G) Battn.   -do-
(8) 11th Battalion M.G.C.
(9) 1st Infantry Brigade
(10) 2nd Infantry Brigade
(11) 3rd Infantry Brigade
(12) 1st Division "G"
(13) 1st Division "Q"
(14) War Diary
(15) War Diary
(16) File.

SECRET.　　　　　1ST BATTALION, MACHINE GUN CORPS.　　　Copy No.
　　　　　　　　　　　　　　ORDER NO.34.
　　　　　　　　　Reference BETHUNE combined Sheet.

(1) "A" Company plus 1 gun will relieve "C" Company plus 1 gun in the CAMBRIN Section on the 18th instant.

(2) All details of relief will be arranged between O.C.Coys concerned direct.

(3) O.C."C" Coy. will hand over 2 guns complete to O.C. "A" Company.

(4) On completion of relief "C" Coy. will proceed to billots in BARLIN.

(5) "A" Coy. will move by train leaving BARLIN at 1.30.p.m.
"C" Coy. will move by train leaving SAILLY LABOURSE at 7.p.m.

(6) Copies of receipted Trench Store lists will be forwarded to this Office by 9.a.m. 20th instant.

(7) Completion of relief will be reported to Battalion H.Q. by the code word "BOLSHO" and to 3rd Infantry Brigade direct.

(8) On completion of relief Group Commander Left Group will be CAPT.A.DU...

　　　　　　　　　　　　　　　　　　　　Captain and Adjutant,
Issued at 10.p.m. 16/7/18　　　　　　　　1st Battalion, Machine
　　　　　　　　　　　　　　　　　　　　　Gun Corps.
　　　　　　　　　　　Distribution overpage.

Copies issued to:- (1) "A" Company
                    (2) "B" Company
                    (3) "C" Company
                    (4) "D" Company
                    (5) Battalion H.Q.
                    (6) 55th Battalion, M.G.C.
                    (7) 1st Infantry Brigade
                    (8) 2nd Infantry Brigade
                    (9) 3rd Infantry Brigade
                    (10) 1st Division "G"
                    (11) 1st Division "Q"
                    (12) War Diary
                    (13) War Diary
                    (14) File

SECRET.   1st BATTALION, MACHINE GUN CORPS.   Copy No. 15

Order No. 35.

Reference BETHUNE combined sheet.1/40,000

1) "D" Coy. less 4 guns will relieve "B" Coy. less 4 guns in the HOHENZOLLERN Section on the 24th inst.

2) All details of relief will be arranged between O.C.Coys. concerned direct.

3) On relief "B" Coy. will proceed to billet in BARLIN.

4) "D" Coy. less 4 guns will move by train leaving BARLIN at 1.30 pm.
"B" Coy. less 4 guns will move by train leaving SAILLY LABOURSE at 7.pm.

5) Copies of receipted Trench Store Lists will be forwarded to Battalion Headquarters by 9 a.m. 25th inst.

6) Completion of relief will be reported to Battalion Headquarters by the Code Word "BOLSHEVIK", and to 1st Infantry Brigade direct.

7) On completion of relief Group Commander, Right Group will be Major T.G.ANSON

8) ACKNOWLEDGE.

Captain & Adjutant.
1st Battalion, Machine Gun Corps.

Issued at 7.0 p.m. 22/7/18.

Distribution normal, and to:-

"A" Coy. 3rd (R.H.G.) Battn. Guards, M.G.Regt.
11th Battalion, Machine Gun Corps.

SECRET.   1st BATTALION, MACHINE GUN CORPS.   Copy No. 14

Order No. 38.

Reference BETHUNE combined sheet.

(1) "C" Coy. plus 1 gun will relieve "A" Coy. plus 1 gun in the CAMBRIN Section on the 26th inst.

(2) All details of relief will be arranged between O.C. Companies concerned direct.

(3) O.C. "A" Coy. will hand over 1 gun complete to O.C. "C" Coy.

(4) On completion of relief "A" Coy. will proceed to billets in BARLIN.

(5) "C" Coy. will move by train leaving BARLIN at 1.30 p.m.
    "A" Coy. "   "   "   "   "   SAILLY LABOURSE at 7 pm.

(6) Copies of receipted Trench Store Lists will be forwarded to this Office by 9 am. 28th inst.

(7) Completion of relief will be reported to Battalion Headquarters by the Code Word "MARNE", and to 3rd Infantry Brigade direct.

(8) On completion of relief Group Commander, Left Brigade Group will be Capt. T. MORGAN.

(9) ACKNOWLEDGE.

                                                    Capt. & Adjutant.
                                                    1st Battalion, M.G. Corps.

Issued at 7.0 p.m. 24/7/18.

                    Distribution overpage.

Copies issued to:-
(1) "A" Company.
(2) "B"   "
(3) "C"   "
(4) "D"   "
(5) Battalion H.Q.
(6) 55th Battalion, R.G.C.
(7) "D" Coy. 3rd (R.H.G) Bn., Guards M.G.Regt
(8) 1st Infantry Brigade.
(9) 2nd Infantry Brigade.
(10) 3rd Infantry Brigade.
(11) 1st Division "G".
(12) 1st Division "Q".
(13) War Diary.
(14) War Diary.
(15) File.

SECRET.   1st BATTALION, MACHINE GUN CORPS.   Copy No. 16

ORDER No. 37.

Reference BETHUNE combined sheet.

(1) "B" Coy. 1st Battalion, M.G.C. will relieve "D" Coy. 3rd (R.H.G) Battalion, Guards M.G.Regt. in the HOHENZOLLERN Section on 1st August.

(2) All details of relief will be arranged direct between Officers Commanding Companies concerned.

(3) On completion of relief "D" Coy., 3rd (R.H.G) Bn. will rejoin 3rd (R.H.G) Bn. Guards, M.G.Regt.

(4) "B" Coy. will move by motor lorries, details of which will be notified later.

(5) Copies of receipted Trench Store Lists will be forwarded to this Office by 9.0 a.m. 3rd proximo.

(6) Completion of relief will be reported to Battalion H.Q. by the Code word "RASPBERRY", and to 1st Infantry Brigade direct.

(7) On completion of relief Group Commander, Right Group will be Major T.G. ANSON.

(8) ACKNOWLEDGE.

Issued at 10.0 a.m.
31/7/18.

for Captain & Adjutant.
1st Battalion, Machine Gun Corps.

Distribution overpage.

Copies issued to:-

(1) "A" Company.
(2) "B" Company.
(3) "C" Company.
(4) "D" Company.
(5) Battalion, H.Q.
(6) 11th Battalion, H.G.C.
(7) "D" Coy. 3rd (R.H.G.) Bn. Guards M.G. Regt.
(8) 1st Infantry Brigade.
(9) 2nd   "   "
(10) 3rd   "   "
(11) 1st Division "G".
(12) 1st Division "Q"
(13) War Diary.
(14)   "   "
(15) File.

WAR DIARY or INTELLIGENCE SUMMARY

Army Form C.2118.

1ST BATTALION MACHINE GUN CORPS.

Place	Date	Hour	Summary of Events and Information	Remarks and references to Appendices
BARLIN K.32.d S.4.E	1/8/18		Situation normal. B. Coy (less W.M.G.) relieved "D" Coy 3rd K.R.R. Regt. Guards Bn. G. Regt. in the HOHENZOLLERN Sector. Relief complete 11:30pm. Harassing fire carried out 5700 rounds being fired on gaps on. in L.L.R. and 4000 rds in LA BASSEE Road. Verey lights fired and flares observed at intervals.	Appendix A.
"	2/8/18		Situation normal. Enemy artillery quiet. Harassing fire carried out 4700 rounds being fired on our Allies front. At 9.1.30. fired from hostility.	J.R.
"	3/8/18		Situation normal. Enemy artillery quiet. Harassing fire carried out 5/2 rounds on I.O.R. and BRICK STACKS being [illeg] and 4000 rounds [illeg] on LA BASSEE Road.	J.R.
"	4/8/18		Situation quiet. Enemy artillery normal. Our Coy stn in Reserve Village line firing the night 12 000 rounds fired by M.G. on Gaps on wire in Kings Keep sector.	J.R.
"	5/8/18		Situation unchanged. Enemy artillery quiet. Harassing fire carried out by the infantry firing [illeg] at gaps in wire and 10,000 rds by heavy M.G. MG's firing thro the flying [illeg] Above was thought from in Enemy lines. The MG's of the CAMBRIN Sector claim.	J.R.
"	6/8/18		Refraction unchanged. Enemy artillery quiet. Harassing fire carried out by firing fired on LA BASSEE Road, AUCHY ALLEY and other enfilade targets. B Coy reported to "A" Coy (no Guns) Guns "D" Coy (1 gun) in the CAMBRIN Section appr rest.	Appendix A.
"	7/8/18		Situation normal. Enemy artillery quiet. Our survey M.G. active during morning at 11:45am Enemy parties of the enemy attempted to rush our HOHENZOLLERN Section. M.G. was brought up again at 1:05 am. with heavy burst of M.G. fire and Lewis gun Harassing fire was carried out 380 rounds were fired at E.A.	J.R.
"	8/8/18		Situation unchanged. Inspected 2 uneventful wound was carried out at 12:15am on enemy trenches by 10th Coy 3/9 I.R. was captured and five prisoners are known to have been killed one [illeg] with 106 got. 7th Casualties were 1 officer and 1 NC slightly wounded. Our [illeg] put a barrage round the area to H. Harassing fire too rounds harassing out. Our guns firing the [illeg]trenches to harass enemy ration parties at [illeg] and [illeg] belts.	Appendix A.
"	9/8/18		Situation normal. Enemy artillery quiet. Harassing [illeg] Coming [illeg] 15,000 rounds being fired.	J.R.

WAR DIARY or INTELLIGENCE SUMMARY

Army Form C. 2118.

(Erase heading not required.)

1st BATTALION MACHINE GUN CORPS
No. ....
Date ....

Place	Date	Hour	Summary of Events and Information	Remarks and references to Appendices
BERLIN K.32 & SK.44	10/8/18		Situation unchanged. Slight E/A aerial activity tried to read our S/L in report but were driven off by Rifle & M.G. fire. Enemy artillery quiet. Our M.G's fired 6000 rounds on AUCHY ALLEY and target in A.29.a. & FARE PROOF.	JR
"	11/8/18		Situation unchanged. Fast enemy artillery activity about normal. From 10.30 a.m. to 3 p.m. NOEUX-LES-MINES heavily shelled. PONT-FIXE, ANNEQUIN and SAILLY also shelled. E/A very active during night. Trench mortars active on SAILLY and NOEUX-LES-MINES. Our M.G's fired 18,000 rounds harassing fire on roads and tracks.	JR
	12/8/18		Sit. unchanged. Enemy art. also normal. Chiefly back areas. Our M.G's fired 18,900 rounds on harassing targets.	JR
	13/8/18		Sit. unchanged. E. art. slight. One M.G. fired 1500 rds. on pt. target.	JR
	14/8/18		Sit. unchanged. E. art. slight. 23,000 rounds fired on harassing targets.	JR
	15/8/18		Sit. unchanged. Several reports received enemy front line. E. art. slight. M.G. fired 31,000 rds. on ground targets.	JR
	16/8/18		D. relieved A Coy in CAMBRIN subs. & O.Coy relieved 15. Coy in HOHENZOLLERN subs. A Coy fired 3 guns on tgt. FACTORY. Sit. unchanged. M.G. fired 16000 rds. on tgts.	Appendix x?
	17/8/18		Sit. unchanged. Enemy slight. Our M.G fired 18000 rounds on tgts.	JR
	18/8/18		Sit. unchanged. En. artillery slight. Our M.G fired 16000 rounds on harassing tgts.	JR
	19/8/18		Sit. unchanged. En. artillery less active. Our M.G fired 36000 rds. on tgts. M.G's active on pt. targets.	JR
	20/8/18		A Coy. Coys 3 guns & B Coy 5 guns BARLIN & E.P.S. Sit. unchanged. Our artillery & Cn. Extension more active on harassing ideas. Bn M.G. fired 19000 rds. on pt. targets.	JR
	21/8/18		A Coy 16th Bn relieved D.Coy. in CAMBRIN sector. D.Co. proceeded to E.P.S. Sit. unchanged. E. art. slight. Our M.G. fired 21000 rds. on pt. tgts.	JR
	22/8/18		B.Coy. 16th Bn relieved C.Co. in HOHENZOLLERN sector. Bn. H.Q. & C.Co. proceeded to E.P.S. War 3 gun & A Coy. Sit. unchanged. This subpt. but NOEUX fired on by H.V.	JR

Army Form C. 2118.

WAR DIARY
or
INTELLIGENCE SUMMARY.
(Erase heading not required.)

Instructions regarding War Diaries and Intelligence Summaries are contained in F. S. Regs., Part II. and the Staff Manual respectively. Title pages will be prepared in manuscript.

1ST BATTALION
MACHINE GUN CORPS
No. A 219
Date

Place	Date	Hour	Summary of Events and Information	Remarks and references to Appendices
E P S	23/8/18		Training at E.P.S.	J.f.B
	30/8/18		Orders received to move to ARRAS area. Tini entrained at AMVIN by tactical train. Transport moved to new area by road.	J.f.B
	31/8/18		Strength of Batt's at beginning of month: Officers 47, O.R. 867	
			Strength at end of Aug: Officers 50, O.R. 892	
			Casualties: Offs. nil, O.R. nil	
			Reinforcements: Offs. nil, O.R. nil	

1st BATTALION, MACHINE GUN CORPS.

Order No. 38.

Copy No. 17

Reference BETHUNE combined sheet.

(1) "A" Coy. (16 guns) will relieve "C" Coy. (16 guns) and "D" Coy. relieve 1 guns at V.47 in the CAMBRIN Section on the 6th inst.

(2) All details of relief will be arranged between Officers Commanding Companies concerned direct.

(3) On completion of relief "C" Coy. will proceed to billets in BARLIN.

(4) "A" Coy. will move by train leaving BARLIN at 1.30 p.m.
"C" Coy. will move by train leaving SAILLY LABOURSE at 7.0 p.m.

(5) Copies of receipted Trench Store Lists will be forwarded to this Office by 9.0 a.m. 8th inst.

(6) Completion of relief will be reported to Battalion H.Q. by the Code word "POTATO", and to 2nd Infantry Brigade direct.

(7) On completion of relief Group Commander, Left Group, will be Major C.C.L. Fitzwilliams.

(8) ACKNOWLEDGE.

Issued at 10.0 a.m.
4/8/18.

Captain & Adjutant.
1st Battalion, Machine Gun Corps.

Distribution overpage.

Copies issued to:-
(1) "A" Company.
(2) "B" Company.
(3) "C" Company.
(4) "D" Company.
(5) Battalion Headquarters.
(6) 55th Battalion, M.G.C.
(7) 1st Infantry Brigade.
(8) 2nd Infantry Brigade.
(9) 3rd Infantry Brigade.
(10) 1st Division "G".
(11) 1st Division "Q".
(12) War Diary.
(13) War Diary.
(14) File.

WAR DIARY
INTELLIGENCE SUMMARY

Army Form C. 2118.

Place	Date	Hour	Summary of Events and Information	Remarks and references to Appendices
MASSEMY	26/9/18		Bn Headquarters returned to MASSEMY. The situation was unchanged and fairly quiet. Relieved W.D. Coy 61st Bn M.G. Corps. Many wounded received by A Coy. Relieve A Coy by the 1st Hert. Bn M.G.C. Casualties 3 O.R.	Appendix APP13 do
MASSEMY	27/9/18		Situation unchanged. One fairly quiet. A Coy relieved before 8 Hert. Bn M.G.C. in the left section which Bn Buried four, wounded 5 Six. Casualties nil	do
MASSEMY	28/9/18		Situation unchanged. Considerable activity on the right. Orders received that the Division would attack in co-operation with the 46th Div on the left and the 6th Division on the right. Casualties 3 O.R.	do
MASSEMY	28/9/18		Moved B Coy into Bivouacs to the CANHAINCOURT area.	
MASSEMY	29/9/18	5.30AM	The 1st Division attacked at 5.30AM in conjunction with the 46th on the left & the 6th on the right. The objective was in the first place to form a defensive flank and for the 46 Div to attack through the GREEN LINE was taken by the 46th Division to secure the high ground in MAGNY, THORIGNY and THANT Hill. A Coy cooperating with 1st Bde rendered significant assistance to the advance and C Coy and B Coy of D Coy supported the advance of the 2nd Bde. The attack was successful the advance reached the Woods N of THORIGNY. B Coy remained in Wells at CAULAIN COURT.	do
MASSEMY	30/9/18		Battalion Headquarters advanced moved forward to M15C 3.3 and Near Bn Hqs moved to MASSEMY. The Division continued to advance and reached THANT Hill and the THORIGNY – SEQUEHART Ridge. A Coy did excellent work in assisting the advance of the 2 Bde forward troops Ridge. Casualties 2Lt R.W.H. BAKER & A Coy wounded and 3 O.Rs	do

Nucey 18 Bn M.G. Corps.

SECRET.   1st BATTALION, MACHINE GUN CORPS.   Copy No. 18

ORDER No. 57.

Reference BETHUNE combined sheet.

(1) "B" Coy. 1st Battalion, M.G.C, will relieve "D" Coy. 3rd (R.H.G) Battalion, Guards M.G.Regt. in the HOHENZOLLERN Section on 1st August.

(2) All details of relief will be arranged direct between Officers Commanding Companies concerned.

(3) On completion of relief "D" Coy., 3rd (R.H.G) Bn. will rejoin 3rd (R.H.G) Bn. Guards M.G.Regt.

(4) "B" Coy. will move by motor lorries, details of which will be notified later.

(5) Copies of receipted Trench Store Lists will be forwarded to this Office by 9.0 a.m. 3rd proximo.

(6) Completion of relief will be reported to Battalion H.Q. by the Code word "RASPBERRY", and to 1st Infantry Brigade direct.

(7) On completion of relief Group Commander, Right Group will be Major T.G. ANSON.

(8) ACKNOWLEDGE.

for Captain & Adjutant.
1st Battalion, Machine Gun Corps.

Issued at 12.0 a.m.

Copies issued to:-
- (1) "A" Company.
- (2) "B" Company.
- (3) "C" Company.
- (4) "D" Company.
- (5) Battalion, H.Q.
- (6) 11th Battalion, R.G.C.
- (7) "D" Coy. 3rd(R.H.G.)Bn. Guards M.G.Regt.
- (8) 1st Infantry Brigade.
- (9) 2nd   "   "
- (10) 3rd   "   "
- (11) 1st Division "Q".
- (12) 1st Division "Q"
- (13) War Diary.
- (14)   "   "
- (15) File.

SECRET

1ST BATTALION, MACHINE GUN CORPS
ORDER NO. 38. 39

Copy No. 14

Reference BETHUNE combined Sheet 1/40,000

(1) The following reliefs will be carried out on the 16th inst.

"D" Coy. will relieve "A" Coy. in the CAMBRIN Section.
"C" Coy. will relieve "B" Coy. in the HOHENZOLLERN Section.
"A" Coy. will relieve 3 guns of "D" Coy. at FACTORY BATTERY.

(2) All details of relief will be arranged between Officers Commanding Companies concerned direct.

(3) On completion of relief "B" Coy., and "A" Coy. less three guns will proceed to billets in BARLIN where,

"A" Company less 3 guns will be Company in Support.
"B" Company will be the Company in reserve.

(4) "C" and "D" Coys. will move by train leaving BARLIN at 1.30.p.m.
"A" and "B" Coys. will move by train leaving SAILLY LABOURSE at 7.p.m.

(5) Copies of receipted Trench Store Lists will be forwarded to this Office by 9.a.m. 18th instant.

(6) Completion of relief will be reported to Battalion H.Q. by the code word "GAELIC" and to Infantry Brigades concerned direct.

(7) On completion of relief Group Commanders will be:-

Left Group,   Major T.G.Anson.
Right Group,   Major F.G.Gurney, M.C.

(8) Acknowledge.

Captain and Adjutant,
1st Battalion, Machine
Gun Corps.

Issued at 10.p.m. 13/8/18

Distribution overpage.

Copies issued to:-
- (1) "A" Company
- (2) "B" Company
- (3) "C" Company
- (4) "D" Company
- (5) Battalion Headquarters.
- (6) 55th Battalion, M.G.C.
- (7) 11th Battalion, M.G.C.
- (8) 1st Infantry Brigade.
- (9) 2nd Infantry Brigade.
- (10) 3rd Infantry Brigade.
- (11) 1st Division "G"
- (12) 1st Division "Q"
- (13) War Diary
- (14) War Diary
- (15) File.

SECRET.

1ST BATTALION, MACHINE GUN CORPS.
ORDER NO. 40.

Copy No. 17.

1st Battalion Machine Gun Corps. No. 3903

Reference BETHUNE combined Sheet, 1/40,000.
and Sheet 44.B. 1/40,000.

(1) Reference this Office No.3892 "WARNING ORDER" issued to Companies this day, the following reliefs will be carried out on the 19th instant.

One Company 16th Battalion, M.G.C. will relieve "A" Company less 3 guns in Support at BARLIN.
One Company 16th Battalion, M.G.C. will relieve "B" Company in Reserve at BARLIN.

The 3 guns of "A" Company at Factory Battery will be relieved under orders to be issued later.

(2) All details of relief will be arranged between Officers Commanding Companies concerned direct.

O.C. "A" Company will hand over to relieving Company all details of his role as Support Company and all Defence Schemes Maps and Trench Stores.

O.C. "B" Company will hand over to relieving Company all orders and details in connection with the reconnaissance of MINX Locality and the BEUVRY-CAMBRIN Road and LAUNDRY Lines and also all Defence Schemes Maps and Trench Stores of the Reserve Defences.

N.B. No Maps Sheet 44.b. 1/40,000; Lens, 1/100,000, or Hazebrouck, 1/100,000, will be handed over.

(3) Copies of receipted lists of Trench Stores, Defence Schemes Maps etc. handed over will be forwarded to this Office immediately on completion of relief.

(4) On completion of relief, dismounted personnel, "A" and "B" Companies will move to billets in EPS by bus, details of which will be issued later.

(5) Transport and mounted personnel of "A" and "B" Companies will move to new area by march route under 2/Lieut. Spary M.C. by the following route:-

BARLIN - HAILLICOURT - BRUAY - CALONNE RICOUART - PERNES - SAINS-LES-PERNES - EPS.

The head of the column will pass the starting point at K.20.c.2.2. (cross-roads) by 9.a.m. 19/8/18.

(6) On completion of relief the 2 Companies of 16th Battalion, M.G.C. come under the orders of the 1st Division.

(7) Completion of relief will be reported direct to this Office.

(8) ACKNOWLEDGE.

Captain and Adjutant,
1st Battalion, Machine
Gun Corps.

Issued at 10.p.m. 18/8/18.

Distribution overpage.

Copies issued to:-
(1) "A" Company
(2) "B" Company
(3) "C" Company
(4) "D" Company
(5) Transport Officer.
(6) Battalion Headquarters.
(7) 16th Battalion M.G.C.
(8) 1st Infantry Brigade.
(9) 2nd Infantry Brigade.
(10) 3rd Infantry Brigade.
(11) 1st Division "Q"
(12) 1st Division "G"
(13) A.P.M. 1st Division.
(14) S.S.O. 1st Division.
(15) War Diary
(16) War Diary.
(17) File.

SECRET.   Copy No. 14

1st BATTALION, MACHINE GUN CORPS
ORDER No. 41.

Reference BETHUNE combined sheet, 1/40,000
and Sheet 44.B. 1/40,000.

1. "D" Coy. 1st Bn., M.G.Corps will be relieved by "A" Coy. 16th Bn., M.G.Corps, on the 21st inst.

2. (a) All details of relief will be arranged between Officers Commanding Companies concerned direct.

   (b) All Defence Schemes, details of work on hand, etc. and all maps except 44.B., LENS 1/100,000, HAZEBROUCK 1/100,000, will be handed over.

   (c) O.C. "D" Coy. will also hand over all Trench Stores at the following positions (at present unoccupied) and obtain receipts for same.
   N.M.G. 14.   Princes Post (1 gun position)
   N.M.G. 18.   (Moir Pillbox)

3. O.C. "D" Coy. will leave the following personnel in the line until 4.0 p.m. on 22nd inst., when they will proceed to Battalion Headquarters by road.
   1 Officer at Coy. H.Q.,   1 N.C.O. per Section.

4. Copies of receipted list of Trench Stores, Maps, etc. will be forwarded to Battalion Headquarters by 9.0 a.m. 23rd inst.

5. "A" Coy. 16th Bn., M.G.Corps will proceed by train leaving BARLIN at 12 noon 21st inst. Detraining station:- SAILLY LABOURSE.

6. Dismounted personnel of "D" Coy. 1st Bn., M.G.Corps, will move to new area by BUS, embussing at K.24.c.5.7. at a time to be notified later, and debussing at BOYAVAL.

7. Transport and mounted personnel of "D" Coy. 1st Bn., M.G.Corps will move to new area by march route under Lieut. KAUFFMANN, by the following route :-
   BARLIN-HALLICOURT-BRUAY-CALONNE RICOUART-PERNES-
   -SAINTS-LES-PERNES-EPS.

   The head of the column will pass the starting point at K.20.c.2.2. (cross roads) at 0.0 p.m. 21/8/18.

8. On completion of relief "A" Coy. 16th Bn., M.G.Corps will come under the orders of the 1st Division, and Group Commander, Left Group will be Major B.H.JONES.

9. Completion of relief will be reported to Battalion Headquarters by the Code phrase "Your A.S.321 Noted", and to 2nd Brigade direct.

10. ACKNOWLEDGE.

Captain & Adjutant.
1st Battalion, Machine Gun Corps.

Issued at 7.0 p.m., 20/8/18.

Copies issued to :-

(1) "C" Coy.   (6) 16th Bn., M.G.C.   (11) 1st Div. "G"
(2) "D" Coy.   (7) 2nd Inf. Bde.   (12) A.P.M.
(3) "A" Coy. 16th Bn.   (8) 3rd Inf. Bde.   (13) S.S.O.
(4) Transport Officer. (9) 55th Bn. M.G.C.   (14) War Diary.
(5) Battalion, H.Q.   (10) 1st Div. "Q"   (15) File.

SECRET.   Copy No. 14

1st BATTALION, MACHINE GUN CORPS.
ORDER No. 42.

Reference Sheet 44.B.

1. "C" Coy. 1st Bn., M.G.Corps will be relieved by "B" Coy. 16th Bn. M.G.Corps in the HOHENZOLLERN Section on the 22nd inst., and 3 guns of "A" Coy. 1st Bn., M.G.Corps at FACTORY POST will be relieved by 3 guns of "C" Coy. 16th Bn., M.G.Corps.

2. (a) All details of relief will be arranged between Officers Commanding Companies concerned direct.
   (b) All Defence Schemes, Schemes of work, Trench Stores and all maps, except 44.B., LENS 1/100,000 & HAZEBROUCK 1/100,000, will be carefully handed over.
   (c) Trench Stores at the following positions (at present unoccupied) will also be handed over and receipts obtained.
       VALLEY Battery. BULLY Bty. (2 positions) 4 positions at ANNEQUIN.

3. O.C. "C" Coy. will leave the following personnel in the line until 4.0 p.m. on the 23rd inst., when they will be withdrawn under arrangements to be notified later.

4. Copies of receipted Trench Store Lists will be forwarded to Battalion H.Q. by 3.0 p.m. on 23rd inst.

5. "B" Coy. 16th Bn., M.G.Corps will proceed to SAILLY LABOURSE BY
   (a) train leaving BARLIN at 8.0 a.m. 22/8/18.
   (b) 100 yards distance will be maintained between each transport vehicle moving up to SAILLY LABOURSE.

6. Dismounted personnel of Battalion Headquarters & "C" Coy. 1st Bn., M.G.Corps will move by BUS from embussing point at a time to be notified later, and will debus at EPS.

7. Transport and mounted personnel of Battalion H.Q., will move by march route under Lieut. RAYNER by the following route :-
       BARLIN-HALLICOURT-BRUAY-CALONNE RICOUART-PERNES-
       -SAINS-LES-PERNES-EPS.
   Head of the column will pass the starting point at K.20.c.2.2. (cross roads) at 9.0 a.m. 22/8/18.

8. Completion of relief will be reported to Battalion H.Q. by the Code phrase "Your A.S.330 noted", and to Brigade concerned direct.

9. On completion of relief Group Commander, Right Group, will be Major George.

10. ACKNOWLEDGE.

                                              Captain & Adjutant,
                                         1st Battalion, Machine Gun Corps.

Issued at 2.0 p.m., 21/8/18.

Copies issued to :-

(1) "A" Coy. 1st Bn.	(6) 16th Bn., M.G.C.	(11) 1st Division "Q"
(2) "C" " -do-	(7) 47th Inf. Bde.	(12) A.P.M. 1st Div.
(3) "B" " 16th Bn.	(8) 2nd " "	(13) S. S. O.
(4) Transport Officer.	(9) 11th Bn., M.G.C.	(14) War Diary.
(5) Battalion H.Q.	(10) 1st Div. "G"	(15) File.

SECRET. 1ST BATTALION M.G.C. Copy No.
ORDER No. 43
REF. MAP. LENS 1/100,000

1. The Battalion will move tonight 31 Aug/1st Sept. into the ARRAS area.

2. Dismounted personnel will move by bus. Transport mounted personnel by route march.

3. Transport & mounted personnel will move by route march under Lieut. Rayner by the following route. EPS - ANVIN - FLEURY - CROIX - RANNECOURT - MONTS - EN - TERNOIS, thence to SAVY where it will stage for the night. Time of starting 1 pm. Advance billeting party will meet the transport at the road junction ½ mile due S. of the Y in SAVY, at 10 pm tonight & conduct them to billets & horse lines. Rations & forage for the 1st Sept. will be carried.

4. The Battalion less transport will parade on the EPS - ANVIN Rd facing S. at 6.30 pm in the following order HQ. a. B. C. D Coys ready to move off* and will embus on the ANVIN - BERGUENEUSE Rd at 7.0 pm. The battalion will debus at FAUBOURG DE BAUDIMONT & billeting parties will meet the Battalion at the Cross Rds ½ mile N. of the S. in ARRAS.

5. Billeting parties have gone forward under separate orders & will meet the battalion at place stated in para. 4. at 10 pm. tonight.

6. Rations for the 1st Sept. will be carried by the men and all water bottles must be filled.

7. Transport & mounted personnel will rejoin the battalion on the 1st. Sept. under orders to be issued later.

8. 3 signallers have been sent to each Coy and they will be rationed by them until further orders.

9. No transport or mounted personnel will move E. of a line drawn N. & S. through GAUCHINLEGAL before 8.30 pm.

10. Coy Comdrs will report arrival to Battalion HQ by the code word "completed".

11. Acknowledge.

*Head of columns at School Bldgs.

Issued at 2 pm 31/8/18   [signature] Captain & Adjutant,
1st Battalion Machine Gun Corps.

Copies issued to:
(1) (2) (3) (4) Coys.
(5) T.O.
(6) 1st Div S.
(7) 1st Div "Q"
(8) 1st Bde
(9) 2nd Bde
(10) 3rd Bde.
(11) War Diary
(12)
(13) File

WAR DIARY or INTELLIGENCE SUMMARY

Army Form C. 2118.

BATTALION: MACHINE GUN CORPS

Place	Date	Hour	Summary of Events and Information	Remarks and references to Appendices
ARRAS	1/9/18		Battalion less transport. Battalion arrived in ARRAS detraining at 10AM. Transport moving by road arrived at 6pm. Orders received on the Battalion to move up taking the 4th Canadian Division into were effective	APPENDIX A
			the DROCOURT-QUEANT line the following morning. A,B & C Coys were attached to 1st, 2nd & 3rd Inf. Bde respectively and attacked at Zerohour under their orders. D Coy moved with transport. Situation to a position of assembly just W. of WANCOURT. Battalion Headquarters moved WANCOURT. was quiet and no casualties occurred.	
WANCOURT	2/9/18		The 4th Canadian Division attacked at dawn and were successful. The battalion received orders were 15th Round. Bn. Headquarters Reopened to Trefile at O.20.C.5.9 and D Coy. advanced 5 the Gunmen from line in O.20 & 21. A Coy advanced to the area of STRIPECOPSE in O.21.d, B Coy to O.26.a.1 and C Coy to O.30.C with their respective Bdes. Casualties 2 O.R.	
FOSSE FARM. N.12.a.0.6.	3/9/18		My Division relieved the 4th British Division in the DROCOURT-QUEANT line from Southern Quick line J.P.15. to ETAING inclusive. Battalion Headquarters moved to FOSSE FARM N.12.a.0.6. A Coy in 1st Bn line was disposed as follows: 4 guns in RECOURT WOOD. H guns RECOURT QUARRY, 8 guns in support in DROCOURT-QUEANT line. B Coy with 2nd Inf Bde, the positions of guns: C Coy H.Q and 12 guns in Reserve at P.13.d.N.3, H Guns at P.3.d.5.2, 4 guns in P.9.a, 2 guns B6.a.35 and 12 guns P.H.c.5.a. C Coy was with 3rd Bde in reserve and were lulting in the area of VISEN AVENUE. D Coy relieved Coy 14th Bn. Can E.E.F. Rgt. in WOOD in P.7a. The battalion remained in these dispositions from evening dulling in the neighbourhood of ETAING, RECOURT WOOD and the LECLUSE WOOD the battalion was again. Casualties 6 O.R. Holding the line taken over from 4th Division. Situation normal. Casualties nil	
FOSSE FARM N.12.a.0.6	4/9/18		- do -	
- do -	5/9/18		- do -	
- do -	6/9/18		C Coy moved with 3rd Inf Bde to Huts by the Blangy area. Warning orders receiving that the Division was being relieved by 52nd Division normal in the line evacuating 3rd	
- do -	7/9/18		A Coy relieved by A Coy 156th Bn M.G.C. and moved farther Ruinives in the FEUCHY area by march route.	
			B Coy relieved by B " " " " " moved by bus via ARRAS to TILLOY with 2nd Bde. D Coy " " D " " " "	
			C " " C " " " " moved by march route to Ehmuirs in N.34.	APPENDIX A
- do -	8/9/18		Battalion Headquarters A & D Coys with transport moved to HUT ETRUN by march route via ARRAS. B & C Coys TILLOY & HERMAVILLE respectively.	APPENDIX A

WAR DIARY
or
INTELLIGENCE SUMMARY.
(Erase heading not required.)

Army Form C. 2118.

Place	Date	Hour	Summary of Events and Information	Remarks and references to Appendices
HUTS E FARM	9/9/18		Resting and cleaning up in huts. Orders received that the Division were move in Starting train to another army.	
-do-	10/9/18		Battalion Headquarters and D Coy went with transport entrained at MAROEUIL to move to MARCELCAVE. A Coy, B Coy and C Coy entrained both B Coy and D Coy detraining at MAROEUIL HQ and Battn respectively. entrained at MAR. CELCAVE and moved by buses by MORCOURT area.	APPENDIX A
MORCOURT AREA	11/9/18		Battalion at MAR CELCAVE and billeted in MORCOURT AREA. B Coy moved billets in PROYART and C Coy detrained and moved by bus to CAIX AMIENS Area.	
MORCOURT AREA	12/9/18		Battn HQ A B + D Coy resting and cleaning up in billets. C Coy under orders of 3rd Bde relieved the 33rd Bn MGC Sections (North of the) on the Hinden. Line from Peronne to BR.	
MERAUCOURT	13/9/18		Battn Headquarters A B + D Coys moved by bus to MERAUCOURT A Coy to TERTRY, B Coy to ATHIES. D Coy detrained at ATHIES and marched & relieved A Coy 2nd Bn MGC in the alarm lines of Runasine from @2 g.d to W.G.b. and placed an additional 2 guns in the line. A Coy were placed in mobile reserve at R.36 C. C Coy in the line with 3rd Bde engaged the enemy and were withdrawn.	APPENDIX A
CAULAINCOURT	14/9/18		Bttn HQ moved to CAULAINCOURT. A Coy moved to billets in CAULAINCOURT. B Coy Rifles to TERTRY. C Coy operating with 3rd Infantry Brigade who were advancing captured many prisoners and sept. down the enemy line ... about Russian section that were knocking out a machine gun and Machine Gun nests in Reserve Chown rifle fire which was impeding the advance of the 1st Gloster Regt. D Coy in reserve with 2 sections in close support of gun Bde and 2 sections in support at R.34.C.D.7 south Coy SP.	
CAULAINCOURT	15/9/18		C Coy continued to support the advance of 3rd Bty, who this had reached Rd C.P.5 - N.1E J. MASSEMY R.36.a.62 Harassing line was brought to bear on posts 14.K.5 and the sunken road in R.II b.re and reinforcement were engaged throughout the day. D Coy was divided into 2 subgroups left B.W.group with 4 guns in R.15 d. my gun Rd2d and right wing subgroup with 8 guns at R.22 central. D Coy fired 3000 rds harassing fire on supporting Brigade.	

WAR DIARY or INTELLIGENCE SUMMARY

Army Form C. 2118.

Place	Date	Hour	Summary of Events and Information	Remarks and references to Appendices
CAULAINCOURT	16/9/18		C Coy in the line with 2nd Infantry Brigade, continued to carry out harassing fire with enemy and engaged enemy targets throughout the day. D Coy remained in the positions they were yesterday.	APPENDIX A
			A Coy moved from CAULAINCOURT to the Rly EMBANKMENT E. of VERMAND	
			B Coy moved from TERTRY to CAULAINCOURT. 2nd Bde was relieved by 1st & 2nd Bdes but remained in for operations tomorrow.	APPENDIX A
CAULAINCOURT	17/9/18		Orders were received that the division was to attack in conjunction with the 4th Australian Division to the N and that the positions on the divisional sector were noted later. M.G. Corps were attached to 1st and 2nd Bdes respectively and detailed orders (see Appendices to O.O. H.Q.)	
			were issued on C and D Coys. Reconnaissances were carried out by the Commanding Officer and all Coy Cmdrs. All preparations for the attack were made. S.A.A. dumps to zero area Corps were moved up to positions of assembly during the night.	
CAULAINCOURT	18/9/18		The Division attacked in conjunction with 1st Australian Division on the right and the 1st Division on the left. Zero Hour 15-20 Appendix "B" gives the operation message and shows on the attached map Appendix "C". By 10-15 am the final objective had been gained everywhere, and C Coy has withdrawn to its position of assembly in R.25 a.? to R.24 a.8. The attack progressed onto extreme left. M.Gs were held up on the right throughout the attacks the consolidation of objectives. C.Coys successfully with the infantry took during the attacks their co-ordination of objectives. Detailed reports of the batteries are shown in Appendix B. Casualties 1 O.R.	APPENDIX B
CAULAINCOURT	19/9/18		The advance was continued and the line FOURMI RANCH - Sunken Rd N. of VILLERET - ENERGIE TRENCH - a Minor Tank from FOURMI TRENCH to E. end of BERTHACOURT. An enemy counter-attack air barrage against the line E. of BERTHACOURT QUARRY was repulsed. The Guns of B. Coy caused 30 casualties to the enemy. Casualties 3 O.R.	APPENDIX B
MASSEMY	20/9/18		Battalion Headquarters advanced to Battalion at MASSEMY. Several attempts to locate the A B C Coys. Many a time ? top the enemy targets and carrying out harassing fire. Casualties 2 OR	APPENDIX C

WAR DIARY
or
INTELLIGENCE SUMMARY.
(Erase heading not required.)

Army Form C. 2118.

Place	Date	Hour	Summary of Events and Information	Remarks and references to Appendices
MASSEMY	21/9/18		Situation normal. Harassing fire carried out by the guns in the line and enemy trench engaged. Ammunition was fairly active. B. Sec. and 8 divs. of D. Sec. were relieved by 112th Brigade R.G.A. and proceeded to CATHEMCOURT Area. E. Sec. relieved C. Sec. of 5th Bath. T.M. Corps under orders from 3rd Brigade. Casualties 16 O.R.	
MASSEMY	22/9/18		Situation normal. Enemy was rather quiet and 117th division on the left were out to be relieved this night. All preparations made and orders issued for the attack and the attack was to take place outh 24th. A & D Corps were engaged with hostile batteries during the afternoon stage. The attack under the orders of 2nd & 3rd Brigades.	APPENDIX A
MASSEMY	23/9/18		During the night B. Sec. of Ours & B. T. C. were detailed to operate under the orders of 2nd & 3rd Brigades. The situation was quiet, water Battery positions, that Question allowed moves to R3c 5.5 where they were in Battery positions. Ours & A & D Corps advanced with all Battery positions. Communication was good & B. Sec. B. T. C. and with all Battery positions. Active throughout the night but did not fire any rounds. Casualties 1 OR.	
R30c.5.5	24/9/18		The Division attacked at 5 a.m. under cover of a creeping barrage, in Conjunction with 117th Division on the left and the 6th Division on the night. The objective being FRESNOY le PETIT and GRICOURT. B. Section & this attack mostly over the marsh line. Matters of A & D Corps had a very successful barrage which much assisted the advance of the Infantry. On completion of the barrage the guns of A & D Corps advanced in support of the Infantry. Ours & B. D. Corps advanced in support. The gunner Battery accounts with Ours & D. Corps all did excellent work in these counter attacks, and shown escorting the consolidation objectives and engaging enemy trips. The attack was very active throughout. Effective and very active throughout. Enemy's artillery was very active throughout. Casualties 16 O.R. Own 800 prisoners were taken by the Division during these operations	APPENDIX C APPENDIX D
R30c.5.5	25/9/18		Situation unchanged and fairly quiet. Few minor changes were made in the dispositions of guns. Casualties 1 Offr. H. O.R.	APPENDIX B

SECRET.

1ST BATTALION M.G.C
ORDER NO. 43
REF. MAP. LENS 1/100.000

Copy No.

1. The Battalion will move tonight 31 Aug/1st Sept. into the ARRAS area.

2. Dismounted personnel will move by bus. Transport & mounted personnel by route march.

3. Transport & mounted personnel will move by route march under Lieut. Rayner by the following route. EPS – ANVIN – FLEURY CROSS – RONNECOURT – MONTS – EN – TERNOIS. thence to SAVY where it will stage for the night. Time of starting 4 pm. Advance billeting party will meet the transport at the road junction ½ a mile due S. of the Y in SAVY at 6 pm tonight & conduct them to their horse lines. Rations & forage for the 1st Sept. will be carried.

4. The Battalion less transport will parade on the EPS – ANVIN Rd facing S. at 6.30 pm in the following order H.Q. A.B.C.D Coys ready to move off* and will embus on the ANVIN – BERGUENEUSE Rd at 7.0 pm. The battalion will debus at FAUBURG DE BAUDIMONT & billeting parties will meet the Battalion at the Cross Rds ½ mile N. of the S. in ARRAS.

5. Billeting parties have gone forward under separate orders & will meet the battalion at place stated in para. 4. at 10 pm. tonight.

6. Rations for the 1st Sept. will be carried by the men and all water bottles must be filled.

7. Transported & mounted personnel will rejoin the battalion on the 1st Sept. under orders to be issued later.

8. 3 signallers have been sent to each Coy and they will be rationed by them until further orders.

9. No transport or mounted personnel will move E. of a line drawn N. & S. through GOUVINLEGAL before 8.30 pm.

10. Companies will report arrival to Battalion HQ by the code word "completed"

11. Acknowledge.

*Head of column at School Bldgs.

Issued at 2 pm 31/8/18

[signature]
Captain & Adjutant,
1st Battalion Machine
Gun Corps.

Copies issued to:
(1) to (4) Coys.
(5) T.O.
(6) 1st Div. G
(7) 1st Div. "Q"
(8) 1st Bde
(9) 2nd Bde
(10) 3rd Bde.
(11) War Diary
(12)
(13) File

1ST BATTALION MACHINE GUN CORPS.
No. 4168
Date.

SECRET.   1ST BATTALION, MACHINE GUN CORPS.   Copy No.
                      ORDER NO.44.
              Reference Map Sheet, 41.B.

(1)   The 1st Battalion, British M.G.Corps will be relieved by
the 56th Battalion, British M.G.Corps between now and NX
10.a.m. on the 9th instant.

(2)   "B" Company, 1st Bn.British M.G.Corps will be relieved under
arrangements of 2nd British Infantry Brigade.

(3)   "A" Company 1st Bn.British M.G.Corps will be relieved by
"A" Company 56th Bn.British M.G.Corps on the night of
7th/8th September 1918.

(4)   "D" Company, 1st Bn.British M.G.Corps willmbe relieved by
"C" Company 56th Bn.M.G.Corps on the afternoon of the 7th Sept.

(5)   All details of relief will be arranged between O.C.Companies
concerned direct.

(6)   On completion of relief "A" Company will proceed by march
route to FOSSE FARM N.12.a.0.3. where guides will meet them and
conduct them to accommodation which is being prepared.

(7)   On the night of the 8th/9th inst. on relief of 1st British
Infantry Brigade, "A" Company will rejoin the 1st Infantry
Brigade Group under orders to be issued later.

(8)   On completion of relief "D" Company less Transport, will
proceed by march route to ROHART FACTORY, 0.15.c.8.5. at which
point they will embus at 7.30.p.m. 7/9/18.   Details of
destination of "D" Company and move of "D" Company Transport
will be issued later.

(9)   Lieut.J.BULLPITT will be at the Road Junction at 0.14.a.0.7.
at 4.30.p.m. to guide "C" Company 56th Battalion, M.G.Corps.

(10)   Completion of relief will be reported to Battalion Headquarters
by the code phrase "Your A.S.25 noted."
        "A" Company will also report completion to 1st British Infy.
Brigade direct.

(11)   ACKNOWLEDGE.

                                            Captain and Adjutant,
                                          1st Battalion, British Machine
Issued at 9.p.m. 6/9/18   Gun Corps.

Copies issued to:-   (1) "A" Company, 1st Bn.Br.M.G.C.
                     (2) "B" Company   -do-
    (3) "C" Coy.1st Bn.Br.M.G.C.   (4) "D" Coy.1st Bn.Br.M.G.C.
    (5) 56th Bn.M.G.C.   (6) 1st British Infy.Bde.
    (7) 2nd British Infy.Bde.   (8) 3rd British Infy.Bde.
    (9) Q.M.1st Bn.Br.M.G.C.   (10) Battn.H.Q.1st Bn.Br.M.G.C.
   (11) 1st British Division "G"   (12) 1st British Division "Q"
   (13) 56th Division "G"   (14) A.P.M. 1st British Division.
   (15) S.S.O.1st British Division   (16) War Diary.
   (17) War Diary.   (18) File.

SECRET.

AMENDMENT NO.1 TO 1ST BATTALION, BRITISH
M.G.C. ORDER NO.44.
Reference Map Sheet 41.B. 1/40,000.

Copy No.

(1) Delete para.8. and substitute:-

"On completion of relief "D" Company less Transport will proceed by march route to FOSSE FARM N.12.a.0.3. where guides will meet them and conduct them to accommodation which is being prepared."

(2) Para.9. for 4.30.p.m. read 4.0.p.m.

(3) Add para.8.a. "Transport of "A" and "D" Companies will move to the area in N.3.d. on the 7th instant.

Shanks.
Captain and Adjutant,
1st Battalion, British Machine
Gun Corps.

Issued at 11.a.m. 7/9/18.

Copies issued to all recipients of 1st Bn.Br.M.G.C.Order No.44.

SECRET.

1ST BATTALION, MACHINE GUN CORPS
ORDER NO. 45.

Copy No.

Reference Map Sheet LENS 11, 1/100,000.

(1) Battalion Headquarters and "A" and "D" Companies, 1st Battalion, Machine Gun Corps will move by march route from present billeting area in N.3.d. to "Y" Huts N.W. of E. of ETRUN.

(2) Battalion Headquarters, "A" and "D" Companies with Transport will parade ready to move off at 2.p.m. 8/9/18 in the order stated, head of the column at the cross roads at N.3.b.8.2.

(3) Battalion Headquarters will close at FOSSE FARM N.12.a.0.6. at 1.p.m. on 8/9/18 and will re-open, on arrival, at "Y" Huts N.W. of "E" in ETRUN.

(4) ACKNOWLEDGE.

Captain and Adjutant,
1st Battalion, Machine Gun Corps.

Issued at 10.a.m. 8/9/18.

Distribution normal.

SECRET. **1ST BATTALION, MACHINE GUN CORPS.** Copy No.
ORDER NO. 46.

Reference Maps LENS 11, and AMIENS 17, 1/100,000.

(1) Battalion Headquarters and "D" Company will entrain at MAROEUIL Station to-day to move to another Army.

(2) Transport of Battalion Headquarters and "D" Company will move under Lieut. Kauffmann and will be at MAROEUIL Station at 1.10.p.m.

(3) O.C. "D" Company will detail 1 Officer, 4 N.C.Os. and 30 men as loading party to be at MAROEUIL Station at 1.10.p.m.

(4) Battalion Headquarters and "D" Company will parade ready to move off at 2.15.p.m. on the road opposite the huts of their respective lines.

(5) No Transport or personnel is to enter the Station Yard without permission of the R.T.O.

(6) Lieut. A.H. Smyth is detailed as Battalion entraining officer. He will report to the R.T.O. at 1.p.m.

(7) O.C. "D" Company will render full entraining states to Battalion Headquarters at 12 noon to-day.

(8) All billets must be left clean and in a sanitary condition and a certificate to this effect will be rendered to Battalion Headquarters by 12 noon to-day.

(9) Details regarding billets will be issued later.

(10) Battalion Headquarters will close at "Y" Huts ETRUN at 12.1.p.m. to-day and will re-open at a place and time to be notified later.

(11) ACKNOWLEDGE.

Captain and Adjutant,
1st Battalion, Machine
Gun Corps.

Issued at 10.a.m. 10/9/18.

Copies issued to:—
(1) to (4) Companies.
(5) Battalion Headquarters.
(6) Transport Officer.
(7) 1st Division "G"
(8) 1st Division "Q"
(9) A.P.M. 1st Division.
(10) S.S.C. 1st Division.
(11) War Diary
(12) War Diary
(13) File.
(14) File.

1ST BATTALION, MACHINE GUN CORPS.

SECRET.   ORDER NO.47.   Copy No.

Reference Map AMIENS 17, 1/100,000 and Map Sheet, 62.C. 1/40,000.

(1) The 1st Battalion British M.G.C. will relieve the 32nd Battalion M.G.C. between now and the night 13th/14th inst.

(2) Moves and reliefs of "A" "B" and "C" Companies will be carried out under the orders of the 1st, 2nd, 3rd British Infantry Brigades respectively.

(3) Transport and mounted personnel of Headquarters and "D" Coy. will move under Lieut. Kauffmann as under:-

Date.	From.	To.	Hour of Starting.	Route.
12/9/18	Present area.	O.32-33 U.2.3	1.p.m.	To be notified later.
13/9/18	O.32-33 U.2-3	MONTECOURT Area.	To be arranged by Lieut.B. Kauffmann.	No restrictions as to route. To be at MONTECOURT by 2.p.m.

(4) Dismounted personnel of Battalion H.Q. and "D" Company will move by bus to MONTECOURT Area on the 13th inst. details of which will be notified later.

(5) Detailed orders regarding "D" Companies relief will be issued later.

(6) On arrival of Battalion Headquarters in the new area, location will be notified to Companies. On receipt of this location Os.C.Coys. will send an orderly to Battalion H.Q. with location of their Company H.Q.

(7) ACKNOWLEDGE.

                             Captain and Adjutant,
                             1st Battalion, Machine Gun Corps.

Issued at 11.a.m. 12/9/18.

Copies issued to:-
     (1) to (4) Companies.
     (5) Battalion H.Q.
     (6) Quartermaster.
     (7) 1st Division "G"
     (8) 1st Division "Q"
     (9) S.S.O. 1st Division.
     (10) A.P.M. 1st Division.
     (11) War Diary
     (12) War Diary
     (13) File
     (14) File

SECRET.

1ST BATTALION, MACHINE GUN CORPS.
ORDER NO.48.

Copy No.

Reference Map Sheet 62.C. 1/40,000.

(1) "D" Company will relieve 4 guns of "A" Company, 32nd Battalion, Machine Gun Corps in the Main Line of Resistance, which consists of the line of uncompleted trenches and wire running from Q.29.d. to W.6.9. between the Divisional Boundaries, on the 13th instant as soon as possible after arrival in the new area.

(2) O.C. "D" Company will arrange to get into touch with O.C. 32nd Battalion, Machine Gun Corps whose Headquarters are at W.8.b.7.4.

(3) All details of relief will be arranged between Officers Commanding Companies concerned direct.

(4) O.C. "D" Company will place 8 guns in positions so as to cover the Divisional Front of Main Line of Resistance. He will keep 8 guns mobile in a position of readiness, and will reconnoitre for a suitable location for these guns, probably under cover of the wood in R.36.c.

(5) These 8 mobile guns will be prepared to give immediate support to the advanced Brigade. O.C."D" Company will arrange to have a liaison officer at or near 3rd Brigade H.Q. at W.5.a.4.8. These guns will not be used until the sanction of Divisional Headquarters is obtained.

(6) "D" Company Transport will be at MONTIECOURT at 2.p.m. under existing arrangements. Further orders will be issued regarding meeting Transport on receipt of the embussing orders from Division.

(7) Completion of relief and dispositions of guns will be reported to Battalion Headquarters by runner.

(8) Acknowledge.

(Signed) A. Shanks,

Captain and Adjutant,
1st Battalion, Machine
Gun Corps.

Issued at 11.p.m. 12/9/18

Distribution normal.

1ST BATTALION, MACHINE GUN CORPS

SECRET.　　　　　　ORDER NO. ~~45~~ 49.　　　　　Copy No. 2

Reference Map Sheets, 62.C.S.E. 62.B.S.W. 62.B.N.W.
1/20,000.

(1) **GENERAL INFORMATION.**

   (a)   The 1st Division will attack in conjunction with the 6th Division on the right and the 4th Australian Division on the left on a date (Z) which will be notified later.

   (b)   Zero hour will be notified later.

   (c)   The 1st Infantry Brigade will attack on the right in touch with the 16th Infantry Brigade, 6th Division, and the 2nd Infantry Brigade will attack on the left in touch with the 12th Australian Infantry Brigade.

   (d)   Objectives and boundaries between Brigades will be as shown on the 1/20,000 Map A. issued (to "C" and "D" Companies only) herewith.

   (e)   The 1st Objective (Green Line) and the 2nd Objective (Red Line) will be gained under cover of a creeping barrage. The 3rd Objective (Blue Line) will be gained by exploitation after the Red Line has been reached.
        Infantry forming up line and the hours of reaching and leaving objectives will be as shewn on attached Map A.

(2) **ACTION OF MACHINE GUNS.**

   "A" and "B" Companies will operate under the orders of 1st and 2nd Brigades respectively.

(3) **"C" COMPANY**

   (a)   "C" Company will remain in action in its present positions covering the Divisional front, until Zero plus 2 hours, when it will assemble in the approximate area R.23.c. and d. and R.29.a. and b. and will come into reserve.
        O.C. "C" Company will be personally with his guns from Zero hour onwards, with an officer representative at Brigade Headquarters at VERMAND.
        He will be informed by this Officer directly the Green Line has been taken.
        Having assembled his Company, O.C. "C" Company will keep in touch with the new advanced Brigade Headquarters in MAISSEMY at which place further orders can be sent to him as required.

   (b)   If the situation allows he will get his fighting limbers up to the assembly area and should be prepared to move in any direction immediately on receipt of orders.

   (c)   4 guns will be kept mounted to deal with low flying enemy aeroplanes.

   (d)   "C" Company will maintain communication direct to Battalion Headquarters by runner.

(4) **"D" COMPANY**

   (a)   "D" Company will be organised into 2 sub-groups of 8 guns each, to be known as Left and Right Sub-Groups, operating north and south of the river respectively.

   (b)   O.C. "D" Company will appoint an officer to command each sub-group.
        O.C. "D" Company will keep in touch with 1st and 2nd Infantry Brigades starting at VERMAND and moving forward to the new Advanced Brigade Headquarters, MAISSEMY, at the same time as Brigades

(continued overpage)

(4) "D" COMPANY (continued)

    (b) (continued)

        The Sub-Group Commanders will keep in touch with Officers Commanding Reserve Battalions of Infantry Brigades on whose front they are operating: i.e. Left Sub-Group Cmdr. at H.Q. 1st Battalion Northants Regiment, Right Sub-Group Commander at H.Q. 1st Black Watch.

    (c)   The Sub-Groups will be assembled at Zero roughly as follows:-

        Left Sub-Group, R.20.b.
        Right -do- R.33.b.

    (d)   They will advance by sections at Zero plus 3½ hours using fore portions of limbers and pack saddles, to positions between the RED and GREEN Lines. Mounted officers will reconnoitre forward to keep in touch with the situation and send back information.

        The Left Sub-Group will advance along the line of the road leading through R.21 central - R.16 central - R.11 central.

        The Right Sub-Group will advance along the line of the road through VILLECHOLLES - MAISSEMY thence along the line of FOURMOY Alley, if possible, as far as M.14.c.5.3. From this point the guns etc. will have to be carried.

    (e)   Owing to the possibility of mining of roads and clearly defined gaps in the wire, Sections, where possible, should move off roads and if necessary, cut gaps through weak parts of the wire.

(5) THE MAIN TASK OF "D" COMPANY WILL BE.

    (a)   By increasing the depth of the attacking Brigade formations to ensure protection for the flanks.

    (b)   To bring harassing fire to bear on selected parts of the ground in front of the BLUE Line in event of an S.O.S. and during Z.A. night.

        The guns will be disposed in batteries of 4 guns each, roughly in the positions, M.21.b.0.9. M.15 central, M.1.d.5.8. and R.11.b.8.7. to be known respectively as "A" "B" "C" and "D" Batteries.

        These positions are only approximate and Officers Commanding each Sub-Group must chose exact positions, paying special attention to fields of fire to the flank.

    (c)   Directly batteries have reached their positions, they should be prepared to answer an S.O.S. Batteries will concentrate their fire as shown on attached maps.

        The extent of indirect fire will be limited by the ammunition it has been possible to get up.

        At least a minimum of 2,000 rounds per gun will be kept for direct fire.

    (d)   At least one shovel per gun team will be carried and every opportunity will be taken to consolidate the Battery positions.

    (e)   "D" Company will establish a rear Headquarters at R.31.c.0.7.

    (f)   O.C. "D" Company will send progress reports to Battalion Headquarters through the Brigade Headquarters with whom he is in touch.

(6)   Battalion Headquarters will remain at W.4.b.9.3. CAULAINCOURT.

(7)   Detailed Administrative Instructions will be issued later.

(8)   ACKNOWLEDGE.

                                Captain and Adjutant,
                                1st Battalion, Machine
Issued at 4.p.m. 17/9/18.   Gun Corps.

Distribution overpage.

Copies issued to:- (1) to (4) Companies.
(5) Battalion Headquarters.
(6) Quartermaster.
(7) 1st Infantry Brigade
(8) 2nd Infantry Brigade
(9) 3rd Infantry Brigade
(10) 1st Division "G"
(11) 1st Division "Q"
(12) 4th Australian Battalion M.G.C.
(13) 6th Battalion, M.G.C.
(14) 1st Division Signals.
(15) War Diary.
(16) War Diary.
(17) File.

SECRET   ADDENDUM NO.1 TO   Copy No. 22

1ST BATTALION, MACHINE GUN CORPS ORDER 49.

(1) To paragraph (5) add, sub-para. (g)

    The guns of "D" Company have been allotted the above tasks by Divisional Headquarters and although they are disposed in Brigade Groups they are on no account to be moved unless for urgent tactical reasons.

                                           Captain and Adjutant,
                                           1st Battalion, Machine
Issued at 5.30.p.m. 17/9/18   Gun Corps.

Copies issued to all recipients of 1st Battalion, M.G.C. Order No.49.

SECRET.

1ST BATTALION, MACHINE GUN CORPS.
ORDER NO. 50.

Copy No.

Reference Map Sheets, 62.C.S.E. 62.B.S.W. 62.B.N.W.
1/20,000.

(1) **GENERAL.**

    (a) On a date to be notified later the 1st Division will attack in conjunction with 6th Division on the right and 46th Div. on the left.

    (b) The 3rd Infantry Brigade will attack on the right in touch with the 16th Infantry Brigade, 6th Division.
2nd Infantry Brigade will attack on the left.

    (c) Objectives, boundaries between Brigades, and Infantry forming up lines will be shown on the 1/20,000 map issued herewith. *with copies (1) to (6)*

    (d) All objectives will be gained under a creeping barrage. Three sections of tanks will co-operate.

(2) **ORGANISATION OF 1ST BATTALION, MACHINE GUN CORPS.**

    (a) "B" and "C" Companies will be attached to the 2nd Infantry Brigade and 3rd Infantry Brigade respectively, and will receive all orders from them.

    (b) "A" and "D" Companies will be organised into batteries as follows:-

      "A" Company.   4 guns, M.20.a. 8. 3.   ("W" Battery)
                         12 guns, M.26.a. 5. 5.   ("X" Battery)

      "D" Company.   8 guns, M.26.c. 7. 5.   ("Y" Battery)
                         8 guns, M.26.b.55.70.   ("Z" Battery)

(3) **ACTION AND ROLE OF MACHINE GUNS.**

    (a) "B" and "C" Companies with 2nd and 3rd Brigades will consist of Forward and Rear Guns.

    ROLE of the Forward Guns.

      (a) To assist the advance of the Infantry and engage any target that presents itself over the sights.

      (b) To assist in the consolidation of the final objective.

    Role of the Rear Guns.

      (a) In conjunction with Brigadier's wishes will co-operate with the Divisional Machine Gun Barrage by shooting on previously selected areas.

      (b) After capture of final objective will advance to commanding positions by sections, where they will,

        (i) Engage any enemy targets that present themselves
       (ii) Shoot on previously selected areas.
      (iii) Carry out harassing fire mon ZA night.
      (iv) By defence in depth, protect the flanks.

(continued overpage)

(2)

(4) "A" and "D" Companies organised in Batteries as in para.(2)

(a) Will fire a barrage on FRESNOY - GRICOURT Valley.

(b) On capture of final objective, "W" "X" and "Y" Batteries will be prepared to shoot on S.O.S. Lines.

(c) "Z" Battery will advance by sections to the high ground in R.16.d. and R.28.c. where they will,

   (i) Assist in the defence.
   (ii) Engage at once with direct fire any enemy machine guns that are harassing our infantry.

(d) All clearances etc. have been increased considerably above normal safety angles.

(e) All barrage batteries will have sentries 100 yards in front of batteries in order to warn Infantry reserves who may be straying into the immediate danger area of the Battery.

(5) COMMUNICATIONS.

Battalion Headquarters will be at R.30.c.5.5. and will be in direct communication with 2nd and 3rd Infantry Brigades at R.29.d.9.6. and R.35.b.7.7. respectively.

"B" and "C" Company Headquarters will be in the neighbourhood of Brigade Headquarters.

"A" and "D" Companies in the neighbourhood of Battalion H.Q.

Each barrage battery will have at least two guns detailed for to deal with low flying enemy aeroplanes.

Fighting maps will be at each battery position and switches on to enemy concentrations can be arranged as ordered by G.O.s.C. Infantry Brigades.

Communications will be maintained at all Batteries by telephone and visual.

Detailed instructions as to rate of fire, S.O.S., Administrative instructions etc. will be issued direct to Companies concerned.

                            Captain and Adjutant,
                            1st Battalion, Machine
                              Gun Corps.

Issued at 2.p.m. 23/9/18.

Copies issued to:- (1) to (4) Companies.
                (5) Battalion Headquarters.
                (6) Quartermaster.
                (7) 1st Infantry Brigade
                (8) 2nd Infantry Brigade
                (9) 3rd Infantry Brigade
                (10) 1st Division "G"
                (11) 1st Division "Q"
                (12) 4th Battalion, M.G.C.
                (13) 6th Battalion, M.G.C.
                (14) 1st Division Signals.
                (15) War Diary
                (16) War Diary
                (17) File.

SECRET.

1ST BATTALION, MACHINE GUN CORPS.

Copy No.

ORDER NO.51.

Reference Map Sheets 62.C.&S.E. 62.B.N.W. 62.B.S.W.

(1) Reliefs will take place as follows:-

   (a)   On the night 26th/27th September 1918 "C" Company, 1st Battalion, M.G.C. will be relieved by a Company of the 6th Battalion, M.G.C. and on relief will proceed to VERMAND (area to be allotted by 3rd Brigade)

   (b)   On the night 27th/28th, "A" Company, 1st Battalion, M.G.C. will relieve a Company of the 46th Battalion, M.G.C.

   (c)   All guns of "D" Company, 1st Battalion, M.G.C. in 3rd Brigade Area, if not relieved will be withdrawn to R.29.b.

   (d)   All guns in 2nd Brigade sector will remain as at present.

(2)   All details of reliefs will be arranged between Officers Commanding Companies concerned direct.

(3)   ACKNOWLEDGE.

                                                        Captain and Adjutant,
                                                        1st Battalion, Machine
                                                            Gun Corps.

Issued at 4.p.m. 26/9/18.

Distribution overpage.

Copies issued to:- (1) to (4) Companies
                  (5) Battalion H.Q.
                  (6) Quartermaster.
                  (7) 1st Division "G"
                  (8) 1st Division "Q"
                  (9) 1st Infantry Brigade
                  (10) 2nd Infantry Brigade
                  (11) 3rd Infantry Brigade
                  (12) 46th Battalion, M.G.C.
                  (13) 6th Battalion, M.G.C.
                  (14) 1st Division Signals.
                  (15) War Diary.
                  (16) War Diary.
                  (17) File.

SECRET.   Copy No. 16

1st BATTALION MACHINE GUN CORPS.

ORDER No. 52.

Reference Map Sheets 62.c.S.E., 62.B.N.W., 62.b.S.W.

(1) "C" Company, 16 guns, will relieve "B" Company on the Right Section of the Divisional Front on the 28th inst.

(2) All details of relief will be arranged between Officers Commanding Companies concerned direct.

(3) On completion of relief "B" Company will proceed to billets in VERMAND.

(4) Completion of relief will be reported to Battalion H.Q. by the Code Word "PEAR" and the 3rd Infantry Brigade direct.

(5) ACKNOWLEDGE.

for Captain & Adjutant,
1st Battalion, Machine Gun Corps.

Issued at 10.0 a.m. 28/9/18.

Distribution overpage.

Copies issued to :-

      (1) to (4) Companies.
      (5) Battalion H.Q.
      (6) Quartermaster.
      (7) Signalling Officer.
      (8) 1st Division "G".
      (9) 1st Division "Q".
    (10) 1st Infantry Brigade.
    (11) 2nd Infantry Brigade.
    (12) 3rd Infantry Brigade.
    (13) 4th Battalion, M.G.C.
    (14) 6th Battalion, M.G.C.
    (15) 1st Division Signals.
    (16) War Diary.
    (17) War Diary.
    (18) File.

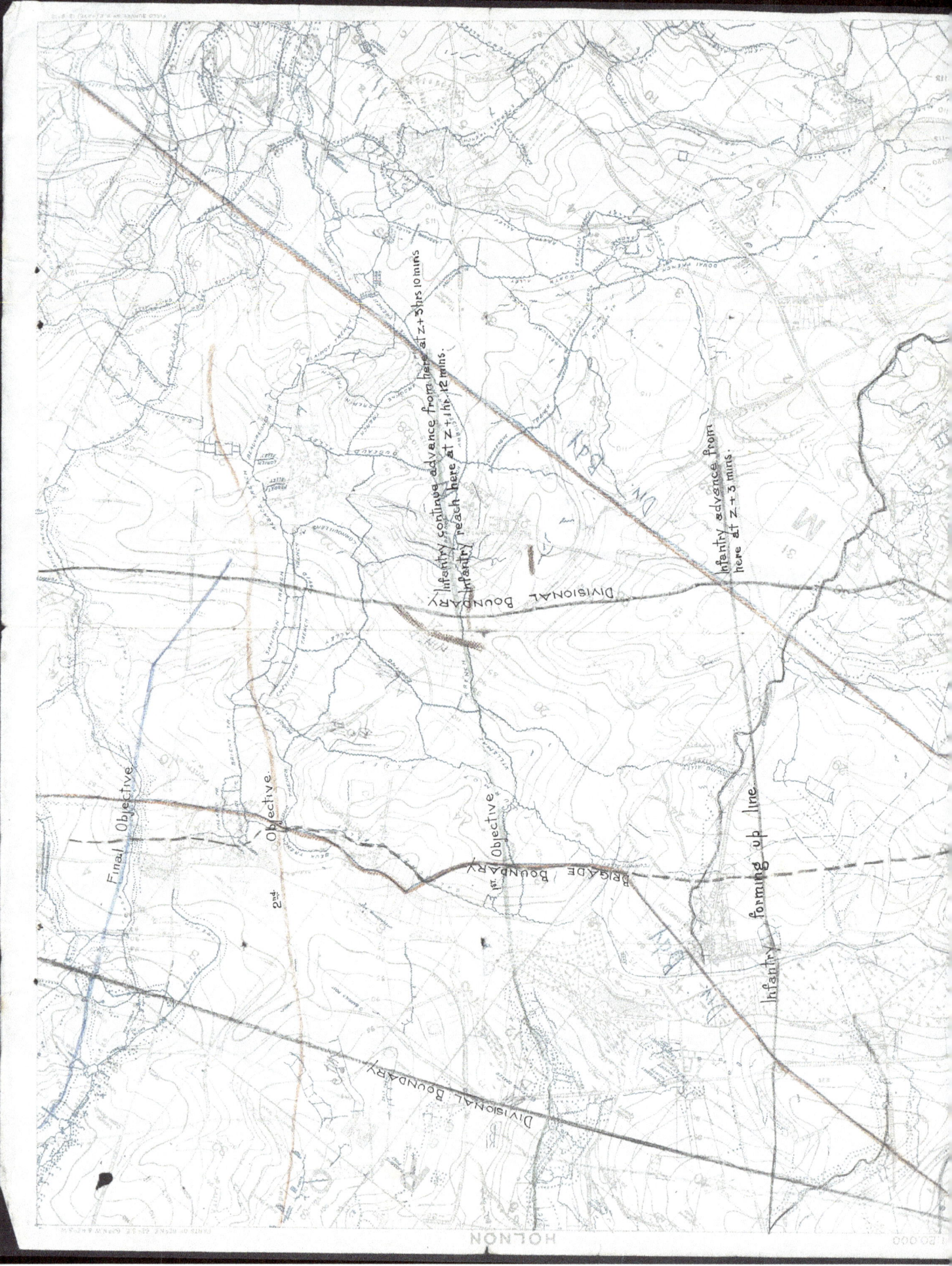

MESSAGE FORM.

_____ Division.

Map Reference or Mark
on Map at Back.

_____

1. I am at _____ and am consolidating.
2. I am at _____ and have consolidated.
3. I am at _____
4. Am held up by M.G. at _____
5. I need: Ammunition
         Bombs
         Rifle Grenades
         Water
         Verey Lights
         Stokes Shells
6. Counter-attack forming up at _____
7. I am in touch with _____ on Right at _____
                        on Left at _____
8. I am not in touch on Right.
                       Left.
9. Am being shelled from _____
10. I estimate my present strength at _____ rifles.
11. Hostile {Battery / Machine Gun / Trench Mortar} active at _____

Time _____ m.   Name _____
                     Platoon _____
Date _____   Company _____
                     Battalion _____

APPENDIX B.
TO
WAR DIARY
SEPTEMBER,
1ST BATTALION, MACHINE GUN CORPS.

"A" Company.

18/9/18. 1st Brigade attack.

    In the Line;- Lieut.Taylor.
           Lieut.Melville M.C.
           Lieut.Berra.
           Lieut.Canning.

    Coy.H.Q.   Major Fitzwilliams.
           Captain A Dukes.

    Wagon Lines.   2/Lieut.Bryan (O.C.Details)
           2/Lieut.Baker.
           Lieut.Sharpe (Transport)

    Leave to U.K. 2/Lieut.G.E.Shead, M.C.

   Reveille 3.30.a.m. for Company H.Q. and Nos.1 and 2 Sections. Breakfasts 4 a.m. No.1 Section, Lieut.W.H.Canning, and No.2 Section, 2/Lieut.Berra, stood to from 5 a.m. onwards in readiness to move. At 5.20.a.m. preliminary bombardment began. Retaliation feeble on back areas. At 8.45.a.m. O.C. "A" Company returned from 1st Brigade Headquarters with orders for forward move. March Route to MAISSEMY via VILLECHOLLES. At 10.30.a.m. Company Headquarters re-opened at MAISSEMY, R.23.b.5.4., the village at this time being lightly shelled. Nos.1 and 2 Sections in sunken road due south of the village.
   Meanwhile the attack of the 1st Brigade had been vigorously opposed. The first objective (green line, 1300 yards to 1800 yards N.E. of MAISSEMY) was not gained until about noon by both battalions. Machine guns from ARBOUSSIERS WOOD held up a further advance on the right, but BERTHACOURT was captured on the left, and several hundred prisoners passed through the Divisional cage. At 7.10.p.m. Lieut.Melville, (No.4 Section) reported the disposition of his guns as follows:-

   Section H.Q. and 2 guns at M.14.c. 5. 4.
        2 guns at M.20.b. 8. 9.

   Enemy was seen approaching our line via ESSLING ALLEY at 4.p.m. one of these guns opened fire and four of the enemy were seen to fall. Enemy also counter-attacked twice at BERTHACOURT, and were driven off.
   At 9.30.a.m. 19th, Lieut.Taylor reported his dispositions as follows:-

    2 guns at M.20.a. 7. 5.
    1 gun at M.20.d. 5. 4.
    1 gun at M.20.d. 7. 1.
 Section H.Q. with guns at M.20.a. 7. 5.

   No.3 Section fired about 500 rounds during the day of 18th September at enemy light Machine Guns in ARBOUSSIERS WOOD. Enemy guns moved frequently in consequence. Harassing fire from this wood enfiladed our whole front during the night. At 9.30.a.m. ARBOUSSIERS WOOD was reported clear of the enemy. This proved doubtful later. Following casualties in No.3 Section:- Sergeant Culley, Pte.Bowley, Pte.McLeod,(wounded) Pte.Maroney, Pte.Clark (wounded, remained at duty)

      (continued)

(2)

In No.4 Section:- Pte.Hughes (wounded) sent to Wagon Lines.

At 2.p.m. Major Fitzwilliams took 2/Lieut.Berra and 2 guns from No.2 Section forward. They were reported at 4 p.m. to be in position at M.20.b.75.80. and touch was established with sections 3 and 4. At 7.a.m. 19th dispositions had been improved as follows:-

1 gun at M.14.d. 9. 6.
1 gun at M.20.b.75.80.

These guns were with 1st Camerons and 1st Black Watch respectively.

The remaining two guns of No.2 Section (Sgt.Morrison) and 4 guns of No.1 Section (Lieut.Canning) were held in reserve in sunken road south of MAISSEMY.

The battle area and MAISSEMY Village were heavily bombed during the night until rain again stopped operations.

19/9/18.
Rainy morning until 9.a.m. Messages from all officers in the line were received. By 10.a.m. dispositions of guns at noon:-

No.4 Section, 2 guns at M.14.c. 5. 4.
2 guns at M.20.b. 8. 9.

No.3 Section, 2 guns at M.20.a. 7. 5.
1 gun at M.20.d. 5. 4.
1 gun at M.20.d. 7. 1.

No.2 Section, 1 gun at M.14.d. 9. 6.
1 gun at M.15.c.44.05.

No.1 and remainder of No.2 still in reserve. Consolidation continued. O.C. "A" Company visited the guns as above in the course of the day. At 5.30.p.m. the two remaining guns of No.2 Section under Sgt.Morrison, were sent up to 2/Lieut.Berra to be established on high ground in M.14.d. 8. 2. The reserve section(No.1) stood to to move at dawn. The night was quiet and cold no rain fell.

20/9/18.
At 5.a.m. Lieut.Canning with 4 guns of No.1 Section moved up to M.26.a. 7. 7. and established a battery at this point for indirect fire on ESSLING ALLEY, range 2,000 yards 2,600 yards. Grid bearing 54 degrees.

2/Lieut.Berra's Headquarters and gun at M.20.b.75.80. were heavily shelled from 4.30. to 5.30.a.m. One gun and tripod were blown up. Sgt.Whyatt was killed. 2/Lieut.Berra reported discovery of an enemy field gun 77 mm. camouflaged at M.15.c.25.25. and claimed capture of this gun at 6.a.m. 1st Brigade informed. Dispositions of guns at 9.a.m. 20/9/18. (Right to left)

4 guns at M.26.a. 7. 7.
2 guns at M.20.d. 3. 0. and 6. 0.
2 guns at M.20.a. 7. 5.
1 gun at M.20.b. 7. 7.
2 guns at M.14.d. 8. 2.
1 gun at M.14.d. 9. 5.
2 guns at M.14.c. 7. 3.
2 guns at M.14.c. 1. 9.

At 12 noon Lieut.Taylor reported one of his guns at M.20.a. 7. 5. hit by shell and out of action. This gun, and Lieut.Berra's (destroyed) were immediately replaced. About 7.p.m. numerous hostile planes flew over Company Headquarters at a low altitude, and Pte.Norris (driver, No.1 Section) was wounded in the calf by their fire. The night was quiet MAISSEMY lightly shelled at intervals.

(continued)

(3)

21/9/18.   At 6.a.m. we opened an intense bombardment on the left and a concentration of all artillery on PONTRUET was observed. All section officers reported the night quiet in the line with the exception of harassing machine gun fire from FRESNOY and a slight increase of enemy trench mortar activity. Casualties nil.
Dispositions of guns at 9.a.m. 21/9/18.

       4 guns at M.26.a.65.75.
       1 gun at M.26.a.80.95.
       1 gun at M.20.c.75.05.
       2 guns at M.20.a. 8. 4.

No.2 and 4 Sections as before.

    Later all section officers reported the day quiet, but Company Headquarters in MAISSEMY received salvos of light shelling (77 mm. and 4.2s) at intervals of about 1 hour from 12.45 onwards. Horses and limbers were moved about 300 yards north west of the village. Towards dusk a proportion of gas shells were used. One of our horses was killed and another wounded at 9.30.p.m. MAISSEMY was shelled at intervals throughout the night and bombing planes were active. Forward areas, valleys and wagon lines were also shelled.

22/9/18.   Morning quiet. Dispositions of guns at 9.a.m. - unchanged. 2/Lieut.Berra (No.2 Section) Reported an apparent enemy withdrawal from trench in front of FRESNOY WOOD. Very lights being fired from ridge behind this line. During the night 21st/22nd September the 1st L.N.Lancs (Right Battalion) and 1st Camerons (Left Battalion) changed over. Lieut.Melville M.C. now with North Lancs, Lieut. Taylor now with Camerons. Situation quiet during theday. 30 filled belts were sent to Lieut.Canning at 6.p.m. in preparation for barrage fire from M.26.a. 7. 7. At 7.30.p.m. S.O.S. wemt up on right, and left divisional fronts and both artilleries were active, but no action developed. Rainy evening.

23/9/18.   MAISSEMY was somewhat heavily shelled from 2.a.m. to 4.a.m. Reports received from Section Officers shewed that the enemy had counter-attacked near BERTHACOURT at 7.30.p.m. 22/9/18 but was repulsed. The day was spent in preparation for barrage fire of 16 guns, "A" Company, during attack of 2nd and 3rd Brigades. At 6.p.m. Nos. 2 and 4 Sections were relieved by "B" Company, 1st Battalion, M.G.C. and withdrew their guns to Company Headquarters at MAISSEMY , prior to occupying battery positions in M.26.a. Position of guns in battery formation:-

       No.3 Section 4 guns at M.20.a.93.40 leftgun.
       No.1, 2 and 4 Section 12 guns, M.26.a.72.90. left gun

    The above prepared positions were occupied at 10.p.m. Targets:- FRESNOY Cemetary, COURNOUILLERS WOOD and Trench Junctions of the advanced Hindenburg Line. Rates of fire - about one and a half belts per minute from zero to zero plus forty. Then one belt per minute from zero plus forty to zero plus sixty. After this hour - special targets and S.O.S.

24/9/18.   The night was lively. MAISSEMY and Company H.Q. was shelled by 4.2s and 5.9s from 12 midnight to 4.a.m. At 5.a.m. (zero) the bombardment opened. Our low flying planes were active on this fine morning. The German S.O.S. signal was observed 2 minutes after opening of bombardment and the greater part of the enemy artillery opened to be smothered, although numerous bursts were fired on back areas.

(continued)

(4)

Our battery guns (16) fired 50,000 to 60,000 rounds on targets as on page (3). All objectives were gained at an early hour and a large number of prisoners were taken. By 9.a.m. the situation had become very quiet on the whole front. Day normal. Prisoners taken by first Division in this attack were over 800.

25/9/18. Day quiet to normal. Positions of guns unchanged.

26/9/18. Positions of guns unchanged at 9.a.m. Arrangements were made to relieve "A" Company 46th Battalion, M.G.C. in the PONTRUET Sector. Relief was postponed until 27th/28th.

27/9/18. The 16 guns and 4 sections were withdrawn at 1.p.m. to sunken road south of MAISSEMY, and afterwards relieved 8 guns each of "A" and "B" Companies, 46th Battalion, M.G.C. in the PONTRUET Sector. Guns and sections as follows:-

No.1 Section, 4 guns at M. 2.b. 2. 5.
No.2 Section, 4 guns at M. 2.c. 1. 9.
No.3 Section, 4 guns at M. 7.b. 9. 8.
No.4 Section 4 guns at M.13b. 9. 3.
Company H.Q. MAISSEMY, R.23.b. 4. 4.
Wagon Lines as before.

Relief was complete at 11.10.p.m.

28/9/18 At 5.a.m. a salvo of 5.9s fell upon Lieut.Melville's guns at M.13.b.9.3. causing 6 casualties, 4 other ranks killed 2 other ranks wounded. At about the same hour one gun of No.3 Section was damaged and put out of action. The day was spent in preparation for IX Corps attack. Officers of No.1 2 and 3 Sections reconnoitred their battery and forward positions.

29/9/18 Bombardment opened at 5.30.a.m. Positions of guns at this hour:-

No.3 Section, with 1st L.N.Lancs about G.33 central.
Nos.1 and 2 Sections, in FOURMI Trench, M.3.a. and .c. firing a barrage upon FOURGANS and FLUTE Trenches, east and north-east of PONTRUET.
No.4 section in Brigade reserve at M.13.b.9.3.

A dense mist covered the field until 11.a.m. when considerable progress was reported. 1st Brigade threw out a defensive flank towards the canal at BELLENGLISE, while 46th Division crossed canal and captured this village and MAGNY LA FOSSE. Nos1 and 2 Sections fired about 30,000 rds in support of these operations. and prisoners afterwards reported the great effet of this fire. No.3 Section co-operated with L.N.Lancs informing the defensive flank and Lieut.Baker who had pushed his guns out boldly to protect the infantry was wounded, together with his section sergeant. By 12 noon our guns were left considerably in rear of operations. No.3 Section was withdrawn to Brigade reserve at M.14.d.3.3. where advanced Company H.Q. was also established. At 6.p.m. No.4 Section joined 1st Camerons in PONTRUET. The night was rainy.

30/9/18. At 11.a.m. Nos.1 and 2 Sections were moved up from M.3 central to FANFARONS Trench in M.12 and N.7 in support of our right flank. No.4 Section was also in this area. Advanced Company H.Q. moved with Brigade to M.11.b.7.9. near Canal. At 7.p.m. Nos.1 2 and 4 Sections were ordered across the Canal joining the L.N.Lancs and Camerons, and during the night and following day were disposed as follows:-
No.2 Section(L.N.Lancs) 2 guns at N.14.c.0.6. 2 guns at N.14.b.3.9.
No.1 Section 4 guns at N.8.b.5.7. No.4 section 4 guns at N.3.c.4.7. No.3 Section. in reserve at M.11 central.

Report of action 18th to 20th September 1918.

"B" Company.

Attack commenced at 5.20.a.m. 18/9/18.

No.3 Section advanced with K.R.R.C. On the attack being held up in M,13.d. Lieut.Harriss went forward with a gun to assist in overcoming the opposition. As he arrived at the forward waves the enemy resistance weakened and our infantry were able to get into the first objective (VILLEMAY TRENCH) The section then pushed forward to about M.14 central where several targets were engaged. In the afternoon as the infantry had only got to BERTHACOURT and the guns were under heavy artillery and machine gun fire the latter were withdrawn to VILLEMAY Trench. From here numerous targets were engaged. During the night one gun was destroyed by shell fire.

No.1 Section advanced with the Royal Sussex. 2 guns being with the right Company and two with the left. They kept well up with the front wave and reached the objectives almost at the same time. On arrival at the final objective the guns took up positions near the tumulous in M.1.d. From this point numerous targets were engaged. Sgt.Hopkins V, dealt very effectively with several hostile machine guns which were holding up the 2nd.K.R.R.C. on the right flank thereby enabling the infantry to advance.

Nos. 2 and 4 Sections moved forward about 11 a.m. to consolidate the first objective at about R.11. About 12 noon these sections moved forward to consolidate the final objective taking up positions, No.4 Section about M.1.b.9.8. And No.2 Section about M.7.b.8.8. Both these sections moved by limber up to about R.11.b.7.7. Company Headquarters moved about 11 a.m. to MAISSEMY R.15.c.9.2.

On 19/9/18 No.3 Section gave covering fire into PONTRUET and beyond for the attack at 9.a.m. which however was held up. All sections engaged various targets during the day.

On 20th September several targets were engaged during the day. Company was relieved in the evening by "A" Company, 46th Battalion, M.G.C.

Report of Action 24th to 28th September 1918.

At zero 5.a.m. 24/9/18 No.2 Section advanced with 2nd R.Sussex and took up positions about M.21.b.8.7. No.4 Section went forward with the 2nd Northants and got into position with two guns about M.15.a.7.5. and two guns about M.15.b.4.4. During the two counter attacks about noon the guns at M.15.a.7.5. got into action and inflicted many casualties. Later the two guns in M.15.b.4.4. moved to M.9.c.8.4. Nos.1 and 3 Sections fired a barrage on a line from M.16.a.7.2. to M.16.a.72.10. from zero plus 10 to zero plus 20 and on a line from M.16.b.0.9. to M.16.b.0.1. from zero plus 20 to zero plus 30. 20,000 rounds were fired. On completion of the barrage No.1 Section moved forward to about M.15.d.7.4. No.3 Section moved forward and took up positions about M.15.a.8.6. During the two enemy counter attacks about noon these latter guns inflicted many casualties on the troops advancing on the ridge in M.17.a. and in PONTRUET (M.10.a.) Numerous other targets were engaged during the day. Each section had one gun put out of action.

On the 25/9/18 two guns of No.2 Section were moved up to about M.16.c.4.4.

On 26/9/18 No.2 Section handed over one gun to No.1 Section and took over two guns from No.4 Section at M.9.c.8.4. under Lieut.Chester. No.4 Section handed over one gun to No.3 Section and were then withdrawn to Company Headquarters. On 27/9/18 No.4 Sec. moved up 2 guns to M.15.c.1.4. No.1 Section moved two guns to this point all under Lieut.Browne.

On 28/9/18 Lieut.Browne and two guns from No.4 Section relieved Lieut.Dines and two guns from No.1 Section. Company relieved by "C" Company 1st Battalion, M.G.C.

"C" Company

16/9/18.	Engaged parties of enemy with direct fire. Carried out harassing fire during night on enemy roads.
17/9/18.	Engaged enemy trenches and roads till dawn.
18/9/18.	Brigade advanced and the Company was left at MAISSEMY in reserve until night of the 21st.
21/9/18.	No.1 Section relieved No.1 Section of "C" Company, 6th Battalion, M.G.C. at M.27.d.0.2. and Lieut.Barker M.C. took up positions at M.25.d.9.1. He had four casualties going up.
22/9/18.	The above two sections remained in position and 2 and 3 Sections remained resting at MAISSEMY as they were detailed to Battalions for the attack on the 24th.
23/9/18.	Lieut.Hedley relieved Lieut.Barker M.C. who was proceeding on leave.
24/9/18.	Attack on FRESNOY arrangements for:-

No.1 Section under Lieut.Hart was to advance after the attacking Battalion support Company and engage FRESNOY from South thereby supporting the left attacking battalion. This section will in no way be under the infantry but has a special function that is to push forward to FRESNOY Trench and take up a defensive position in that trench. No.2 Section will be under the command of O.C. 1st Gloucesters No.3 Section will be under the O.C.Welsh Regt. No.4 Sect. will be move to quarry before zero whene it will be in reserve and will move forward to defensive positions in FRESNOY Trench north of No.1 Section for the defence of the Village. After the attack all sections will take up defensive positions and lay out S.O.S. lines on enemy approaches.

Attack on FRESNOY:-

As arrange Nos.2 and 3 Sections followed attacking infantry and took up defensive positions. Lieut.Marks M.C. also mounted two enemy guns for defence. 2/Lieut.McLean went forward with two guns into FRESNOY Cemetery. The situation was not clear and a pocket of the enemy held up the attack of the left battalion, so, as this section had gone in advance of this pocket it was withdrawn it having a rough time having lost one gun and one team gassed. No.4 Section took its place for the time being, and, not being able to get into FRESNOY Trench owing to the strong point, went into defensive positions in FRESNOY Cemetery for the night with one platoon of infantry of the S.W.Bs. No.2 Section had then two guns south west of the village and one gun in reserve at quarry. No.1 Section was able early in the day to take up its defensive position and was the means of capturing some prisoners. The villages of FRESNOY and GRICOURT fell into our hands.

25/9/18.	Guns of No.2 and 3 Sections went forward to defend GRICOURT
26/9/18.	On the evening of this date the Company was relieved by "D" Company 6th Battalion, M.G.C. getting to billets in MARTEVILLE about 5.a.m. 27th.
27/9/18.	Remained in MARTEVILLE.
28/9/18.	Men had baths and we relieved "B" Company 1st Battalion M.G.C. H.Q. at MAISSEMY. 4 sections in line with 3rd Infantry Bde.
29/9/18.	General attack, guns moved forward with infantry.
30/9/18.	Enemy retired and te infantry followed up. Guns of No.4 Section followed S.W.Bs. Nos.2 and 3 formed defensive flanks to south. Transport ordered up to become mobile. No.4 Section took up defensive positions with S.W.Bs. in front line and engaged targets at GLAMO Trench M.26.b. and sunken road Many hits were claimed having direct enfilade fire on sunken road. Two more guns were put into action by 6.p.m. The remaining guns were assembled with transport ready for next advance. TALANA HILL was reconnoitred for gun positions but the fields of fire were not good and Lewis Guns could do the job. So the remaining guns remained in reserve.

"D" Company.

15/9/18. Weather fine and sunny. Nos.1 and 2 sections in positions forming the left sub-group with 4 guns R.15.a. and 4 guns in reserve R.21.a. under control of Infantry Commander. Nos.3 and 4 Sections in positions at R.28 central forming the right sub-group. Situation normal during day. At night intermittent shelling, gas and H.E. on right. Operations. 3,000 rounds harassing fire by right sub-group during night. Casualties, nil, Transport sent with sections under O.C. sub-group.

16/9/18. Weather sunny, situation normal during day, intermittent hostile shelling during night. E.A. active during the day and night. Casualties, nil.

17/9/18. Situation normal. Preparations made for operations on 18th instant. S.A.A. dumps of 50,000 rounds established at R.15.c.4.5. and X.4.d.10.25. respectively. Hostile artillery active during the night chiefly with gas. Some E.A. active during the day. Casualties 3 other ranks wounded.

18/9/18. Forward Company H.Q. with 1st and 2nd Brigades, Rear H.Q. remaining at R.31.c.0.8. Nos.1 and 2 Sections forming left sub-group were in reserve to 2nd Brigade. Nos.3 and 4 Sections forming right sub-group were in reserve to 1st Brigade. Operations commenced at 5.20.a.m. during heavy rain storm and dense mist which cleared up during the morning. Sections commenced moving forward at 9.15.a.m. when Infantry were believed to have secured first objective. Left sub-group under Lieut.Strover reached forward positions at 12.30.p.m. Right sub-group under Lieut.Browne were held up at MAISSEMY. Forward Company H.Q. were moved to MAISSEMY about midday moving with 1st and 2nd Brigades. About 7.30.p.m. Lieut.Carr with No.2 Section was occupying positions on right of Tumulous and Lieut.Strover on left. Hostile artillery active day and night. Casualties. 1 O.R. wounded.

19/9/18. Right sub-group moved forward and occupied positions about 1000 yards in front of MAISSEMY, guns being disposed to protect right flank of Divisional front. After dusk Lieut. Strover occupied a Battery position on right of No.2 Section in order to be in readiness to deal with enemy counter attacks which were then developing on the right brigade front. Casualties, 3 O.Rs wounded.

20/9/18. Batteries occupying positions as previously stated. Lieut. Strover slightly wounded whilst visiting guns at stand-to but remained at duty. Sniping gun was pushed forward about 700 yards by left sub-group at 11.30.a.m. and remained out until 5.30.p.m. Good results were obtained by Lieuts.Strover and Carr (Left sub-group) by direct fire on PONTRUET about 1200 rounds being expended. At 8.p.m. Left sub-group was withdrawn to Coopers Quarry where they remained during the night.

21/9/18. Left sub-group moved to MAISSEMY at 1.p.m. to Forward Company H.Q. Situation normal during the day. Harassing fire was carried out at night by Right sub-group between 7.30.p.m. and 5.a.m. 12,000 rounds fired on selected targets. Forward Company Headquarters heavily shelled by H.E. and Blue Cross Gas.

22/9/18. Weather continues dull and showery. Situation normal 200,000 rounds of S.A.A. drawn and dumped with the Right sub-group commander in preparation for the operations. Enemy aeroplanes active during the day. Hostile artillery harassing forward areas intermittently day and night. Casualties 1 other ranks wounded slightly. At midday Company H.Q. moved to trench in R.29.b. owing to heavy shelling.

23/9/18. At dusk No.1 and 2 Sections under Lieut.Strover moved up and occupied Battery positions at M.26.b.55.30.and Nos. 3 and 4 Sections under Lieut.Brown moved to Battery positions at M.26.c.75.70 ready for operations on the morning of the 24th. Forward Company Headquarters moved to R.30.c. established battle headquarters there with Battalion Headquarters.

(continued)

24/9/18.	Operations commenced at 5.a.m. Each battery fired foregoing according to Barrage Time Table. Lieut.Strover in command of "Z" Battery carried out programme as required and formed a reserve of 8 guns when infantry had advanced beyond range. Lieut.Browne in command of "Y" Battery carried out firing according to programme being heavily shelled with gas and H.E. after zero plus 90. 4 guns under Lieut.Streets moved forward to M.20.b.65.60. and came under 2nd Brigade helping to defend this flank. 2 guns under the command of Lieut.Browne went forward to M.28.b. and came within the 3rd Brigade area engaging any likely targets. The remaining two guns under 2/Lieut.Copley were withdrawn to R.29.b. where they remained for the night. At dusk 4 guns under Lieut.Carr moved forward to R.16.d. to consolidate infantry posts there front line GRICOURT having been captured. These guns assisted in repelling local enemy counter attacks during the afternoon.
25/9/18.	Two gun teams of 2/Lieut.Copley relieved two gun teams of Lieut.Browne which returned to R.29.b. on relief. Four gun teams of Lieut.Strover relieved four gun teams of Lieut.Carr at dusk. Teams on relief returning to R.29.b.
26/9/18.	The two gun teams under Lieut.Copley were withdrawn from 3rd Brigade front and held in reserve.
27/9/18.	The 8 gun teams in reserve moved back to rear Company Headquarters in VERMAND at 9.a.m. There they had a hot bath and were issued with clean clothing. Lieut.Streets carried out harassing fire from dusk to dawn firing 8,000 rounds.
28/9/18.	At dusk Lieut.Strover was relieved by four gun teams of Lieut.Browne and Lieut.Streets relieved by one gun team by Lieut.Carr. Teams on relief returned to rear Company H.Q. at VERMAND. Harassing fire was carried out by Lieut.Carr. 5,000 rounds being fired.
29/9/18.	During the morning a certain amount of firing was carried out by Lieut.Brown who was assisting the 3rd Brigade in their advance. At night these guns were withdrawn to M.20.b. forming a reserve of 8 guns with those of Lieut.Carr. Casualties 1 Sgt.Killed and 1 other ranks wounded.
30/9/18.	About 2.p.m. these 8 guns were moved forward to SAMPSON Trench in M.16.c. Forward Company Headquarters moved to sunken road by MUGUET WOOD IN M.15.b. The remaining 8 guns and teams together with Rear Company H.Q. occupied vacated positions in R.30.c. The company remained in these positions during night of the 30th and 1st October.

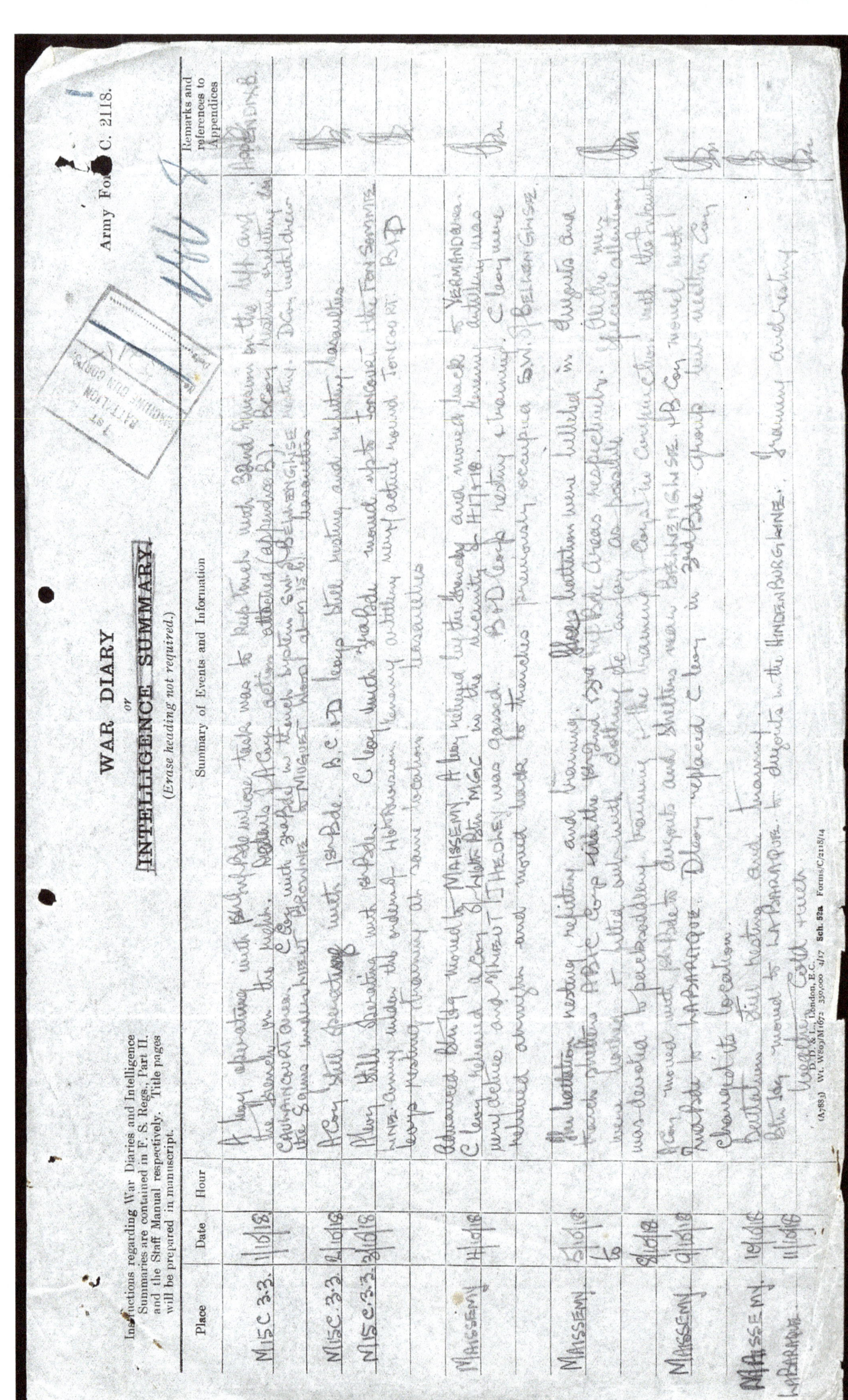

Army Form C. 2118.

WAR DIARY
or
INTELLIGENCE SUMMARY
(Erase heading not required.)

Instructions regarding War Diaries and Intelligence Summaries are contained in F.S. Regs., Part II. and the Staff Manual respectively. Title pages will be prepared in manuscript.

Place	Date	Hour	Summary of Events and Information	Remarks and references to Appendices
M15.C.3.3.	1/3/18		A Coy operating with Rifle Brigade whose task was to hold trench with 2nd Gunners in the left and the trench in the right. Relieved A Coy action attached (Appendix B). B Coy resting & shelling in CAUCHICOURT QUARR. C Coy with 2nd Bde in trench system Sh.51.B BELLENGLISE NELLU. D Coy with the Same Brigade NE of BROWVILZ & MUGUET Wood at M.15.B BELLENGLISE NELLU.	Hope Lieut DMB
M15.C.3.2.	2/3/18		A Coy still operating with 1st Bde. B, C, D Coys still resting and refitting BASINVILLE	
M15.C.3.3.	3/3/18		Very still operating with 18th Bde. C Coy went forward to relieve Hd Ft SERVINS B.A.D. M15 Coy under the command of 1st Brown Bavarian Company Artillery went before going forward to location BASINVILLE Coys resting training at Same location	
MAISSEMY	4/3/18		Advance Bty HQ moved to MAISSEMY A Coy relieved by Bn Seneffe and moved back to VERMANDEN. C Coy relieved A Coy & Hdt Bn MGC in the vicinity of H.17-18. Known activity was very active and MUGUET & THOREY was ceased. B,D Coys resting & training. C Coys were relieved & formation and went back to trenches previously occupied Sh.51 B BELLEN GHISE.	
MAISSEMY	5/3/18 to 8/3/18		Bn battalion resting, refitting and training. These battalions were billeted in dugouts and various places A.B.C Coys were the 2nd and 3rd with the areas respectively. Orders were given to entrain - with dummies were busy as possible, also we were devoted to preparing training of the various Coys in connection with the trenches.	
MAISSEMY	9/3/18		A Coy went with Pamphlets to dugouts and shelters near BELLENZI GHISE. B Coy moved with troops to LAPARANQUE. D Coy relieved C Coy in 3rd Bde Group this relief Coy changed its location.	
MAISSEMY LAPARANQUE	10/3/18 11/3/18		Battalion still resting and training. Bn Hqs moved to LAPARANQUE - Dugouts in the HINDENBURG LINE. Training and resting	

WAR DIARY
or
INTELLIGENCE SUMMARY

Army Form C. 2118.

(Erase heading not required.)

Place	Date	Hour	Summary of Events and Information	Remarks and references to Appendices
LA BARQUE	12/4/18		Battalion resting and training. Weather fine	
do	13/4/18		do do Weather warmer	
do	14/4/18		Battalion training. Fine day	
do	15/4/18		Commanding Officers attended a conference at Division and received verbal instructions regarding attack to be made by the Division on 17th. By Bohain. Orders received in the evening known as "Bohain Order No. 1". M.B.Coys were given orders of 1st and 2nd Objectives respectively and C & D Coys forming under Battalion Arrangements. (Vide Appendix A + 3051).	APPENDIX A
BOHAIN	16/4/18		Battalion bivouacked in C D Coys moved by march route to Bohain and were billeted in the town. A B Coys moved with their Bdes. Heads for area NW of BOHAIN (Vide appendix A) Orders were issued regarding the attack (Vide appendix A 3053).	APPENDIX A
BOHAIN	17/4/18		At 3 AM Advanced Battalion Headquarters was established with 1st & 2nd Inf Bde HQs. At Zero hour 05.20 the 6th & 18th Divisions attacked and gained the 1st objective line (Shown in ORANGE on sketch) where the Division passed through them. The enemy resistance was very stiff but by the Division captured LANPLUAZ MURATRE and ANDIGNY les FERMES. Along Barestine with 12th Bde Bohard and a long hung in support of the attack and had heavy direct temple Bloom forming with our Infantry Brigade Mouillon. The enemy Snipers and Knuckel out several guns M.G.s C.D loops remaining hidden watching. There was little to record they reach their Battery positions reversely shown as the advance did not proceed for enough to ensure their true Coys were the Subject of the attack and carried out harassing fire with even	APPENDIX B

WAR DIARY or INTELLIGENCE SUMMARY

Army Form C. 2118.

Place	Date	Hour	Summary of Events and Information	Remarks and references to Appendices
VAUX ANDIGNY	17/10/18		Battalion Headquarters (advanced) move forward to VAUX ANDIGNY. Beaurevoir. 7 ORs.	B.
	18/10/18		The Division resumed the attack at 11.30 hours and gained all objectives capturing the latter village. The attack was carried out by 137th Infantry Bde. & 139 Infantry Bde. A Coy & & part of D Coy operated with 15th Bde and Bn. Coys with 3rd Bde. A successful barrage was put up in the initial stage of the attack and enemy trench targets were engaged by the guns during the advance. Bn. assisted during the consolidation and harassed enemy from tracks used during the night. The attack was completely successful and over 700 prisoners taken. B Coy casualties resumed in the afternoon. Casualties: 1 Off. O.R.	Appendix A. A.
LAVAQUERIE MOLAIN	19/10/18		The attack was resumed at 0550 the line RESTET - BEAUREPIO - MARETZ - MARETZ - SIX were reached. 137 Bde - 139 Bde came into reserve. A Coy withdraws KATHALEZ MOLAIN. B Coy attaches to 2nd Bn. moved up in the evening to relieve the American Brigade on the left of the Division. In doing so casualties were incurred, namely 11 Officers & 60 O.Rs. Battalion Hq. moved to LAVAQUERIE MOLAIN Casualties: 1 Off O.R.	A. Appendix B. Appendix B.
LAVAQUERIE MOLAIN	20/10/18		A Coy in reserve at LA VAQUERIE MOLAIN. B Coy in the line with 2nd Bde. C & D Coys were relieved by 2 companies 8 2nd (Rif. Guards) Bn. McQuardo, and moved back & billets in VAUX ANDIGNY and MOLAIN respectively. Harassing fire was carried out during the day and night. Casualties. 1 O.R.	Appendix A. do. B.
LAVAQUERIE MOLAIN	21/10/18		A. C. & D Coy in billets resting and refitting. B Coy and Rifle Guards in the line carried out usual approach harassing fire. Enemy artillery was very active. Casualties. 2 O.R.	Appendix. B.

WAR DIARY
or
INTELLIGENCE SUMMARY

Army Form C. 2118.

Place	Date	Hour	Summary of Events and Information	Remarks and references to Appendices
LAVENTEE MUNATRE	22/4/18		D Coy relieved B Coy in the line the latter returning billets in VAUX ANDIGNY. B'n in much same position the line was advanced slightly. Usual harassing fire carried out. Enemy were issuing and allowances approach to the attack which had been issued + Battalion was prepared Divisional conferences and in Divisional instructions issued. (see SS No 109T.) Casualties 1 OR.	Appendix # B
LAVENTEE MUNATRE	23/4/18		The Division attacked in conjunction with the 6th Division on the left Ahr 01.30 aug the Battalion was [?] outflanking Canal the SAMBRE & ahorse warranted. D Coy 1st guns + the Battalion over stays of good. (One Coy) 2 LTMG Quando Co operated in this center + first in through stages of the attack a most successful barrage and after suffered casualties 8 ORs.	Appendix ND 49/3 B
LAVENTEE MUNATRE	24/4/18		The position was unchanged but enemy artillery warring active. Usual harassing fire was carried out with the enemy on enemy forward AH Coys taking quint. [?] in VAUX ANDIGNY VAUX 212 MOHATRE VAUX ANDIGNY AMNAM indentifier the enemy carried out some heavy but [?] with fire carried out. Casualties from heavy shellfire too much the M.T. trains + transport, heaving 4 [?] A war warring Day in the evening	Appendix 14
LAVENTEE MUNATRE	25/4/18		My Eind in situation was the same. Other 3 Coys PATROL later grande warriors in the consolidation and during the evening carried out harassing fire. Thereafter	Appendix 17
LAVENTEE MUNATRE	26/4/18		Situation unchanged in the line except for infantry patrol [?] in highway different areas. 2 LT G Philipino carried out harassing fire on all enemy posts in stands AHR+ loop [?] in rush + carried out heavily rifle refied fire in gun run	Appendix B
LAVENTEE MUNATRE	27/4/18		No change in the situation. The usual harassing fire was carried out. Enemy attackr heavy [?] with salt from Battalion canadiis 2 ORS.	B

WAR DIARY or INTELLIGENCE SUMMARY
Army Form C. 2118.

(Erase heading not required.)

Instructions regarding War Diaries and Intelligence Summaries are contained in F. S. Regs., Part II. and the Staff Manual respectively. Title pages will be prepared in manuscript.

Place	Date	Hour	Summary of Events and Information	Remarks and references to Appendices
LA VALLEE MULATRE	28/10/18		During the summer country attacks launched by the enemy were 2nd Battalion the Queens. A Coy fired a barrage & defense. 30,000 rds and the guns of 2nd (H.G. Jumbo Btn) MG Guards also co-operated. In the afternoon the 3rd (R.H.G.) Btn MG Guards relieved the Coy of 2nd (H.G.) Btn MG Guards, & D Coy us in the new situation on the Divisional front. Lesauvillie 1st R.	APPENDIX #B
-do-	29/10/18		The Commanding Officer proceeded on leave. Major N.B.N. Green M.C. took over command temporarily. In the line there were no change in the general situation and usual harassing fire was carried out. Lesauvillie 2nd R.	B
-do-	30/10/18		01-05:30 SOS sent up with line - throughout. A Coy fired a barrage in which the guns of B Coy 3rd (R.H.G.) Btn MG Guards co-operated. So were two posts of 2nd Port Bn had been driven in by the enemy in the enemy raid at 05:30 a small counter attack was successfully carried out at 12:10 d. which A Coy 1918 B Coy 3rd R.H.G. Btn co-operated firing an excellent barrage necessary in its consolidation. Lesauvillie: Lieut S.C. Bryan wounded. 1st R Ralia	MAZZINI B B
-do-	31/10/18		The situation was quiet in the line. D Coy relieved A Coy, B Coy relieving C Coy in the forward area. A & C Coys proceeding Kulluls in MOHAIN and NAS AMBIGNY respectively. Lesauvillie mel.	MAZZINI B A

SUMMARY OF OPERATIONS FROM 17TH TO 27TH OCTOBER 1918.

"A" Company, 1st Battalion, M.G.C.

17/10/18. 1st Division took part in IX Corps attack. Zero hour for this attack was 05.20. 1st and 2nd Brigades were to pass through Brigades of the 6th and 46th Divisions who were to capture a line running south of MOLAIN to ANDIGNY. Sections place and hour of assembly as follows:-

No.2	V.29.c.	05.20	)
No.3	V.29.c.	05.20	) Ref. Map Sheet,
No.1	V.28	05.40	) FORET D'ANDIGNY
No.4	V.28	05.40	) (62.B. N.E. and 57.B. S.E)

Tasks:- No.2 and 3 Sections advancing behind L.N.Lancs to protect the right flank of the 1st Brigade resting on the Foret d'Andigny. No.1 Section to pass through these sections to the neighbourhood of WASSIGNY and to protect the eastern extension of this flank. No.4 Section in Brigade reserve. All sections were under the control of O.C. "A" Company and were not attached to Battalions. The morning was fine but misty and the smoke of heavy bombardment added to the difficulty of keeping touch. All sections advance with limbers and mounted orderlies. Nos.2 and 3 Sections became engaged about 09.00 firing from the neoghbourhood of BELLEVUE RIDGE and LES GOBELETS upon direct targets. Over 6,000 rounds were fired by these sections and many of the enemy were seen to fall. Nos. 1 and 4 Sections advanced to W.26.a. and about 15.00 No.1 Section moved up in support of an attack by 1st Camerons but did not become engaged. Numerous prisoners were taken during the day and an advance of 4,000 yards was made, although all objectives were not attacked. Company H.Q. moved to BECQUIGNY at 06.00 hours and to Quarry near VAUX ANDIGNY at 11.00. Position of guns at 18.00 hours.
No.3 Section 2 guns at E.4.d.5.5. and 2 guns at E.4.c.3.9
No.2 Section 2 guns at E.4.d.9.9. and 2 guns at W.20.d.9.2.
No.1 Section 4 guns in W.28.b.
No.4 Section 4 guns in W.26.a.
Our casualties in these operations were 4 other ranks wounded. Company H.Q. moved at 18.00 hours to a house in VAUX ANDIGNY.

18/10/18. Fine morning. 1st Division resumed the attack at 11.30. At 10.00 Nos. 2 and 3 Sections were relieved by "A" Coy. 46th Bn.M.G.C. and withdrawn to W.26. No.4 Section were detailed to advance behind the 1st Black Watch and move off at Zero. No.1 Section remained in W.29 central. Nos.1 and 2 Section gave covering fire (about 12,000 rounds) in support of the initial stage of the attack. Excellent progress was made in this attack WASSIGNY being captured with many prisoners. At 16.00 O.C. "A" Company moved with 1st Brigade to LA VALLEE MULATRE and Company H.Q. and Transport to sunken road between ANGIN FARM and MALASSISE FARM. No.4 Positions of guns at 18.00. 3 Sections at MALASSISE FARM No.4 Section advancing with the Black Watch. At 21.00 No.2 Section was ordered to X.26.b.(WASSIGNY) and No. 4 Section to WASSIGNY Station. Night firing was carried on by these sections on ARROUAISE FARM and the railway S.E. of WASSIGNY. 11,000 rounds were fired during the night. Casualties 4 Other ranks wounded.

19/10/18. Morning misty. Attack was resumed by 1st Brigade at 05.20 under a heavy protective bombardment. 1st Black Watch in the line. No.2 Section advance behind this Battalion and occupied positions near ARROUAISE FARM upon which they had fired at 2700 yards range throughout the night. At 15.00 this section with No.4 was withdrawn to WASSIGNY. 1st Brigade came into support. Meanwhile at 09.00 Company H.Q. and Transport with 1 and 3 Sections had moved to LA VALLEE MULATRE W.24.c.4.6. Billets here were good. Casualties 2 other ranks wounded.

20/10/18 to 23/10/18	Company Resting. Locations of sections unchanged.

24/10/18. Arrangements made for the relief of "D" Company, 1st Battn. M.G.C. for the morning of 25/10/18. Lieut. Taylor reconnoitred the line with Major Anson. No.2 Section moved to LA VALLE MULATRE.

25/10/18. The Company (16 guns) relieved 12 guns of "D" Company, 1st Battalion, M.G.C. on the CATILLON front as follows:-
No.1 Section, 4 guns relieved 2 guns in R.29.c.
No.3 Section, 4 guns relieved 4 guns in R.22.d. and R.28.b.
No.2 Section, 4 guns relieved 2 guns in R.33.d. (2) and X.3.b. (2)
No.4 Section, 4 guns relieved 4 guns in R.33.a.
Company H.Q. in MAZINGHIEN R.33.d.0050
Transport and Quartermasters Stores remained in LA VALLEE MULATRE. (Sheet 51.B. S.E. Edition 2)
Nos. 1 and 4 Sections started firing indirect overhead fire on exits in CATILLON ~~on exist from CATILLON~~ in R.23.b. and d. at about 18.30 at request of C.O. 1st Battn. Black Watch. Casualty 1 Other rank wounded.

26/10/18. 11,000 rounds were fired during the night 25/26th. The enemy shelled the forward sections intermittently throughout the 24 hours.

27/10/18. 4,000 fired on night of 26/27th on southern exits from CATILLON. Intermittent shelling by the enemy of all areas and cross roads in MAZINGHIEN received considerable attention. The two left guns of No.1 Section at R.29.a.5.1. were shifed north to R.21.a.5.5. in order to cover the valley between the two roads. No.3 Sections guns were shifted and placed as follows:-
1 gun at R.22.d.90.10 - 1 gun at R.22.d.8.2. - 1 gun at R.22.d.6.7. - 1 gun at R.22.d.55.75. Hostile artillery was again active during the night on all areas. No night firing owing to infantry relief. Casualty 1 O.R.Killed in A.

28/10/18. On the night of the 27th 28th the enemy pushed in one or two posts of the 1st Northants. just South of CATILLON. On the morning of the 28th the Northants counter-attacked and regained their posts. In conjunction with this operation two guns of No. 4 Section and 4 guns of No. 2 Section fired a barrage on the Southern exit of CATILLON. 19,500 rounds were fired including harassing fire during the night.
Casualties:- One O.R. rank wounded.

29/10/18. Two guns of No. 4 Section went forward with the 1st Northants. and took up positions at R.35.a.6.3. and R.35.c.7.4. respectively. No. 2 Section moved up into a Battery position in R.34.d. and fired 6,000 rounds during the night on exits of CATILLON. During the night the S.O.S. Signal went up.
No. 1 Section had two guns firing to M.32.a.c. & D (BOIS DE L'ABBAYE) during the night. 16,000 rounds were fired in all.
Casualties:- Two O.R's wounded.

30/10/18. At about 05-30 the S.O.S. Signal went up again and the Battery position openede up at once, 5 minutes rapid, and continued with long bursts for ten minutes. The Battery was then withdrawn to its old position. At 11,00. orders were received to fire a Barrage on to CATILLON in conjunction with the counter-attack being made by the Northants who had had one or two posts thrust in. Zero hour was 12,00. The Battery was again moved forward and was in position and ready to fire by 11.30. At 11.40 the CO.Northants under orders from B.G.C. 2nd Inf. Bde. ordered all rear guns to move forward at once. This order was confirmed by Group Commander. Orders were sent forthwith to stop Battery firing and pack up ready to move forward. The two guns of No. 4 Section left behind, also moved forward. Positions were taken up as follows. No. 4 Section:- 1 guns at R.29.d.95.20.

1 Gun at R.30.c.65.20., 1 Gun at R.30.c.8.6. and 1 Gun at R.30.a.9.0.
No. 2 Section again took up a Battery position at R.55.b.1.5. This was done as it was considered unnecessary to place any more guns forward as the fields of fire were restricted by the hedges. Lieut.Bryan, when putting his guns into position came under direct M.G. fire at close range and was wounded in 3 places. One O.R. who was with him was killed.
Casualties :- One Officer wounded, One O.R. killed.

31/10/18. The day was fairly quiet. The Company was relieved by "D" Company, 1st Battalion, Machine Gun Corps, in the afternoon and evening, and marched to billets at MOLAIN.

SUMMARY OF OPERATIONS FROM 17TH TO 20TH OCTOBER 1918.

"B" Company, 1st Battalion, M.G.C.

17/10/18. The 2nd Brigade attacked on the 17th October from east of VAUX ANDIGNY with the object of reaching a line (the green line) N. and S. just east of WASSIGNY and then exploiting east of this line. The 1st Northants were on the right and the 2nd K.R.R.C. on the left with the 2nd Royal Sussex in reserve prepared to exploit. The Company was attached to tge 2nd Brigade for this operation and its role was as follows:-
No.1 Section attached 1st Northants.
No.4 Section attached 2nd K.R.R.C.
These two sections were to act as batteries of opportunity No.2 and 3 Sections were in Brigade reserve their task being (i) to move forward as soon after zero as possible and take up positions about W.23.b. to carry out harassing fire on RIBEAUVILLE and the exits therefrom. and (ii) on completion of this firing to move forward to positions to protect the left flank and the green line as follows:-
No.3 Section to about MILL FARM X.20.d.
No.2 Section to about X.14.a.
Company H.Q. was to remain during the operations with the H.Q. of the Royal Sussex.
The Company was assembled at 04.00 as follows:-
No.1 with 1st Northants in W.23.d.
Company H.Q. and remaining sections W.23.c.4.1. Owing to the nature of the ground where the 2nd K.R.R.C. assembled No.4 Section was not able to assemble with them but had orders to move forward as soon after zero as possible to join them. All sections assembled with their fighting limbers and retained them to the end of the days proceedings. The assembly was carried out without incident or interference by the enemy.
The attack commenced at 05.20 h At first the air was clear but very shortly afterwards a dense mist supervened which restricted visibility to about 10 yards. No.1 Section moved off with the Northants. 2 guns being attached to "C" Company and 2 guns in Battalion reserve. They moved along the north of the Railway. The remaining three sections and Company H.Q. moved up about 06.00 in rear of the 2nd R.Sussex. Movement was very slow on account of the thick mist but these three sections proceeded via VAUX ANDIGNY to the sunken road in W.15.c. Here they were held up by the M.G. fire from MOLAIN and from about W.15.b.5.3. No.4 Section therefore got into action and silenced the gun at W.15.b.5.3. As the situation in MOLAIN still remained obscure Lieut.Chester and Lieut. Brown reconnoitred forward and captured three of the enemy who were still holding out. After removing various obstructions they took their sections to the eastern outskirts of the village. Meantime hostile machine gun fire from the direction of W.23.b.1.8. was causing trouble. No.3 Section was therefore ordered to move forward to endeavour to neutralise it. Before they were able to do so however Sgt.Folwell advanced with his two guns up the high ground in W.22.b. and silenced the enemy guns. No.3 section were therefore ordered to move forward and endaevour to carry out their original programme. About 10.15 in spite of a certain amount of machine gun fire Nos.3 and 4 Sections were ready to move forward to W.17.c.3.1. From this vicinity No.4 Section got into action with two guns and silenced enemy machine guns firing from the railway and hedges in W.18.a. No.3 Section also got into action here with four guns and brought heavy fire to bear on the railway embankment in W.18.a. and on DEMILIEU. They then worked forward round the hedges and engaged at close range a hostile Machine gun about W.17.b.1.2. killing or wounding the whole of its

crew. Nos.2 and 4 Sections then, and later No.3 Section, moved up to about 23.b.2.8. (time about 11.30) from this point these two sections engaged numerous targets particularly about BELLEVUE and DEMILIEU. About noon orders were received from Brigade to place up to four guns of the reserve guns at the disposal of 2nd K.R.R.C. Lieut.Chester was therefore ordered to get into touch with O.C. K.R.R.C. and place himself at his disposal. As however the situation had become more or less stabilised he was not required and remained in his position. At about 16.30 orders were received for an attack at 17.10 on BELLEVUE and the road in W.13.b. and d. For this operation No.2 Section were ordered to advance with the Royal Sussex and No.3 Section with the Northants. No.2 Section advanced beyond the Railway in W.8.a. but finally took up positions about W.18.a.25.25. No.3 Section advanced as far as W.24 central but as the attack did not progress as expected took up positions at W.23.b.4.3.

18/10/18 In conjunction with an attack by the Americans at 05.30 on the left 4 guns of No.4 Section fired on the wood in X.7.d. up to 07.30 afterwards from 10.30 to 11.30 onwards Nos. 1 3 and 4 Sections fired on BELLEVUE and areas in vicinity during forming up of the 3rd Brigade. From 11.30 when the attack commenced to 11.50 No.4 Section and 2 guns of No.1 Section barraged the woods W and E. of the road about W.13.d.95.00. During these operations altogetjer about 20,000 rounds were fired and as the 3rd Brigade appeared to meet little opposition in the way of machine gun fire it would seem that this fire was very effective.

19/10/18. Company assembled at 05.30 about W.23.b.1.9. prepared to take part in operations of the 3rd Brigade. Company took over sector occupied by 119th and 120th American Regiments 36 casualties were incurred going into the line so that only 11 guns could be manned and these were disposed as follows.   No.1 Section 4 guns W.33.b. 4.5.
No.3 Section 4 guns W.33.a. 4. 7.
No.2 and 4 Sections 3 guns W.32.d.4.6.

20/10/18. An additional gun was sent up to W.32.d.4.6.

21/10/18. Company relieved by "D" Company 1st Battalion, M.G.C. and returned billets in VAUX ANDIGNY.

SUMMARY OF OPERATIONS FROM 17TH TO 19TH OCTOBER 1918.

"C" Company, 1st Battalion, M.G.C.

17/10/18. The Company moved from BOHAIN with orders to occupy Battery positions in copse W.24.a.4.3. and to support advance from Red Line to Green Line by firing on to Foresters House LES MARCONNIERS (F.1.b.) and WASSIGNY STATION from Z plus 307 to Z plus 350. Moved by road to VAUX ANDIGNY. (road was under hostile machine gun fire at about W.25. central from the right) Thence across country from to MOLAIN. Road barricaded in W.15.b. This was moved whilst a reconnaissance was made. Heavy machine gun fire in W.17.c. and W.23.a. Position forward uncertain but hostile machine guns reported from VALLE MULATRE Area firing. These were fired on by the forward guns of "B" Company which had advanced forward to crest about W.17.c.0.3. Company with fighting limbers on East side of MOLAIN at 10.30. Men under cover of banks in W.16.a. and c. Positions for guns found at about W.17.c.(sunken road) and hedge W.23.a.3.8. At 14.30 instructions were received from O.C. 1st Battalion M.G.C to move forward occupying these positions as rear line of defence and to carry out any ~~Infantry~~ supporting and harassing fire required by infantry.

    Dispositions:- 8 guns W.23.a. 4. 7.
               8 guns - 4 at W.17.b.3.2.
                     4 at W.17.c.9.3.
Company H.Q. VAUX ANDIGNY.
Fired 7,000 rounds harassing fire on to RIBEAUVILLE-BELLEVUE and X.25.

18/10/18. Attack of 3rd Infantry Brigade supported by overhead fire from 11.35 to 11.55.

    Dispositions:- 8 guns in copse, W.24.a.3.4.
               4 guns W.17.b.3.2.
               4 guns W.17.c.9.3.
Fired 16,250 rounds on to RIBEAUVILLE and MILL FARM and to East of Farm and 500 rounds direct overhead fire. At 14.00 8 guns moved to X.13.a. and c. to support 1st Gloster Regt. on defensive flank. 8 guns moved to X.20.a.3.6. up to WASSIGNY copse. Company H.Q. LA VALLEE MULATRE.

19/10/18. 8 guns at X.20.a.3.6. remained in position. 8 guns from defensive flank moved into position at X.16.a.4.5. (4 guns) and X.9.d.9.1. (4 guns) These were already in position. 4 guns of "D" Company at X.9.b.8.3. - X.10.a.3.3. and 4 guns ("D" Coy.) on crest about S.19.a. - S.20.c. Company H.Q. WASSIGNY.

    Casualties, 3 Other ranks wounded.
               4 horses wounded.
               1 gun destroyed by shell fire.

SUMMARY OF OPERATIONS FROM 17TH TO 23RD OCTOBER 1918.

"D" Company, 1st Battalion, M.G.C.

17/10/18. Company with "C" Company moved from BOHAIN 06.30 and proceeded to take up battery positions at W.24.a.8.8. going was rather difficult owing to the bad state of the roads and country and hostile shelling. On reaching MOLAIN the Americans were encountered who informed us the attack had not progressed according to time table. Major Gurney and Captain Catchpole proceeded to reconnoitre forward to ascertain the situation leaving Companies and Transport in MOLAIN under cover to avoid hostile artillery fire. 2nd Bn.Royal Sussex were found held up about W.16.a. by hostile machine gun fire. Battery positions which we intended to occupy were therefore still in enemy hands, finally the two sections of "D" Company were sent to 1st Cameron Highlanders and attached to them for duty. The Commanding Officer decided to use these eight guns for defensive work and they established themselves on defensive lines through W.28.b. and d. Remainder of the Company was withdrawn to VAUX ANDIGNY with Company Headquarters at W.20.a.1.1.

18/10/18. 1st Infantry Brigade attacked at dawn on the morning of the 18th. The 8 guns attached to the Cameron Highlanders supported the advance by bringing harassing fire to bear on selected targets about 6,000 rounds were fired from positions in W.28.d.7.7. After the attack these 8 guns were withdrawn to Company Headquarters at VAUX ANDIGNY by order of C.O. Orders received about 24 hours 23.50 for two sections to accompany 3rd Infantry Brigade in an attack to take place next morning (19th) about 10.30.

19/10/18 After consultations with C.Os of Welsh Regiment and S.W.Bs 2/Lieut.Graham and Lieut.Browne attached their sections to Welsh Regiment and S.W.Bs respectively. During the attack they moved forward with the infantry giving covering fire en route, and engaging any suitable targets which presented themselves. Attack reported going well and defensive positions were occupied during the afternoon about 04.00. No.2 Section at W.21.c. central, and No.3 Section at W.13.a.3.1.
Casualties 3 other ranks wounded.
During morning "D" Company less 2 Sections moved with Battalion Headquarters to LA VALLEE MULATRE W.23.d.75.25 Rear Company H.Q. and Transport advanced to the vicinity of MOLAIN, W.16.a.7.9. At 03.30 Nos.1 and 4 Sections moved to MAZINGHIEN, one section to X.4.c. Central and 1 Section to R.33.d. The eight guns came under the command of Major Snowball, Group Commander. Nos.2 and 3 Sections moved forward during the afternoon with the advancing infantry of the 3rd Brigade and finally occupied positions as follows:-
No.2 Sections in defensive positions in S.13.c.
No.3 Sections in harassing fire positions in X.10.a.2.2. in which they fired about 300 rounds.

20/10/18. During the day No.4 Section carried out harassing fire on selected targets. About 2,500 rounds were expended. No.2 Section fired about 100 rounds at low flying enemy aircraft. Company was relieved during the afternoon by the 2nd Life Guards M.G.Bn. and on relief was sent to billets in VAUX ANDIGNY.

21/10/18. Company rested during the day and refilling was carried out as far as possible.

22/10/18. At 7.30 Major Anson attended a conference at Bde.H.Q. re operations to be carried out on the following day. During the morning 16 guns of "D" Coy. relieved the 11 guns of

"B" Company. No.3 Section (4 guns.) was attached to Royal Sussex. No.4 Section was attached to North Lancs. These 8 guns were to go forward with the advancing infantry. next day. Eight guns under Lieut. Browne M.C. were in barrage slits in R.32.d.

23/10/18. Operations commenced at 01.20, 12,000 rounds were fired from barrage positions. These guns then moved forward about 1,000 yards and took up defensive positions in R.33.a. remaining guns moved forward with the infantry and finally dug in. No.2 Section at R.22.d.50.20 on high ground from where they were able to sweep western entrance to CATILLON. No.4 Section had two guns in R.33.d. and two forward guns in R.29.c. which could also command these entrances.

OPERATIONS FROM 24TH TO 31ST OCTOBER 1918.

24/10/18. During the morning four of the eight guns which were in R.33.a. were moved to forward positions about R.22.d.2.9. from where they were able to command the western entrances to CATILLON. These guns were very heavily shelled and sniped at by enemy machine guns. Remainder of guns stayed in positions previously occupied.

25/10/18. During early morning Company was relieved by "A" Company. Kit for forward guns was taken right up to positions on pack mules and own kit brought back on them. Company on relief proceeded to billets in MOLAIN which had been vacated by "C" Company.

26/10/18 Company resting. Overhauling of kit and refitting etc.
to   Baths. Church parade etc.
29/10/18.

30/10/18 Preparing for the line.

31/10/18. During the afternoon "D" Company relieved 16 guns of "A" Coy. 4 at R.23.c. 4 at R.29.c. and 4 at R.30.c. 4 at R.35.b. No operations were carried out during night.

SECRET.

W. Diary.

1ST BATTALION, MACHINE GUN CORPS.
ORDER NO.53.

Copy No.

Reference Map Sheets 57.B. and 62.B. 1/20,000.

(1) The 1st Division is attacking on a date "Z" which has been given out verbally. II American Corps and XV French Corps will be attacking on Left and Right respectively.

(2) Attached map shows First Objective, RED DOTTED, 2nd Objective RED, Third Objective, GREEN.

(3) On the Corps front the RED DOTTED Objective is being taken by the 46th Division on the right and the 6th Division on the left. Inter-Divisional boundary is shewn on the attached map.
The 1st Division will pass through the 6th Division on the RED DOTTED Line and capture the RED and GREEN objective.

(4) General plan of 1st Division Operations:-

(a) 1st Brigade will attack on the right.
2nd Brigade will attack on the left.
3rd Brigade will be in Reserve.

(b) (i) There will be a halt of ½ hour on the RED DOTTED Line.
(ii) There will be a halt of 3 hours on the RED Line.
(iii) In order to straighten the line for the advance from the RED Line at an hour to be notified later the 1st Brigade and the Right Battalion of the 2nd Brigade will advance from the RED Line to the line roughly, N.&.S.Grid running through X.19 and X.25 centrals
(iv) Attacking Brigades will exploit success towards the Canal de la Sambre.

(5) Action of Machine Guns will be as follows:-

(a) "A" Company will operate under the orders of B.G.C.1st Inf.Bde
(b) "B" Company will operate under the orders of B.G.C.2nd Inf.Bde
(c) "C" Company (16 guns) will proceed to the Wood in W.24.a. and from this position will assist the advance from the RED to the GREEN Line by shooting on selected areas. On completion of tasks "C" Company will be assembled with transport, and will be ready to advance to positions to assist the exploitation from the GREEN Line.
(d) "D" Company (16 guns) will proceed to W.24.b. and from this position will assist the advance from the RED to the GREEN Line by bursts and rapid fire on selected areas. On completion of tasks will assemble with transport at W.24.b. and await further orders for assisting exploitation.
(e) Details of the moves and tasks of guns of "C" and "D" Companies will be as shewn on Tables "A" and "B" and Map attached.

TABLE B not attached

(f) In conjunction with the B.G.Cs Infantry Brigades it has been arranged that the tasks of the 8 rear guns of "A" and "B" Coys respectively will be as shewn on attached table "B". The forward guns of "B" Company will cover the advance of the Whippets from the GREEN Line, by shooting on the woods in X.17 and X.18 and engage at once any anti-tank guns etc. that they can see.
(g) All guns employed on barrage will keep a sharp lookout for any visible targets that may show themselves and the Officers in command will at once get as many guns to such targets as may seem necessary. * of

(continued overpage)

(6) Headquarters. Advanced Battalion Headquarters will be with 1st and 2nd Brigade Headquarters.
Rear Battalion Headquarters will be at BOHAIN, D.21.a.8.4.
"C" and "D" Company Headquarters will be with their Batteries in W.24.a. They will move as their Companies advance.

(7) Communications. Communication must be maintained with Battalion Headquarters by runners and mounted orderlies. If necessary the Signalling Officer will arrange for visual.

(8) ACKNOWLEDGE.

Major,
1st Battalion, Machine Gun Corps.

Issued at 22.50, 15/10/18.

Copies issued to:-
(1) to (4) Companies.
(5) 1st Division "G"
(6) 1st Division "Q"
(7) 1st Infantry Brigade
(8) 2nd Infantry Brigade
(9) 3rd Infantry Brigade
(10) C.M.G.O. IX Corps.
(11) 6th Battalion, Machine Gun Corps.
(12) 46th Battalion, Machine Gun Corps.
(13) 27th American Division.
(14) War Diary
(15) War Diary
(16) File.

TABLE "A" to accompany 1ST BATTALION, MACHINE GUN CORPS ORDER 53.

Serial Number	Company	Moving From	Moving to	Time of Arrival	Route	Remarks
1	"C" 13 guns.	D.21.a. (S.W. of BOHAIN)	Wood at W.24.a.4.5.	1½ hours before final advance from RED Line (exact time will be notified later)	At discretion of Company Commander avoiding road wherever possible.	Remain at W.24.a.4.5. awaiting further instructions.
2	"D" 16 guns.	D.21.a. (S.W. of BOHAIN)	-do-	-do-	-do-	8 guns will remain at W.24.a.4.5. awaiting further instructions.
3	"D" 8 guns.	W. of Wood at W.24.a.4.3.	As ordered		-do-	
4	"A" 13 guns.	Will move under orders of B.G.C. 1st Infantry Brigade.				
5	"B" 13 guns.	Will move under orders of B.G.C. 2nd Infantry Brigade.				

TABLE "B" TO ACCOMPANY 1ST BATTALION, MACHINE GUN CORPS ORDER NO.53.

Serial No.	Company.	Battery.	No. of Guns.	Location of guns.	Firing From	Firing To	Location of Target	Nature of Fire	Remarks.
1.	"A"	"Y"	8	LES GOBELETS (E.3.b.)			Road Jcn. at BLANCS FOSSES E.6.c.		Details to be arranged in conjunction with B.Gs.C. 1st and 2nd Inf.Bdes.
2.	"B"	"X"	8	Railway at W.18.d.7.9.			RIBEAUVILLE.		
3.	"C"	"G"	16	Wood at W.24.a.4.5.	307	329	(C.2) FORESTERS HOUSE, LES MARCONNIERS & adjacent road Jcn. (F.1.b.)	Bursts of rapid fire at irregular intervals by all guns.	
4.	"C"	"G"	16	—do—	329	350	(C.1) VASSIGNY STATION.	—do—	
5.	"D"	"A"	8	W.24.b.5.8.	353	362	(A.1) MILL FARM and LEREGET (E. of line N.&S. through X.20.c.7)	—do—	

(2)

Serial No.	Company.	Battery.	No. of Guns.	Location of Guns.	Firing From	Firing To	Location of Target	Nature of Fire	Remarks
6	"L"	"A"	8	W.24.b.3.8.	302	371	(A.2) WASSIGNY (E.) of line N.a.S. thro' X.26.b.2	Bursts of rapid fire at irregular intervals by all guns.	
7	"L"	"B"	8	W.24.a.8.7.	340	344	(B.1) Railway Jcn. (E. of N.a.S.Line through X.25.b.5.)	-do-	
8	"L"	"B"	8	-do-	344	365	(B.2) WASSIGNY (E.) of line N.a.S. through F.20.c.8.)	-do-	

SECRET.

1ST BATTALION, MACHINE GUN CORPS.
ORDER NO.54.

Copy No.

Reference Map Sheets 62.B. 1/40,000.

(1) The Battalion will move from its present Area to the BOHAIN Area to-morrow, 16/10/18.

(2) "A" and "B" Companies will move under orders of 1st and 2nd Infantry Brigades respectively.

(3) Battalion Headquarters and "C" and "D" Companies with Transport will move as follows:-

Order of March	Starting Point.	Hour of Starting	Route.
"C" Coy.	Cross Roads		LEVERGIES, MERICOURT, FRESNOY-LE-GRAND, BOHAIN.
"D" Coy.			
"H.Q"	G.35.c.2.3.	08.45	

The Battalion less "A" and "D" Companies will be formed up ready to move at 08.40. Head of "C" Company at the Cross Roads G.35.c.2.3.

(4) Guides will be at the Railway Crossing at D.14.d.6.2. to-morrow to guide Battalion H.Q. and Companies to billets.

(5) Battalion Headquarters will close at LA BARAQUE at 08.15. 16/10/18 and will re-open at D.21.a.6.4. same day at 14.00

(6) ACKNOWLEDGE.

                                           Captain and Adjutant,
                                           1st Battalion, Machine
                                                     Gun Corps.

Issued at 20.30, 15/10/18.

Copies issued to:-   (1) to (4) Companies.
                          (5) Battalion Headquarters.
                          (6) 1st Division "G"
                          (7) 1st Division "Q"
                          (8) 1st Infantry Brigade
                          (9) 2nd Infantry Brigade
                         (10) 3rd Infantry Brigade
                         (11) S.S.O. 1st Division.
                         (12) 1st Division Signals.
                         (13) War Diary
                         (14) War Diary
                         (15) File.

1ST BATTALION, MACHINE GUN CORPS.
ORDER NO. 55.

SECRET.   Copy No. 12

Reference Map Sheet WASSIGNY, 1/40,000.

(1)　"C" and "D" Companies 1st Battalion, M.G.C. will be relieved to-day and this evening by two Companies of the 2nd Life Guards M.G.Battalion.

(2)　Os.C. "C" and "D" Company, 1st Battn. M.G.C. will arrange to have guides at cross roads at W.24 central (LE TONNELET) at 3.p.m. to-day.

(3)　Os.C. "C" and "D" Company, will each order 3 limbers (empty) to be at cross roads W.24 central to carry gun stores etc. for the Life Guards.

(4)　On completion of relief "C" and "D" Companies will assemble at the cross roads W.24 central and be conveyed by the Life Guards Lorries to billets that have been arranged in VAUX ANDIGNY.

(5)　"C" and "D" Companies will hand over sufficient maps to the incoming Companies.

                                            Major,
                                            1st Battalion, Machine
                                            Gun Corps.

Issued at 13.05.- 20/10/18.

Copies issued to:-   (1) to (4) Companies.
                     (5) Battalion H.Q.
                     (6) 2nd Life Guards M.G.Battn.
                     (7) 1st Division "G"
                     (8) 1st Division "Q"
                     (9) 1st Infantry Brigade
                     (10) 2nd Infantry Brigade
                     (11) 3rd Infantry Brigade
                     (12) War Diary
                     (13) War Diary
                     (14) File.

SECRET.

1ST BATTALION, MACHINE GUN CORPS.
ORDER NO. 57.

Copy No.

Reference Map Sheet OISE CANAL 1/40,000.

(1) GENERAL.

    (a) On a date and at a time to be notified later the Division is attacking - 3rd Brigade on the Right and 2nd Brigade on the left. The front of the attack and the objectives are shown on the map which has been previously issued to all concerned.

    (b) The attack will be delivered under a creeping barrage one section of the 301sr American Tank Battalion will co-operate with the left Brigade.

(2) ACTION OF MACHINE GUNS.

    Machine guns have been allotted as follows.
    (a) 2nd Brigade Group under Major F.G.Anson 1sr Bn.M.G.C.

8 guns "C" Coy. 2nd Life Gds.M.G.Gds.	8
16 guns "D" Coy. 1st Bn.M.G.C.	16
	24

    (b) 3rd Brigade Group under Lieut.Walker 2nd L.G.M.G.Gds.

16 guns "B" Coy.2nd L.G.M.M.Gds.	16
8 guns "C" Coy. -do-	8
4 guns "C" Coy. 1st Battalion, M.G.C.	4
	28

(3) (a) In conjunction with G.Os.C 2nd and 3rd Infantry Brigades tasks have been allotted as follows.

    2nd Brigade Group. 8 guns "D" Company 1st Bn.M.G.C. advance with the 2nd Royal Sussex Regt. on the left and 1st Norhants on the right.   8

    8 guns "D" Company 1st Bn.M.G.C. (a) Barrage LA HAIE TONNAILE FARM (b) Advance to neighbourhood of LA HAIE TONNAILE FARM and be prepared to engage targets in CATILLON or as required.   8

    8 guns 2nd L.G.M.M.Gds. from neighbourhood of RIBEAUCOURT WOOD FARM to barrage road and orchards from A.5.a.3.8.to R.35.c.7.8.   8
     24

    3rd Brigade Group. One section "C" Coy.1st Bn.M.G.C. to advance with 2nd Brigade.Welsh Regt.   4

    12 guns 2nd L.G.M.M.Gds. (a) Barrage canal from S.7.b.3.7. to S.31.d.3.5. from Z to Z plus 30 (b) Be ready to engage areas E. of the Canal as required.   12

    4 guns 2nd L.G.M.M.Gds barrage L'ERMITAGE S.2.d. from Z ro Z plus 60   4

    4 guns 2nd L.G.M.M.Gds. in defensive positions on right of the Brigade front.   4

    4 guns 2nd L.G.M.M.Gds. in Brigade reserve RIBEAUCOURT WOOD FARM.   4
     28

(3) Tasks and time of lifts are shown on tracing attached.

(4) Zero hour will be notified later.

(5) Battalion Headquarters advanced will remain in LA VALLEE MULATRE.

(6) ACKNOWLEDGE.

    (signed)

    Lieut.Colonel,
    Commanding, 1st Battalion,
    Machine Gun Corps.

Issued at 13.10 - 22/10/19.

Copies issued to.
(1) to (4) Companies   (10) 3rd Infy.Bde.
(5) Battalion H.Q.   (11) 2nd Life Gds.M.G.Gds
(6) 1st Division "G"   (12) 6th Battalion M.G.C.
(7) 1st Division "Q"   (13) War Diary.
(8) 1st Infantry Bde.   (14) War Diary.
(9) 2nd Infantry Bde.   (15) File.

* Maps issued to 1st Div."G" and "Q" 1st, 2nd and 3rd Bdes. 2nd L.G.M.GG
"C" Coy. 1st Bn.M.G.C. and "D" Coy. 1sr Bn.M.G.C.

MAP (TO ACCOMPANY 1ST M.G. BATTN. ORDER No. 57)

use with Artillery Maps.

R 22 23

8 GUNS

Z TO Z+30

Z TO Z+60

Z TO Z+60

8 GUNS

12 GUNS 4 GUNS

16 17

SECRET

1ST BATTALION M.G.C.
ORDER NO. 55
Ref. NASSIGNY 1/20 000 Map.

Copy No.

(1) The following reliefs will take place on the night 26th/27th.

(a) B Coy. 1st Bn. M.G.C. (16 guns) under Lieut. Taylor will relieve D Coy. 1/2 Bn. M.G.C. "C" Coy. 2nd L. Gds. M.G. Gds. (12 guns) and ("8" guns), in the Left Sector of the 1st Bde. front. On relief D Coy will take over billets in MOININ at present occupied by "C" Coy.

(b) A Coy. 2nd L.G. M.G. Gds. (16 guns) under Major Phillipson will relieve B Coy. 3rd L.G. M.G. Gds. (16 guns) in the right sector of the 1st Bde. front. On relief the B Coy will proceed as ordered by OC. 3rd L.G. M.G. Gds.

(c) 2 Sections (8 guns) "C" Coy. 1st Bn. M.G.C. will relieve "C" Coy. 2nd L.G. M.G. Gds. in support at X.10.c.4.6. (RIBEAUCOURT WOOD FARM)

(d) "C" Coy 1st Bn. M.G.C. (less 2 sections) will proceed into support at L'ARBRE DE GUISE.

(e) On relief of 3rd Bde by 1st Bde. the section of "C" Coy. at present with 2nd Welsh Regt. will be withdrawn to RIBEAUCOURT WOOD FARM.

(2) All remaining guns will be withdrawn under orders of OC. 2nd L.G. M.G. Gds. and OC D Coy 1st Bn. M.G.C.

(3) Details of relief will be as shown on attached table and will be arranged between Coy. Commanders concerned.

(4) On completion of relief Machine Guns will be disposed as follows –

16 guns B Coy. 1st Bn. M.G.C. in area of 1ST THE BLACK WATCH.
16 " 2nd L.G. M.G. Gds. " " 1ST L.N. LANCS.
8 " C. Coy 1st Bn. M.G.C. at RIBEAUCOURT WOOD FM. (X.10.c)
8 " " L'ARBRE DE GUISE.

(continued overpage)

(2)

(5) HQ will be located as follows:-
Group Comdrs with HQ 1st Inf Bde. (R.22.a.5.0)
OC. A Coy 1st Bn. MGC.   MAZINARIEN
OC. B Coy 2nd L.G. MGdo.   NAZIGNY
OC. C. Coy 1st Bn. MGC.   L'HARRE DE GUISE
Exact location of Coy HQ will be sent to Group Comdrs. HQ as soon as possible.

(6) Completion of relief will be reported to Group Commander at 1st Bde. HQ by code word ROBINSON.

(7) ACKNOWLEDGE.

N Gove
Major.
1st Battalion Machine
Gun Corps.

Issued at
Copies issued to:-
(1) to (4) Coys.
(5) Batalion HQ.
(6) 2nd L.G. MGdo.
(7) 1st Division "G"
(8) 1st Inf. Bde.
(9) 2nd Inf Bde
(10) 3rd. Inf Bde
(11) War Diary
(12) War Diary
(13) File.

Serial No.	Unit	No. of Guns	Will relieve	No. of Guns	Location on completion of relief
1.	"A" Coy. 1st Bn. M.S.C.	4	D Coy. 1st Bn. M.S.C.	4	R.33.b. (MAZINGHIEN)
2.	do.	4	do.	4	R.23.c.1.0.
3.	do.	8	will move to		MAZINGHIEN
4.	"A" Coy L.G's	4	"C" Coy 2nd L.G's.	4	S.5.a (will later take up a position in R.34.c)
5.	do.	4	B Coy. 2nd L.G's.	4	X.11.a (REJET DE BEAULIEU)
6.	do.	4	do.	4	S.14.b. (CAMBRESIS)
7.	do.	4	do	4	S.13.d.
8.	C. Coy 1st Bn M.G.C	8	2 L.G's	8	X.10.c. (RIBEAUCOURT WOOD FARM)
9.	C. Coy. do.	8			L'ARBRE DE GUISE.

SECRET.

1ST BATTALION, MACHINE GUN CORPS.
ORDER NO.59.

Copy No.

Reference Map Sheet WASSIGNY, 1/40,000.

(1) The following reliefs will take place on 31st October 1918. "D" Company (16 guns) will relieve "A" Company 16 guns in the Left Sector of the Divisional Front, and "B" Company (16 guns) will relieve "C" Company (16 guns) in support.
This relief will not affect the dispositions of "D" Company 3rd (R.H.G) Battalion, M.G.Guards who are responsible for the M.G.Defence of the Right Sector of the Divisional Front.

(2) All details of relief will be arranged between Officers Commanding Companies concerned direct.

(3) O.C. "A" and "C" Companies will hand over all details regarding lines of fire and S.O.S. lines to O.C. "D" and "B" Company respectively.

(4) On completion of relief "A" Company will take over billets vacated by "D" Company at MOLAIN and "C" Company billets vacated by "B" Company in VAUX ANDIGNY.

(5) Intervals as laid down in S.S.724 will be maintained between Sections on the march.

(6) On completion of relief M.G.Group Commander will be Major T.G.Anson.

(7) Locations of Headquarters will be:-
    M.G.Group Commander,   X. 2.a.30.95.
    "D" Company,   R.33.d.04. 4.
    "B" Company,   X. 7.b. 9. 7.
    "B" Company, 3rd (R.H.G)   X.26.b. 1. 7.

(8) Completion of relief will, be reported to M.G.Group Commander, who will report relief complete to Brigade and Battalion H.Q. by the code message "your A.S.21 received".

(9) ACKNOWLEDGE. (Companies only)

                        Captain and Adjutant,
                        1st Battalion, Machine
                          Gun Corps.

Issued at 21.30, 29/10/18.

Copies issued to:-   (1) to (4) Companies.
                      (5) Battalion Headquarters.
                      (6) Quartermaster.
                      (7) 3rd (R.H.G) Bn. M.G.Gds.
                      (8) "B" Coy. -do-
                      (9) 1st Infantry Brigade
                      (10) 2nd Infantry Brigade
                      (11) 3rd Infantry Brigade
                      (12) 1st Division "G"
                      (13) 1st Division "Q"
                      (14) S.S.O.
                      (15) War Diary
                      (16) War Diary
                      (17) File.

WASSIGNY

Parts of 57ᵇ 57ᵃ 62ᵇ 62ᵃ Scale 1/40000

To Superimpose on Sheet 62B N.E. 57B S.E.

Army Form C. 2118.

WAR DIARY
or
INTELLIGENCE SUMMARY.
(Erase heading not required.)

1/M.G.C.

Place	Date	Hour	Summary of Events and Information	Remarks and references to Appendices
LA VALLEE MULATRE	10/11/18		Situation in the line unchanged. During the battles available 36(?) Battalion M.G. Company in the line with 3rd Brigade formed a defensive flank in the area near Tupigny whilst McLean Tudy and Bibby in C Company carried on the advance with B Company of the Squadron Moto Cars and Armoured Cars reinforcing for the Cavalry Division in the direction of Avesnes. Casualties 1 O.R. wounded.	Appendix 16 3 O.S.
LA VALLEE MULATRE	11/11/18		Headquarters were held at Battalion H.Q. & it was decided that an advanced guard depart to push attack with Cambrai Division were sent. Advanced Headquarters to H.Q. of the battalion. 4th Battalion M.G.C. the forming of 5th Army was accordingly completed without incurring any casualties. Operation orders were issued regarding the attack. No change in situation in the line in distinction. Company has been ordered to Antwerp. The Corps of the 4th M.G.Bn to 3rd R.H.A. have been withdrawn. N.L.	Appendix 2 A.W.J

WAR DIARY or INTELLIGENCE SUMMARY

Army Form C. 2118.

(Erase heading not required.)

Place	Date	Hour	Summary of Events and Information	Remarks and references to Appendices
LAVALIZ MUKATRA	3/11/18		No change in the situation in the line. During the day personnel of B Coy 1st Battalion and 359 & 360 M.G.Coys Squadrons, 1 Coy HQM.B.M.G.C. moved up to battery position and all details (including Employed A.H.Coys mens who are not in the evening with the 354 Inf & 51 Inf Bgde respectively, B Coy came under orders of B & C 359th Infantry Brigade. Casualties :- Nil.	A.H.S
LAVALIZ MUKATRA	4/11/18		The Division attacked in conjunction with the 32nd (British) Division on the left & the French on the right. At 05.45 hours the attack was completely successful. All objectives being reached and over 1500 prisoners & many Machine Guns were captured according to prisoner statements. The enemy resistance was very intense. The attack was launched in a thick mist and during the day in the late afternoon D Coy 1st Btn. Inf. with 358 Infantry Bgde to VROKMIBIGNY, B Coy 1st Inf Bn KVIAZING then B Coy to RIBEZOVNIZ. Casualties in the line with 359th Infantry Brigade & full guarantee portion of M.G. as attached appendix 5. Casualties :- Killed 2 O.R. Wounded 26 O.R. 1 Officer (2/Lt F.W. McLean) 9 O.R. Wounded and unaccounted	Appendix 3 O.M.R.

WAR DIARY
or
INTELLIGENCE SUMMARY.

(Erase heading not required.)

Army Form C. 2118.

Place	Date	Hour	Summary of Events and Information	Remarks and references to Appendices
A VALLEE MULATRE	5/11/18		Many moved out 12 AM Bn Major HINDGIN O.C. Bn took over from 2/4 Leic. front line to WASSIGNY on Maj Ind a Coy of York Batt. M.G.s. Deployed from Vaux INDIGNY KREMAN and 3rd Mounted Brigade Battalion Headquarters at Bois Marmont in VALLEE MULATRE. All Coys were in Comfortable huts. Billets were bivouac Bn. move to FRESNOY the following day. Casualties 1 O.R. wounded (Gas)	Appendix 4
FRESNOY	10/11/18		The Battalion moved to FRESNOY as per operation order attached. H.Q and Coys moved out [?] and 3rd Infantry Brigade respectively and reached the bottom at FRESNOY Billets were exceedingly good accommodation was good. Lieut Col M.L. Johns D.S.O. returned from Special leave having commanded the battalion. (orders were issued to move to BRANCOURT in ?)	O.A.C.
N[?]ERGIES	11/11/18		Orders received that Hostilities would cease at 11am on 11 SEPT [GEHART?] by which A.S.I.O Corps had Battalion moved from NIVERGIES (SEP GEHART) by which A.S.I.O Corps Army billeted in the former C. Coy in the latter. Both villages badly punished about had fairly comfortable billets was obtained	Appendix 5

Army Form C. 2118.

WAR DIARY
or
INTELLIGENCE SUMMARY.
(Erase heading not required.)

Instructions regarding War Diaries and Intelligence Summaries are contained in F. S. Regs., Part II. and the Staff Manual respectively. Title pages will be prepared in manuscript.

Place	Date	Hour	Summary of Events and Information	Remarks and references to Appendices
LEVERGIES	8/1/18		Day spent in cleaning and washing. Status issued in the Battalion to man to MOLAIN. The following been awarded K Military Medal - No 19574 Corporal (now A/Sgt) W. WILLIAMS and 74102 Pte SPR KENT.	Appx I
MOLAIN	9/1/18		The Battalion moved to MOLAIN 0.2 by approx 6. The weather was cold to march in and the men marched the 14 miles in good spirits. No one falling out on the way. The men were all comfortably settled in billets by 6 p.m. Two Indian Officers joined from the Base. 2/Lieut J.E. NICHOLLS posted to "A" Coy and 2/Lieut RODDICK to "C" Coy	Appx 6. Appx I
MOLAIN	10/1/18		Day spent in washing and cleaning. The following appointments were made. T/Lieut (actg Captain) A.DUKES to command "A" Coy vice Major C.C.L. FITZWILLIAMS to hospital sick. T/Lieut J.C. TAYLOR M.C. to be Captain and 2nd in Command of "A" Coy vice T/Lieut (Acting Captain) A. DUKES to Command	Appx I

WAR DIARY
or
INTELLIGENCE SUMMARY

Army Form C. 2118.

Place	Date	Hour	Summary of Events and Information	Remarks and references to Appendices
MOLAIN	17/11/18		Weather cold and fine. Training was carried out when accommodation in Billets [?] was made during the afternoon. Bath drying baths.	GAS
MOLAIN	18/11/18		Weather was resumed into two Battalion's & move to PRISCHES the following day. Two officers were sent ahead & were to return to billets at PRISCHES with lists to DIRAG who informed them that the Battalion would be billeted at BAZUEL instead. O.C. then was in touch & he was in BAZUEL. Strength of ORS was (was C.O.& C.O. to whom orders went [illegible] ?) Weather fine & fairly cold.	
MOLAIN	19/11/18		Battn. future any more, Reverend Fr. Hen prior to various billets, received by the 1st Bn. Gloucestershire Regt. Orders will be issued in the evening direction to move to O.Rs. the Battalion to move to PRISCHES.	ORS

Army Form C. 2118.

WAR DIARY
or
INTELLIGENCE SUMMARY.
(Erase heading not required.)

Place	Date	Hour	Summary of Events and Information	Remarks and references to Appendices
PRICHES	4/11/18		The Battalion marched to PRICHES (about 7 kilms) (arriving 10.30 a.m.) in column of route and to billet there. On the march (?) "C" Battalion (and "D" (?) The march was (?) in marching order, & rifles and equipment slung. The men were (?) had armbands. Kits carts to Company mess (?) which is billets. 4.5 p.m. The (?) talked to the Regiment who (?) and (?) was held completely (?) After was too short to (?) & tea & to a review of (?) day.	App. 1
FONTAINE S/MS	5/11/18		The march back to NINE continued. The Battalion moved to LEC FONTAINES plus 15 kilms. The weather was (?) to continue the (?) the Bn was (?) (a marching (?) & man (?) with (?) the closest we reach with the (?) and C Coy in the advance guard. ABCD Coy billeted in the village and C Coy in the Regimental (?) of (?) The (?) to see the all(?) being (?) on the (?) land &	(?)

W.J.O.D.D.L. London, E.C. (?) Sch. 52 Forms C2-0114S
(AP001) Wt. W2771/M2031 750,000 5/17

Army Form C. 2118.

WAR DIARY
or
INTELLIGENCE SUMMARY.
(Erase heading not required.)

Place	Date	Hour	Summary of Events and Information	Remarks and references to Appendices
LES FONTAINES	16/11/18		Day spent in the huts and clearing up. Weather still continues fine & very cold, a hard frost every night.	A.D.S.
LES FONTAINES	17/11/18		Arrangements made for Church Parade at 11am. It was being taken by Major - General Sir H Bruce Williams when a message of the kind came through to parade was cancelled. Colonel CHARTERIS An Army Machine Gun Officer visited the Battalion. Orders received that the Battalion would march to RENLIS next day.	G.R.T.
RENLIS	18/11/16		March to the RHINE continues. The Battalion marched to RENLIS. Start 9.5 am. Very smart and steady march kept to along. Half of Coy. was billeted in farms near the town. Second half in huts one mile further on to march. Major Menzies left at 11 to MEAUX wife to Battalion would march to GOOSEROO - LEZ - WALCOURT.	G.R.T.

Army Form C. 2118.

WAR DIARY
or
INTELLIGENCE SUMMARY.

(Erase heading not required.)

Instructions regarding War Diaries and Intelligence Summaries are contained in F. S. Regs., Part II. and the Staff Manual respectively. Title pages will be prepared in manuscript.

Place	Date	Hour	Summary of Events and Information	Remarks and references to Appendices
ROUSSEU LEZ WALCOURT			Battalion billeted in ROUSSEU-LEZ-WALCOURT near 6 miles	Arrived 10.
WALCOURT			[illegible handwritten entries]	
BOUSSEU LEZ WALCOURT			[illegible handwritten entries]	
[illegible]			[illegible handwritten entries]	

WAR DIARY
or
INTELLIGENCE SUMMARY.

Army Form C. 2118.

Place	Date	Hour	Summary of Events and Information	Remarks and references to Appendices
WES-GOMEZEE	20/1/16		10.15 a.m. Battalion left WES-GOMEZEE about 9.15 a.m. and train started about 10 a.m. Marching easy. Large numbers of the enemies' aircraft seen to eastward. Arrived FLAVION about 12 noon & proceeded to billets. Billets fair & battalion to hand that day.	Appendix I.
FLAVION	21/1/16		Battalion marched to FLAVION about 10 a.m. Companies out to watching the silver fire etc to march to the billets in battalion order. Lad three suns leaving HELAIN. The whole Battalion crosses into the new area. Lieut. Col. V. ATCHESON inspected billets for him to U.K.	12
FLAVION	22/1/16		Party of 3 officers and 20 other ranks left & Hospital area. Major F.M. ARKLE, Lieut T.S. SNOWBALL and Major T.E. SNOWBALL joined Battalion from Reserve Depot and Major T.E. SNOWBALL returned from leave. Weather cold & wet.	B.S.

Army Form C. 2118.

WAR DIARY
or
INTELLIGENCE SUMMARY.

(Erase heading not required.)

Instructions regarding War Diaries and Intelligence Summaries are contained in F. S. Regs., Part II. and the Staff Manual respectively. Title pages will be prepared in manuscript.

Place	Date	Hour	Summary of Events and Information	Remarks and references to Appendices
FLANION			*[illegible handwritten entries]*	
FLANION				
FLANION				

Army Form C. 2118.

WAR DIARY
or
INTELLIGENCE SUMMARY.

(Erase heading not required.)

Instructions regarding War Diaries and Intelligence Summaries are contained in F. S. Regs., Part II. and the Staff Manual respectively. Title pages will be prepared in manuscript.

Place	Date	Hour	Summary of Events and Information	Remarks and references to Appendices
FLAVION	6/1/45		Usual training routine during week & afternoon walks and amusements	A/F
			NOTE:- The attached war N.W Europe Not close 1945 taken on to Battalion on its March to the RHINE	Appendix B & C

In keeping with Cmdy (Battalion Medium Gun Corps.)

APPENDIX I.

1ST BATTALION, MACHINE GUN CORPS.

Preliminary Instructions for the Action of Machine Guns in the forcing of the passage of the SAMBRE - OISE CANAL.

Reference Maps, Sheet 51.B. S.E. 1/20,000 and BARZY, 1/20,000.

(1) On a date Z, which has been communicated to all concerned the 1st Division will force the passage of the SAMBRE-OISE CANAL between PETIT-CAMBRESIS and CATILLON. Zero hour will be early in the morning. Simultaneous attacks are being delivered by:-

    33th French Division on the right opposite OISY.
    32nd Division on the left N. of ORS.

(2) 1st Division attack will be carried out by 2nd Infantry Brigade on the Right and 1st Infantry Brigade on the left.
    The 3rd Infantry Brigade will carry out a subsidiary and simultaneous operation to capture CATILLON and form a bridgehead there.

(3) In addition to the 1st Battalion, M.G.C. the following M.Gs will be attached to the Division for the operation.

    3rd (R.H.G) Battalion, M.G.Guards,   3 Companies.
    43th Battalion, Machine Gun Corps.   3 Companies.

(4) ACTION OF MACHINE GUNS.

    (a) "A" "C" and "D" Companies, 1st Battalion, M.G.C. will be attached to 1st, 2nd and 3rd Infantry Brigades respectively and will come under the orders of the B.Gs.C. forthwith.

    (b) "D" Company, 1st Battalion, M.G.C. will put down enfilade barrage on EAST Bank of Canal from about H.31.b.0.1. to H.26.c.0.2. at Zero, and will afterwards put down a creeping enfilade barrage in conformity with the artillery barrage and 100 yards forward of it, up to the limit of their range.

    (c) One Company, 46th Battalion, M.G.C. will fire as in para(B)

    (d) Two Companies, 43rd Battalion, Machine Gun Corps, will put down enfilade barrage on E. bank of Canal from S.7.b.2.5. to S.8.d.1.9. at Zero and afterwards as ordered.

    (e) Three Companies (less 4 guns) 3rd (R.H.G) Bn.M.G.Guards, will put down enfilade barrage on E. bank of the Canal at Zero as follows:-

        One Company will barrage from S. 7.b. 1. 5. to S. 1.d.10.75.
        One Company will barrage from S. 1.d.10.95. to S. 1.b.10.95.
        One Company (less 4 guns)   S. 1.b.10.95. to H.31.b.00.01.

    and will afterwards put down a creeping enfilade barrage in conformity with the artillery barrage and 100 yards forward of it.

    (f) All details of barrage and lifts will be notified later.

(5) ASSEMBLY.

    (a) "A" "C" and "D" Companies, 1st Battalion, M.G.C. will assemble under the orders of the B.Gs.C. 1st, 2nd, and 3rd Infantry Brigades respectively.

(continued overpage)

(2)

(5) ASSEMBLY (continued)

(b) "B" Company, 1st Battalion, M.G.C., 3 Companies 3rd (R.H.G) Bn.M.G.Guards (less 4 guns) and 3 Companies 46th Battalion, M.G.C. will arrange to dump all guns, ammunition, equipment etc. at previously reconnoitred points near barrage positions on X/Y night, under sufficient guard, except 4 guns 46th Battalion, M.G.C. (X.5.a.), 4 guns "B" Company, 1st Battalion, M.G.C. (X.5.c) and 4 guns 3rd (R.H.G) Bn.M.G.Guards in S.13.

The 12 guns mentioned above will proceed to their barrage positions on X/Y night with their personnel and will take over responsibility for the machine gun defence of that section of the front at present held by an equivalent number of guns of "B" Company 3rd (R.H.G) Bn.M.G.Guards.

"B" Company, 3rd (R.H.G) Bn.M.G.Guards less 4 guns, will then move to their new barrage positions.

The remaining 4 guns of "B" Company, 3rd (R.H.G) Bn.M.G.Guards will remain in their present defensive positions in PETIT CAMBRESIS until further orders.

On Y/Z night all the remaining personnel will take up their barrage positions.

Details of times of moves will be notified later.

(6) S.A.A. DUMPS.

Dumps of M.G. S.A.A. will be available as follows:-

K. 4.d. 7. 2. (Estaminet in REJET DE BEAULIEU)
K. 5.a. 2. 2. (FARM)
K.18.c. 3. 8. (Side of track)

(7) Headquarters of "B" Coy. 3rd (R.H.G) Bn.M.G.Guards is at X.26.b.1.5.

(8) ACKNOWLEDGE.

Captain and Adjutant,
1st Battalion, Machine
Gun Corps.

Issued at 23.00, 1/11/18.

Copies issued to:- (1) to (4) Companies.
(5) C.O.
(3) Battalion H.Q.
(7) 3rd (R.H.G) Bn.M.G.Guards.
(8) "B" Coy.   -do-
(9) 46th Battalion, M.G.C.
(10) M.G.Group Commander.
(11) 1st Infantry Brigade.
(12) 2nd Infantry Brigade.
(13) 3rd Infantry Brigade.
(14) 1st Division "G"
(15) 1st Division "Q"
(16) C.M.G.O. IX Corps.
(17) War Diary.
(18) War Diary.
(19) File.

1ST BATTALION, MACHINE GUN CORPS.

SECRET.   ORDER NO.60.   Copy No.

APPENDIX 2

Reference Maps, Sheet 51.E. S.E. 1/20,000 and BARZY, 1/20,000.

(1) In continuation of preliminary instructions for Action of Machine Guns:- On Z day the 1st Division will attack and capture the objectives (dotted blue line, blue line and red line) shown on attached map.

Machine guns will carry out Barrage fire in accordance with the attached table and maps.

(2) The minimum personnel of Companies required to lay out lines of fire will reach barrage positions before dusk. The remainder will move to barrage positions later, but will be E. of N. and S. Grid Lines through W.11 and 12 by 17.00 hours on Y day.

(3) The strictest attention to march discipline and correct distances will be enforced in all assembly movements.

Steps will be taken to ensure that all moves within 3,000 yds of the Canal are carried out silently, and that all troops shall be screened from ground observation in their assembly areas by dawn on Z day, after which time there must be no movement of any sort prior to zero hour.

(4) The Canal will be crossed as follows:-

2nd Infantry Brigade, Main Crossing,   Lock, S.1.d.
                      Subsidiary Crossing, in   S.7.a.
1st Infantry Brigade, Main Crossing in,   M.31.a.
                      Subsidiary Crossing in, M.26.c.

(5) Company Commanders will take steps to ensure that any troops assembling in the neighbourhood of their batteries are warned of the extent of the dangerous area in front of their guns.

Under arrangements with the B.G.C. 3rd Infantry Brigade the area E. of N.&S. grid line through X.12 central to X.18 central, N. of E.&W. grid through X.18 central and S.13 central and W. of a line S.13.b.9.0. to S.8.c.9.9. will be cleared of all troops from Zero - 15 onwards.

(6) Locations of Headquarters will be as follows:-

1st Infantry Brigade, LALOUVIERE FARM.
2nd Infantry Brigade, HOUSE at X.5.a.15.25.
O.C.1st Battn.M.G.C. with 2nd Infantry Brigade H.Q.
O.C. 3rd (R.H.G) Bn.M.G.Guards, O.C.46th Battalion, M.G.C. and O.C. "E" Company, 1st Battalion, M.G.C. will EACH arrange to have 2 runners at 2nd Brigade Headquarters from 23.59 on Y day onwards.

If possible signal communication will be established between O.C. 1st Battalion, M.G.C. and Group Commander, 3rd (R.H.G) Bn. M.G.Guards.

O.C. 1st Battalion, M.G.C. will occupy Battle Headquarters at the same time as 2nd Infantry Brigade, the hour of which will be notified later.

Rear Headquarters, 1st Battalion, M.G.C. will remain at present location, W.25.d.8.2.

(7) Medical arrangements will be notified to all concerned.

(8) Times and places of synchronisation of watches will be notified later.

(9) ACKNOWLEDGE.

Issued at 22.00. 2/11/18.

Captain and Adjutant,
1st Battalion, Machine Gun Corps.

Copies issued to all recipients of 1st Battalion, M.G.C.
Preliminary instructions for action of machine guns.

TABLE TO ACCOMPANY 1ST BATTALION, MACHINE GUN CORPS ORDER NO.60.

Serial No.	Group.	Composition.	No. of Guns.	Location of Directing Gun.	Targets.	Times of Firing.	Rate of Fire.	Remarks.
1	No.1.	1 Coy.(R.H.G) Bn.M.G.Guards.	13	S.13.b.5.1.	See barrage map attached.	Zero to $\frac{1}{4}$ $\frac{1}{4}$ to 5 5 to 17 17 to 29 29 to 52 52 to 64 64 to 79 79 to 87	Max.rate 1 belt per min. 1 belt in 3 mins. 1 belt in 3 mins. 1 belt in 4 mins. 1 belt in 2 mins. 1 belt in 4 mins. 1 belt in 4 mins.	
		-do-	13	S.15.b.20.25.	-do-	Zero to $\frac{1}{4}$ $\frac{1}{4}$ to 5 5 to 17 17 to 29	Max.rate. 1 belt per min. 1 belt in 5 mins. 1 belt in 3 mins.	
		1 Coy.(R.H.G) Bn.M.G.Guards. (less 4 guns)	12	X.18.a.20.35.	-do-	Zero to $\frac{1}{4}$ $\frac{1}{4}$ to 5 5 to 17	Max.rate. 1 belt per min. 1 belt in 3 mins.	
2	No.2.	"C" Company, 43th Bn.M.G.C.	13	X. 5.b.70.75.	-do-	Zero to $\frac{1}{2}$ $\frac{1}{2}$ to 5 5 to 17	Max.rate. 1 belt per min. 1 belt in 3 mins.	
3	No.3.	1 Coy.46th Bn.M.G.C.	13	X. 5.a.95.30. (i) (ii)	S.7.b.9.5. to S.8.a.75.20. S.8.a.75.20 to S.8.d.75.80.	Zero to 5 5 to 15	Max.rate. 1 belt in 4 mins.	
		-do-	13	X. 5.a.95.10.	S.8.a.75.20 to S.8.d.75.80.	Zero to 5 5 to 15	Max.rate. 1 belt in 4 mins.	
4	No.4.	"B" Coy.1st Bn.M.G.C.	12	R.55.c.	See barrage map attached.	Zero to $\frac{1}{4}$ $\frac{1}{4}$ to 5	Max.rate. 1 belt per min.	

Appendix 3.

Narrative of Action of Machine Guns of 1st Division
during the forcing of the passage of the
SAMBRE-OISE CANAL, on 4/11/18.

GENERAL.

(1) In addition to the 1st Battalion, M.G.C. (64 guns) the following guns were attached to the Division for the operations:-

    3 Companies of the 3rd (R.H.G.) Bn.M.G.Guards, (48 guns)
    3 Companies of the 46th Battalion, M.G.C. (48 guns)

(2) With the exception of "D" Company, 1st Battalion, M.G.C. (16 guns) supporting the 3rd Infantry Brigade in the subsidiary operation at CATILLON, all guns were used in support of the main operation as follows:-

    "A" and "C" Companies advanced with the 1st and 2nd Brigades respectively and assisted the operation wherever possible with direct fire, and took up defensive positions to cover the Infantry on the various objectives.

    The remaining 7 Companies* (112 guns) supported the attack with indirect fire within the limits of their range and of these 7 Companies, 3 of the 3rd (R.H.G) Bn.M.G.Guards and "B" Company of the 1st Battalion, M.G.C. were held in readiness to move forward as required, but the necessity for this did not arise.

    3 Companies, 46th Battalion, M.G.C. were attached to the Division for barrage firing.

*less 4 guns remaining in defensive positions.

ACTION OF MACHINE GUNS.

(1) "A" Company, 1st Battalion, M.G.C. with 1st Infantry Brigade. 3 Sections advanced with 1st the Black Watch, 1st L.N.Lancs, and 1st Cameron Highlanders respectively, the 4th Section being held in Brigade reserve. These guns moved with the Battalions and took up positions previously arranged. Two guns on the left Company front of the 1st Camerons were successful in silencing an enemy machine gun and brought down a sniper who had been hindering the advance of our troops, by firing from a tree. No other targets were found. This Company was relieved on the night of the 4th/5th under orders of the B.G.C. 1st Infantry Brigade.

(2) "C" Company, 1st Battalion, M.G.C. with 2nd Infantry Brigade. 3 Sections advanced with the 2nd R.Sussex, 2nd K.R.R.C. and 1st Northants respectively, the 4th section supported the bridging parties with direct fire, afterwards moving forward in rear of the Northants. One gun of the Section with the 2nd R.Sussex fired on an enemy machine gun which was in action to the S. of the Lock. The whole section then moved forward along the FESMY Road and took up positions S.E. of HAUTREUVE near the HAUTREUVE-VIEVILLE Road. Two guns afterwards moved forward to a position on the high ground S. of ROBEHMEYRE to cover the left flank of the Brigade. The section which advanced with 2nd K.R.R.C. came into action on the Route Nationale and succeeded in silencing a machine gun, and scattering hostile infantry in the western end of FESMY. The guns were afterwards disposed along hedges S.E. of SARS POND to assist in forming a defensive flank against FESMY and finally moved to positions along the Road N.W. of VIEVILLE later in the evening.

(continued)

ACTION OF MACHINE GUNS. (continued)

(2) (continued)

One gun of the section with the 1st Northants, engaged and silenced an enemy machine gun which was firing from a house in FESMAY. The section then entered FESMAY and occupied positions at the N.E. end of the village and finally moved to positions in the neighbourhood of VIEVILLE crossroads in the evening. The fourth section after firing in support of the Bridging of the canal advanced and occupied positions about the bend in the road, 500 yards S.E. of the Lock and afterwards advanced to positions S.E. of FESMAY.

The Company was withdrawn on the evening of the 5th under the orders of the B.G.C. 2nd Infantry Brigade.

(3) "B" Company, 1st Battalion, M.G.C. took up positions E. of LALOUVIERE and fired a creeping barrage in support of the left of the 1st Infantry Brigade attack. After firing the barrage they were held in readiness to move forward but this was not required and at 17.00 on the 4th the Company was withdrawn to LA VALLEE MULATRE in accordance with orders received from 1st Division.

(4) 1 Company, 46th Battalion, M.G.C. (16 guns) took up positions N.E. of GORGOUGE from where they put down heavy enfilade barrage on the E. Bank of the Canal in support of the crossing of the 1st Infantry Brigade, and afterwards put down a creeping barrage forward of the artillery barrage to the limit of their range.

2 Companies, 46th Battalion, M.G.C. took up positions to the E. of the LALOUVIERE-REJET DE BEAULIEU Road and put down heavy enfilade fire on the E. Bank of the Canal from bend south of the lock towards the Route Nationale. These 3 Companies came under the orders of the 46th Division at 09.40 on the 4th in accordance with verbal orders received from 1st Division and reported to their own H.Q. for orders.

(5) 3 Companies, 3rd (R.H.G) Bn.M.G.Guards (less 4 guns) took up positions in the hedges to the S. of MALLIOCOURT FARM from which they put down heavy enfilade fire on the E. bank of the Canal from the bend E. of the Lock northwards to the 1st Brigade crossing, and afterwards put down a creeping enfilade barrage forward of the artillery barrage. The remaining 4 guns continued to hold defensive positions in PETIT CAMBRESIS occupied previous to the attack. These three Companies were afterwards held in readiness to move forward but were not required and at 18.00 on the 4th were withdrawn to WASSIGNY in accordance with instructions received from 1st Division.

(6) "D" Company, 1st Battalion, M.G.C. 3 Sections (12 guns) fired a creeping enfilade barrage on, and to the E. of CATILLON in conformity with the artillery barrage. Two of these sections afterwards concentrated their fire on the canal crossing and mainroad running E. and W., N. of CATILLON. The remaining section advanced in rear of the 1st Gloucesters for the purpose of protecting the right flank of the attack. These guns engaged hostile machine guns but these were difficult to locate owing to the mist. They were eventually silenced and the section moved to a position from which guns could fire on the ridge beyond the canal in case of counter-attack.

This Company was withdrawn on the conclusion of the operation under the orders of the B.G.C. 3rd Infantry Brigade.

(7) Battalion Headquarters withdrew from LALOUVIERE to LA VALLEE MULATRE at 17.00 4/11/18 in accordance with orders received from 1st Division.

Appendix 4

SECRET.   1st BATTALION, MACHINE GUN CORPS   Copy No. 16
                      ORDER No. 81.

(1) The Battalion will move from present area to FRESNOY tomorrow, 6th inst.

(2) "A" "C" and "D" Coys. will move under orders of 1st, 2nd and 3rd Infantry Bdes. respectively, and will rejoin the Battalion on arrival at FRESNOY, where they will be billeted under Battalion arrangements.

(3) Battalion Headquarters and "B" Coy. will move as under :-

Order of March.	Starting Point.	Hour of Starting.	ROUTE.
Bn.H.Q. "B" Coy.	Head of column at Road Jnc. W.23.d.8.3. facing South West.	11.30 hours.	MOLAIN, VAUX ANDIGNY, BOHAIN.

(4) Instructions reference billeting parties have been issued.

(5) Details at Quartermaster's Store will join the column at the Road Junction, W.20.c.6.8. at 12.30 hours.

(6) Companies will report completion of move.

(7) Battalion H.Q. will close at LA VALLEE MULATRE at 11.30 hours and will open at FRESNOY at the same hour. (exact location to be notified later)

(8) ACKNOWLEDGE. (Coys only).

                                      Captain & Adjutant.
                          1st Battalion, Machine Gun Corps.

Issued at 11.59 hours
   5/11/18.

                  Distribution normal.

Appendix 5.

1ST BATTALION, MACHINE GUN CORPS.
ORDER NO. 62.

SECRET.   Copy No.

Reference Map Sheet WASSIGNY, 1/40,000.

(1) The Battalion will move to billets in BRANCOURT to-morrow 7th instant.

(2) Companies will march independently as under:-
    "A" Company at 13.00
    "B" Company at 13.30
    "C" Company at 14.00
    "D" Company at 14.30
    Headquarters at 15.00
Route - Direct to BRANCOURT LE GRAND.

(3) Billets from Town Major, BRANCOURT, C.28.a.2.7. Company Commanders will each detail parties to leave Battalion H.Q. under Lieut. Smyth at 09.00.

(4) The strictest march discipline will be observed.

(5) Battalion H.Q. will close at FRESNOY LE GRAND at 15.00 and will re-open at BRANCOURT LE GRAND at the same hour.

(6) ACKNOWLEDGE. (Companies only)

                              Captain and Adjutant,
                              1st Battalion, Machine
Issued at 22.00 - 6/11/18.   Gun Corps.

Distribution normal.

Appendix 6

1ST BATTALION, MACHINE GUN CORPS.

SECRET. ORDER No. 63. Copy No. 13

Reference Map Sheets, 57.D. and 62.B. 1/40,000.

(1) The Battalion will move from its present area to MOLAIN to-morrow, 9th instant.

(2) Companies will move independently as follows:-

Coy.	Hour of Starting.	Route.
"A" and ½ H.Q.	08.50	RAMICOURT-MONTBREHAIN-BRANCOURT-BOHAIN-VAUX ANDIGNY.
"B" and ½ H.Q.	08.45	
"D"	09.00	
"C"	09.00	FRESNOY-BOHAIN-VAUX ANDIGNY.

(3) Haversack rations will be carried.

(4) From 11.30 to 12.00 Companies will halt at suitable points with Company and Transport clear of the road, where haversack ration and tea will be ~~carried~~ consumed.

(5) Arrangements have been made regarding billeting parties. Guides will meet Companies at the Road Junction at W.16.c.1.3.

(6) The Battalion will move in fighting order with S.D. Caps.

(7) Strictest march discipline will be observed.

(8) Battalion Headquarters will close at LEVERGIES at 09.00, 9/11/18 and will re-open at MOLAIN at 12.00. same day.

(9) ACKNOWLEDGE. (Companies only)

Captain and Adjutant,
1st Battalion, Machine Gun Corps.

Issued at 22.00. 8/11/18

Copies issued to:-
(1) to (4) Companies.
(5) Battalion Headquarters
(6) 1st Division "G"
(7) 1st Division "Q"
(8) 1st Infantry Brigade
(9) 2nd Infantry Brigade
(10) 3rd Infantry Brigade
(11) S.S.O.
(12) A.P.M.
(13) War Diary
(14) War Diary
(15) File.

Appendix 7

1ST BATTALION, MACHINE GUN CORPS.
ORDER NO. 34.

SECRET.   Copy No. 8

Reference Map Sheet, WASSIGNY. 1/40,000.

(1) The Battalion will move by march route from its present area to the PRISCHES Area to-morrow, 14/11/18.

(2) Companies will move independently as follows:-

Order of March	Starting Point.	Head of Column to pass starting point at.	Route.
"A" Coy. and ½ H.Q.	W.10.c. 6. 4.	06.10	ST. MARTIN RIVIERE, L'ARBRE DE GUISE-MAZINGHIEM-CATILLON-MEZIERES-LAGOELLE-GROBEART to Road Jen. N.5.c.0.5. where guides will meet Companies and guide them to their billets.
"B" Coy. and ½ H.Q.	W.10.c. 6. 4.	06.20	
"C" Company	W.10.c. 6. 4.	06.30	
"D" Company	W.10.c. 6. 4.	06.40	

(3) Advance billeting parties of 1 Officer mounted and 2 O.R. Cyclists per Company, will parade at Battalion Headquarters at 06.00 and will report to Captain W.F.Wilson, M.C.
Billeting officers will arrange for guides to meet Companies on their arrival at Road Junction N.5.c.0.5.

(4) The Battalion will move in full marching order, S.D. Caps will be worn and steel helmets carried.

(5) Blankets will be carried by motor lorry. Blankets will be tightly rolled in bundles of ten, labelled, and dumped on the road side at each Company Headquarters by 05.30. Loading parties will be provided by Battalion Headquarters, and Companies will not have any loading parties.

(6) Haversack rations will be carried and tea will be provided at a convenient place between 10.00 and 10.30.

(7) Battalion Headquarters will close at MOLAIN at 06.00 on 14/11/18 and re-open at PRISCHES (at a location to be notified later) at 11.00 hours same day.

(8) ACKNOWLEDGE.

Captain and Adjutant,
1st Battalion, Machine
Gun Corps.

Issued at 22.00, 13/11/18.

Distribution normal.

Appendix 8

1ST BATTALION, MACHINE GUN CORPS.

SECRET.   ORDER NO. 65.   Copy No.

Reference Map Sheet 57.A. 1/40,000.

(1) The Battalion will move from present area to LES FONTAINES by march route to-morrow, 15/11/18.

(2) Companies will move independently as follows:-

	Starting Point.	Head of Column to pass starting point at	Route.
"D" Coy.	N.17.a.4.5.	07.45	PRISCHES-CARTIGNIES-LE-DESSOS
"C" Coy.	-do-	07.55	DU MOULIN-GODIN-AVESNES-
"B" and ½ H.Q.	-do-	08.05	VAUDRECHIES-FELLERIES-BEUGNIES-
"A" and ½ H.Q.	-do-	08.15	S. OF SARS POTERIES-LES FONTAINES.

(3) Advance Billeting parties of 1 Officer mounted and 2 O.R. cyclists per Company will report to Captain W.F. Wilson, M.O. at Battalion H.Q. at 07.30. Billeting officers will arrange for guides to meet the Companies on arrival at F.16.d.9.2. TRIANON FM.

(4) The Battalion will move in full marching order.

(5) Blankets will be carried by lorry and will be dumped at the Company Headquarters by 07.00. Loading party will be provided by Battalion Headquarters.

(6) Dinners will be provided on the line of march and Companies will halt for dinners and watering and feeding of animals for a period of 1 hour at 12.00.

(7) Battalion Headquarters will close at present location at 08.15 and will re-open at LES FONTAINES at 17.00.

(8) ACKNOWLEDGE. (Companies only)

Captain and Adjutant,
1st Battalion, Machine
Gun Corps

Issued at 23.50, 14/11/18

Copies issued to:-
(1) to (4) Companies.
(5) Commanding Officer
(6) Adjutant
(7) Quartermaster
(8) Transport Officer
(9) 1st Division "G"
(10) 1st Division "Q"
(11) A.P.M.
(12) S.S.O.
(13) War Diary
(14) War Diary
(15) File

SECRET

Appendix 9

1st BATTALION, MACHINE GUN CORPS.

ORDER No. 63.

Reference Map MAUBR 1/100,000.

1. The Battalion will move from its present area to RENLIES to-day 18/11/18 by march route.

(2). The Battalion will parade at 11-15 hours on the DIMECHAUX-LEZ-FONTAINE-SOLRE le CHATEAU Road in the following order:-

"A" Company, Headquarters, "B" Company, "C" Company and "D" Company, facing East.
Head of "A" Company to be at the Railway Crossing half mile West of SOLRE le CHATEAU. Intervals of twenty yards will be maintained between companies.
Companies will march with the Gun limbers behind each Section.

(3) Guides will meet the Battalion on arrival at the Cross Roads 1,000 yards due North of the T in SUVRY Station.

(4) The Battalion will move in Full Marching Order.

(5) One G.S.Wagon has been attached to each Company for carrying blankets. Companies will arrange to have haversack rations and tea before moving off and dinners on arrival.

(6) Battalion H.Q. will close att 11.00 hours at its present location and reopen at RENLIES at 15.00 hours.

(7) ACKNOWLEDGE.

Captain & Adjutant.
1st Battalion, Machine Gun Corps.

Issued at 09-45, 18/11/18.

Copies issued to :-

(1) to (4) Companies.
(5) Commanding Officer.
(6) 2nd in Command.
(7) Quartermaster.
(8) Transport Officer.
(9) 1st Div. Artillery.
(10) 1st Div. "Q".
(11) 1st Div. "G".
(12) A.P.M.
(13) S.S.O.
(14) War Diary.
(15) War Diary.
(16) File.

Appendix 10

1ST BATTALION, MACHINE GUN CORPS.

SECRET   **ORDER NO.67.**   Copy No.

Reference NAMUR Map, 1/100,000.

(1)   The Battalion will move to BOUSSO-LEZ-WALCOURT to-day 19/11/18.

(2)   The Battalion will parade in full marching order on the RENLIES-VERGNIES ROAD in the following sequence:-

         Battalion H.Q.
         "B" Company
         "C" Company
         "D" Company
         "A" Company

at 09.50. Head of column to be 500 yards E. of the Crossroads ¼ MILES N. of the N. in RENLIES, facing East.

(3)   Advance billeting parties will report to Captain W.F.Wilson M.C. at Battalion Headquarters at 08.45 to-day.
     Billeting officers will arrange to meet Companies on arrival at the Road Junction just S. of the I. in BOUSSO-LEZ-WALCOURT.

(4)   Battalion Headquarters will close at RENLIES at 09.00 and re-open at BOUSSO-LEZ-WALCOURT at 13.00.

(5)   ACKNOWLEDGE.

                           Captain and Adjutant,
                           1st Battalion, Machine
Issued at 04.45, 19/11/18   Gun Corps.

Distribution normal.

Appendix II

1ST BATTALION, MACHINE GUN CORPS.

SECRET.   **ORDER NO. 68.**   Copy No. 8

Reference NAMUR Map Sheet 1/100,000.

(1) The Battalion will move to YVES-GOMEZEE to-morrow 23/11/18.

(2)
Order of March	Starting Point.	Route.
Battalion H.Q.	Road Jcn.	SILENRIEUX-WALCOURT-VOGENEE.
"C" Company	4.E.55.77.	
"D" Company	-do-	Head of Battalion will pass
"A" Company	-do-	the starting point at 09.10.
"B" Company	-do-	

Companies will form up as shown below and will join the column in the above order as it passes them.

"C" Company on road leading from the Square to main BARBENCON-SILENRIEUX Road.
"D" Company on right of main BARBENCON-SILENRIEUX Road opposite Company billets, rear of the column to be clear of the starting point.
"A" Company on the right of main BARBENCON-SILENRIEUX Road, head of column to be at starting point.
"B" Company on road leading from the square to main BARBENCON-SILENRIEUX Road immediately "C" Company are clear of same.

(3) Billeting PARTIES of 1 N.C.O. per Company and 1 NCO from Battalion Headquarters mounted on cycles, will report to Captain W.F.Wilson, M.C. at Battalion Headquarters at 08.15 to-morrow, 23/11/18. Captain Wilson will arrange for guides to meet the Battalion on arrival at the Road Junction 600 yds due N. of the first N. in FONTAINE.

(4) O.C. "B" Company will detail 1 officer and 2 N.C.Os to march in rear of the Battalion to collect stragglers.

(5) Battalion Headquarters will close at its present location at 08.30 and will re-open at YVES-GOMEZEE at 12.00.

(6) ACKNOWLEDGE.

Captain and Adjutant,
1st Battalion, Machine
Gun Corps.

Issued at 22.30, 22/11/18

Distribution normal.

SECRET.

1ST BATTALION, MACHINE GUN CORPS.
ORDER NO. 69.

Copy No. 17

Reference Map Sheet, NAMUR, 1/100,000.

(1) The Battalion will move to-morrow to FLAVION.

(2)
Order of March	Starting Point	Head of Column to pass S.Point.	Route.
Battn.H.Q. "D" Coy. "A" Coy. "B" Coy. "C" Coy.	Road Star ½ mile E. of LA BOTTE.	10.35	ST.AUBIN - FLORENNES - CORENNE.

The Battalion will parade on the road YVES-GOMEZEE to Road Star ½ mile E. of LA BOTTE at 10.30. in the above order. Head of the Column at Road Star ½ mile E. of LA BOTTE facing East. The main FRAIRE - PHILLIPVILLE Road will be left clear until column moves off.

(3) Billeting parties of 1 N.C.O. from Battalion H.Q. and 1 N.C.O. per Company, on cycles, will report to Captain Wilson, M.C. at Battalion H.Q. at 08.30 who will arrange that guides meet the Battalion on arrival at E. house of FLAVION on FLAVION - CORENNE Rd.
The billeting party will report to the S.C.R.A. at the Cross Roads CORENNE at 10.00.

(4) O.C. "C" Company will detail 1 officer and 3 N.C.Os to march in rear of the Battalion to collect any stragglers.

(5) Battalion Headquarters will close at YVES-GOMEZEE at 10.00 and will re-open at FLAVION at 14.30.

(6) Refilling point 24/11/18 - FRAIRE.

(7) ACKNOWLEDGE (Companies only)

Captain and Adjutant,
1st Battalion, Machine
Gun Corps

Issued at 10.00, 23/11/18

Copies issued to:-
(1) to (4) Companies.
(5) C.O.
(6) Second in Command.
(7) Q.M.
(8) Sig.Officer
(9) T.O.
(10) 1st D.A.
(11) 1st Div."G"
(12) 1st Div."Q"
(13) A.P.M.
(14) S.S.C.
(15) War Diary.
(16) File.

WAR DIARY or INTELLIGENCE SUMMARY.

Army Form C. 2118.

1ST BATTALION MACHINE GUN CORPS.

Place	Date	Hour	Summary of Events and Information	Remarks and references to Appendices
FALAËN	1/12/18		Battalion marched to FALAEN about 4½ miles. Quite a little village & were substantially billeted. Kay & Amadie allotted to the Battalion and inspected the comfortable billets. Battalion Headquarters in the Chateau. A fine old building dates back to 1672. Advice received that the march were to be continued next day to MESNIL-ST BLAISE. Weather fine though cold.	A.+C.
MESNIL-ST BLAISE	2/12/16		Battalion marched to MESNIL-ST BLAISE about 10 miles. Every mile or so we had to water the horses & water wretched roads on account of the heavy traffic country lanes when marching through. The River MEUSE was crossed at HASTIERE south of DINANT. Weather cold and dull and inclined to rain.	B.+C.
"			Advice received that the march would be continued next day to HOUYET. (following day)	
HOUYET	3/12/16		Battalion marched to HOUYET about 6 miles. Roads very bad as it was down hill all the way and frozen over. Group Nurse & Guidance in the village. Splendid billets for all. O.C.	3

Army Form C. 2118.

WAR DIARY
or
INTELLIGENCE SUMMARY.
(Erase heading not required.)

Instructions regarding War Diaries and Intelligence Summaries are contained in F. S. Regs., Part II. and the Staff Manual respectively. Title pages will be prepared in manuscript.

Place	Date	Hour	Summary of Events and Information	Remarks and references to Appendices
HOUYET	4/12/16		Day spent in cleaning up. Rainy all day	Appendix
"	5/12/16		Companies training morning and afternoon. Heavy rain	Appendix
"	6/12/16		Training morning & afternoon. Orders received that the Battalion would leave Div HQ Group and come under to orders of 2nd Inf Bde Group as from 7 to 8 PM. Heavy rain	Appendix
"	7/12/16		Training morning & afternoon.	Appendix
"	8/12/16		Sunday Stn.- Company & Battn routine animals orders received that the Battalion would march to HAID next day.	Appendix
HAID	9/12/16		Battalion marched to HAID about 11½ miles. A slight stop was about 3 kilometres long had to be instated on leaving HOUYET. An unpleasant march as it raining most of the time.	Appendix A. Appendix

Army Form C. 2118.

WAR DIARY
or
INTELLIGENCE SUMMARY.
(Erase heading not required.)

Instructions regarding War Diaries and Intelligence Summaries are contained in F. S. Regs., Part II. and the Staff Manual respectively. Title pages will be prepared in manuscript.

Place	Date	Hour	Summary of Events and Information	Remarks and references to Appendices
FRONVILLE	10/11/18		Battalion marched to FRONVILLE about 15 miles. A deep layer of mud on the road made marching difficult. Work of this day the long march to our billets. Battalion H.Q. A + B Coys billeted in FRONVILLE, C + D Coys in NONVILLE about 1 kilometre further on. Thinly populated and a good deal left town & the village	Appendix 5.
SOY	11/11/18		Battalion marched to SOY 5 miles. A'Coy billetes in the outlying farms of W.Y. (about 1 mile march) and arrived in billets by 11.30 P.M. Weather had rained most of the afternoon.	Appendix 6. a.a.o.s
SOY	12/11/18		Cleaning up. Major F.W. PITRIE-HAY M.C. joined battalion as Second-in-Command. Rained all day.	a.a.o.s
SOY	13/11/18		Cleaning up. Weather ruining any training.	a.a.o.s

D. D. & I., London, E.C.
(Af001) Wt. W1771/M2031 750,000 5/17 **Sch. 52** Forms C2. 0/4

WAR DIARY
INTELLIGENCE SUMMARY.

Army Form C. 2118.

Place	Date	Hour	Summary of Events and Information	Remarks and references to Appendices
LA FOSSE and OSTER-LE-BATY	14/12/18		Battalion moved to OSTER-LE-BATY about 10 miles. Bad weather for marching, rained most of the time. "A" & "B" Coys in LA FOSSES A.Q. "C" & "D" in OSTER	Appendix 7 & 8
REGNE	15/12/18		Battalion marched to REGNE about 8 miles. A trying march on account of the steep gradients & rain. H.QRS, "A" & "D" Coys billeted in REGNE. "C" Coy in FRAITURE, "B" Coy in VERLEUMONT.	Appendix 8 & others
BOUVIGNY	16/12/18		Battalion marched to BOUVIGNY, 9 miles. Rained the whole time. On arrival in billets men had to start chopping up of the march past the Divisional Commander tomorrow as we crossed the frontier.	Appendix 9 & others
GERMANY ALDRINGEN			2nd Bde Group crossed the frontier into GERMANY. The Battalion crossed the frontier at 10.15 AM when we marched past the Divisional Commander. Billeted in ALDRINGEN. The Battalion appear to be drill. Major ARKLE assumed command of "C" Coy	Appendix 10 & others

Army Form C. 2118.

WAR DIARY
INTELLIGENCE SUMMARY.
(Erase heading not required.)

Instructions regarding War Diaries and Intelligence Summaries are contained in F. S. Regs., Part II. and the Staff Manual respectively. Title pages will be prepared in manuscript.

Place	Date	Hour	Summary of Events and Information	Remarks and references to Appendices
KRONE SCHONBERG	13/12/18		Battalion marched to SCHONBERG 15 miles. Rained the whole way. Had coupled with the bad roads made marching difficult. No O.R. fell out. 'A' 'B' & 'D' Coy billeted in SCHONBERG, 'C' Coy in ANDLER about 1½ mile away. Both poor billets and billets not very good.	Appendix 11. G. At S.
KRONENBERG	14/12/18		Battalion marched to KRONENBERG about 12 miles. Two stragglers fell during the march. No men fell out. Glorious weather very dusty and disagreeable very old. Have 'B' & 'C' Coys in own billets. 'A' & 'D' Coys in BAASEM & were considerably more comfortable.	Appendix 12. G. At S.
KRONENBERG	20/12/18		Resting. Day spent in cleaning up and carrying in the men, for the future time in German march. Showed	G. At S.
BLANKENHEIMER-DORF	21/12/18		Battalion marched to BLANKENHEIMER-DORF 8 km to wilt. Roads dreadful but which made marching plain. Have A & D Coys in BLANKENHEIMER-DORF, 'B' & 'C' Coys in MULHEIM. No men fell out during march.	Appendix 13. G. At S.

WAR DIARY

INTELLIGENCE SUMMARY.

(Erase heading not required.)

Army Form C. 2118.

Place	Date	Hour	Summary of Events and Information	Remarks and references to Appendices
IVERSHEIM	22/12/18		Battalion marched to IVERSHEIM 15 miles. Hourly day for marching. No one fell out during the march. Township billets allotted to the Battalion. Plenty of room for all. Good billets.	Appendix 14 a.t.c
FLAMERSHEIM	23/12/18		Battalion marched to FLAMERSHEIM 6 miles. Good billets. (and billets for all)	Appendix 15 a.t.c
FLERZHEIM and LUFTELBERG	24/12/18		Battalion marched to FLERZHEIM its final destination about 9 miles. Battn. HQ 'A' & 'C' Coys in FLERZHEIM, 'B' & 'D' Coys in LUFTELBERG about 3/4 mile further off. Plenty of room for all and fairly comfortable billets.	Appendix 16
FLERZHEIM.	25/12/18		CHRISTMAS DAY On account of there not being sufficient time to make the necessary preparations, Christmas was not celebrated today in the Battalion.	a.t.c
FLERZHEIM	26/12/18		Headquarters 'A' & 'C' Coys held their Christmas celebrations. All the men had luncheon in an excellent manner a concert was held in one of the village Schools. The day terminated in a dinner at Sergeants' Mess when the Warrant Officers & Sergeants entertained all the officers here when they proceeded to billets on already	a.t.c

WAR DIARY

INTELLIGENCE SUMMARY.

(Erase heading not required.)

Army Form C. 2118.

Instructions regarding War Diaries and Intelligence Summaries are contained in F.S. Regs., Part II. and the Staff Manual respectively. Title pages will be prepared in manuscript.

Place	Date	Hour	Summary of Events and Information	Remarks and references to Appendices
HERZEELE	27/10/18		Day spent in cleaning up.	a/c
"	28/10/18		Company training during the morning.	a/c
"	29/10/18		Company training during morning. Draft of 112 O.Rs. joined Battalion. Motor bus returned off leave	a/c
"	30/10/18		Company training during morning. Draft of 20 coalminers left for Demobilization.	a/c
"	31/10/18		Company training during morning. Draft of 12 coalminers & 2 long Service men left for Demobilization Centre.	

Moreland Lieut-Col
Cmdg 1st Batt. M.G. Corps

D. D. & I., London, E.C.
(AP001) Wt. W1771/M2031 750,000 5/17 Sch. 52 Forms C2—0/14

SECRET.

1st Battalion, Machine Gun Corps.

ORDER No 70

Reference Map Sheet; NAMUR 1/100000.

1st BATTALION, MACHINE GUN CORPS.
Copy No.
No. 6011
Date..........

(1) The Battalion will move to FALAEN to-morrow 1/12/18.

(2) <u>Order of March</u>   Starting point   Head of column to pass
                                                        Starting point at.

   Battn. H.Q.   Road Jcn.
   "A" Company.   FLAVION:
   "B" Company.   3.I.65.01.   10.15.
   "C" Company.
   "D" Company.

The Battalion will parade ready to move off on the CORENNE-FLAVION Road at 10.05. Head of the column 100 yards west of the starting point facing east.

(3)   Billeting parties of 1 N.C.O. from Battalion H.Q. and 1 Officer and 1 N.C.O. per Company will report at Battalion Headquarters at 08-15 tomorrow, 1/12/18.
    Billeting parties will report to S.C.R.A. at Church, FLAVION at 08-30.
    Guides will meet the Battalion on arrival at the Road Junction at 3.J.45.30.

(4) Refilling Point 1/12/18. ANTHEE.

(5) Battalion Headquarters will close at FLAVION at 09-30 and will re-open at FALAEN at 12.00.

(6) ACKNOWLEDGE. (Companies only.)

                        (signed) A.H.Smyth, Lieut.
                        for Captain & Adjutant,
                        1st Battalion, Machine Gun Corps.

<u>Issued at 17.00 30/11/18.</u>

                   Distribution normal.

Appendix 2
1A

SECRET. **1ST BATTALION, MACHINE GUN CORPS.**
ORDER NO.71. Copy No 14

Reference Map Sheet NAMUR 1/100,000.

(1) The Battalion will move to MESNIL ST.BLAISE to-morrow 2/12/18.

(2) Order of March   Starting Point.   Head of column   Route
                                             to pass starting
   Battn.H.Q.   Road Jcn.   point at.   WEILLON-ONHAYE
   "B" Coy.   FALAEN -   HASTIERE PAR
   "C" Coy.   3.J.63.28.   09.00   DELA-BEAUMONT.
   "D" Coy.
   "A" Coy.

   The Battalion will parade ready to move off at 08.55 as follows:-
   Battalion H.Q. and "B" Company on North Road from FALAEN to starting point. Head of column at starting point. "C" Coy. on South Road from FALAEN to Starting point. Head of Company at starting point. "D" Company in rear of "C" Company. "A" Company will parade outside billets and will follow "D" Company.

(3) Billeting parties of 1 N.C.O. from Battalion Headquarters and 1 Officer and 1 N.C.O. from each Company will report at Battalion H.Q. at 08.00 to-morrow 2/12/18. Billeting parties will report to S.C.R.A. at Road Jcn. at B in BEAUMONT at 09.30, 2/12/18. Guides will meet the Battalion on arrival at the most Westerly House of MESNIL ST.BLAISE.

(4) Refilling point will be notified later.

(5) Battalion Headquarters will close at FALAEN at 08.30 and will re-open at MESNIL ST.BLAISE at 14.00.

(6) ACKNOWLEDGE (Companies only)

                                       Captain and Adjutant,
Issued at 20.00, 1/12/18.   1st Battalion, Machine
                                       Gun Corps.

Copies issued to:- (1) to (4) Companies
                   (5) Commanding Officer
                   (6) Second in Command
                   (7) Q.M.
                   (8) Sig. Officer
                   (9) T.O.
                  (10) 1st.D.A.
                  (11) 1st Div."G"
                  (12) 1st Div."Q"
                  (13) A.P.M.
                  (14) S.S.O.
                  (15) War Diary
                  (16) File.

Army Form W.3766.

GROUP ORGANIZATION CHART.

Reference............ No..........Group. Commanded by............ Group H.Q............. Date............

BATTERY	COMPOSITION	No. OF GUNS	COMMANDER	LOCATION	TARGETS	TIMES		RATE OF FIRE R.P.M.
						FROM	TO	

Signature............ Group Commander.

PRINTED IN FRANCE BY ARMY PRINTING AND STATIONERY SERVICES.   PRESS B. 1988. 13500. 4-18.

SECRET.

1st Battalion Machine Gun Corps.
ORDER No. 72   Copy.No
Reference Map Sheet NAMUR 1/100,000.

(1) The Battalion will move to HOUVET to-morrow 3/12/18.

(2) Order of March.   Starting point   Head of column   Route.
                                                 to pass starting
                                                 point at.
   Battn.H.Q.   Road Jcn. ½ mile
   "C" Company   E. of the 2nd E.   FINNEVAUX
   "D" Company   in MESNIL ST.   MESNIL
   "A" Company   BLAISE.   10.00   EGLISE.
   "B" Company

         The Battalion will parade ready to move off at 09.35
in the above order on the road MESNIL ST BLAISE to starting point
facing E. head of the column at starting point.

(3) Billeting parties of 1 N.C.O. from Battalion H.Q. and 1 Officer
and 1 N.C.O. from each Company will report at Battalion H.Q. at 08.15
to-morrow 3/12/18. Billeting parties will report to S.C.R.A. at
railway station HOUVET at 09.30. Guides will meet the Battalion at
cross-roads ¼ mile South of HOUVET STATION.

(4) Refilling point tomorrow will be at VERRE.

(5) Battalion H.Q. will close at Mesnil ST.BLAISE at 09.30, and will
re-open at HOUVET at 13.00.

(6) ACKNOWLEDGE (Companies only)

                                    (Signed) A.Shanks
                                         Capt and Adjutant,
                                         1st Battalion Machine
                                           Gun Corps.

Issued at 21.30, 2/12/18.

       Copies issued to :-   (1) to (4) Companies.
                             (5) Commanding Officer.
                             (6) Second in Command.
                             (7) Q.M.
                             (8) Sig.Officer
                             (9) T.O.
                            (10) 1st D.A.
                            (11) 1st Div."G".
                            (12) 1st Div."Q".
                            (13) A.P.M.
                            (14) S.S.O.
                            (15) War Diary.
                            (16) File.

War Diary   Appendix 4

1ST BATTALION, MACHINE GUN CORPS.

SECRET.   O.O.M. NO. 73.   Copy No. 15

Reference Map Sheet LAROIE, 1/100,000.

(1) The Battalion will move to HAID to-morrow, 9/12/18.

(2) | Order of March | Starting Point | Head of Column to pass starting point at. | Route |
|---|---|---|---|
| Battalion H.Q. | Bridge at | | HOLT-MUEHIER |
| "D" Company | 4.1.16.50. | | HAID. |
| "A" Company | | 09.00 | |
| "B" Company | | | |
| "C" Company | | | |

The Battalion will parade ready to move off in the above order at 08.50 head of the column at starting point facing East.

(3) Billeting parties of 1 N.C.O. from Battalion Headquarters and 1 Officer and 1 N.C.O. from each Company will report at Battalion H.Q. at 05.00 to-morrow, 9/12/18. Billeting parties will report to representatives of 2nd Brigade Headquarters at 07.30 at the Church, HAID. Guides will meet the Battalion where R.de Molinia cuts road ½ mile S. of HAID.

(4) Refilling point to-morrow will be at HOLT-MUEHIER.

(5) Battalion Headquarters will close at HOUILM at 08.30 and will re-open at 14.00 at HAID.

(6) All G.S. wagons (blankets wagons) will report loaded to Battalion Transport Officer at Battalion Headquarters at 08.30.

(7) ACKNOWLEDGE. (Companies only)

                                        [signature]
                                        Captain and Adjutant,
                                        1st Battalion, Machine
                                        Gun Corps.

Issued at 18.00, 8/12/18

Copies issued to:- (1) to (4) Companies
                   (5) Commanding Officer
                   (6) Second in Command
                   (7) Quartermaster
                   (8) Signalling Officer
                   (9) Transport Officer
                   (10) H.Q. 2nd Infantry Brigade
                   (11) H.Q. 1st D.A.
                   (12) H.Q. 1st Division "G"
                   (13) A.P.M.
                   (14) S.S.O.
                   (15) War Diary
                   (16) File.

SECRET

1st BATTALION MACHINE GUN CORPS.
ORDER NO. 74
Reference Map Sheet MARCHE 1/100,000.

COPY NO. 13

(1) The Battalion will move to FRONVILLE tomorrow, 10/12/18.

(2)
Order of march	Starting point	Head of column to pass starting point at -	Route
Battalion H.Q. "A" Company "B" " "C" " "D" "	Junction of Road and Rly. at 4.C.32.98	09.10	NETTINE - HEURE - NOISEUX - DEULIN

The Battalion will parade ready to move off in the above order at 09.00, head of column at starting point facing East.

(3) Billeting parties of 1 N.C.O. from Battalion H.Q. and 1 Officer and 1 N.C.O. from each Company will report at Battalion H.Q. at 07.00 tomorrow 10/12/18. Billeting parties will report to representative of 2nd Bde. H.Q. at 10.10 at CHURCH, FRONVILLE. Guides will meet the Battalion at cross roads 200 yds. North of E in FRONVILLE.

(4) Refilling point tomorrow will be at SINSIN at 09.30.

(5) Blanket wagons will report to Lieut. Rayner at Battalion H.Q. at 08.30. O.C. "A" Co. will detail 1 Officer and 20 men to report to Lieut. Rayner at the above hour to march with these wagons.

(6) The motor lorry will report to 2/Lt. Johnson at HEURE road fork 3.D.60.58 at 09.30.

(7) ACKNOWLEDGE (Companies only)

Captain and Adjutant
1st Battalion Machine Gun Corps

Issued at 20.30 9/12/18.

Copies issued to:- (1) to (4) Companies
(5) Commanding officer
(6) Second in command
(7) Quartermaster
(8) Transport officer
(9) H.Q. 2nd Infantry Bde.
(10) War diary
(11) File

Appendix 6

1st BATTALION MACHINE GUN CORPS.
SECRET   Order No. 76.   Copy No. 5
Reference Map Sheet MARCHE, 1/100,000

(1) The Battalion will move to SOY tomorrow 11/12/18
     The Battalion will stand fast on December 12th 1918

(2) Order of March Starting point   Head of column   Route
                                      to pass starting
                                      point at :
     Battalion H.Q.
     "C" Coy.   Near the river
     "D" "   crossing 100 yds   10.10   NY - SOY
     "A" "   S. of MELREUX
     "B" "   STATION.

        The Battalion will parade ready to move off in the
     above order at 10.05 head of column at starting point facing
     E.

(3) Billeting parties of 1 N.C.O. from Battalion H.Q. and 1
     Officer and 1 N.C.O. from each Company will report at Battalion
     H.Q. at 07.00 tomorrow 11/12/18. Billeting parties will
     report to a representative of 2nd Brigade Headquarters at SOY
     at 08.10. Guides will meet the Battalion at the 5 km. stone
     HOTTON - SOY Road.

(4) Refilling point tomorrow will be at FRONVILLE at 08.45.

(5) Sick parade tomorrow will be at 07.30.

(6) Blanket wagons will parade as follows: "A" and "B" Coys at
     Battalion H.Q. at 09.00. "C" and "D" Coys. at "C" Coys. H.Q. at
     09.15.
        P.C. "B" Coy. will detail 1 Officer and 20 men to report
     to Lieut. Rayner at Battalion H.Q. at 09.00 hrs. to march with
     these wagons.

(7) The motor lorry will report to 2/Lt. Johnson at HOTTON
     Church at 09.00.

(8) ACKNOWLEDGE (Companies only).

                                      Captain and Adjutant
Issued at 22.00 hrs 10/12/18   1st Battalion Machine Gun Corps.
            Copies issued to (1) to (4) Companies
                             (5) Commanding Officer
                             (6) Second in Command
                             (7) Quartermaster
                             (8) Transport Officer
                             (9) H.Q. 2nd Infantry Bde.
                             (10) War Diary
                             (11) File

SECRET.   1st BATTALION MACHINE GUN CORPS: Copy No. 11
                    Order No. 76.
         Reference Map Sheet MARCHE = 1/100,000   Appendix

(1) The Battalion will move to LA FOSSE and OSTER LE BATTY tomorrow 14/12/18.

(2) Order of March.   Starting point.   Head of column   Route
    H.Q.   to pass starting
    "D" Coy.   6 km stone   point at: GRANDMENI
    "B" "   on SOY - FISENNE
    "C" "   Road
    "A" "   09.20

   The Battalion, less "A" Company, will parade ready to move off in the above order at 09.15, head of column at starting point facing East.

   "A" Company will parade at 09.35 on the WY - FISENNE Road, head of column at road junction in FISENNE 3.C.40.49. and will follow "C" Company as Battalion passes.

(3) Billeting parties of 1 N.C.O. from Battn. H.Q. and 1 Officer and 1 N.C.O. from each Company will report to Battalion H.Q. at 7.15 tomorrow 14/12/18. Billeting parties will take over billets of No. 1 F.A. in OSTER LE BATTY and from 5th R.H.A. in LA FOSSE at 08.30. Guides will meet the Battalion at road junction at 3.H.75.34. N. of LA FOSSE.

(4) Refilling point tomorrow will be at ERZEE at 09.15.

(5) Blanket wagons will report to Lieut. Rayner at Battalion H.Q. at 09.00. O.C. "C" Coy. will detail one officer and 20 men to report to Lieut. Rayner at the above hour to march with these wagons.

(6) The Motor Lorry will report to 2/Lt. Johnson at 09.30 at the 14 km. stone on ERZEE - GRANDMENIL Road.

(7) Sick parade 07.30.

(8) ACKNOWLEDGE (Companies only).

                                           Captain and Adjutant.
Issued at 21.45 13/12/18   1st Battalion Machine Gun Corps.
   Copies issued to: (1) to (4) Companies
                     (5) Commanding officer
                     (6) Second in command
                     (7) Transport officer
                     (8) Quartermaster
                     (9) H.Q. 2nd Inf. Bde.
                    (10) War Diary
                    (11) File

Appendix 10

SECRET.

1st BATTALION MACHINE GUN CORPS.
Order No. 77.
Reference Map Sheet GERMANY 1.E. 1/100,000

COPY No 12

(1) The Battalion will move to ALDRINGEN and ESPELER tomorrow 17/12/18.

(2) The Battalion will march past the Divisional Commander at the frontier. Head of the column will pass the saluting base at 10.20 hours.

(3) Order of March.   Starting point.   Head of column   Route
    H.Q.   to pass start-
    "B" Coy.   ing point at:-
    "C" "   Road junction   BEHO -
    "D" "   1½ km. E. of   08.55   ALDRINGEN
    "A" "   X in BOVIGNY.

    The Battalion will parade on the SALMCHATEAU Road BEHO road at 08.30. Head of column at starting point facing east.

(4) Billeting parties of 1 Officer and 1 N.C.O. from Battalion H.Q. and each Company will report to Battalion H.Q. at 07.15. Guides will meet the Battalion on arrival at Junction of BEHO - ALDRINGEN road. Attention is directed to G.R.O. 3725 regarding billeting in occupied German territory. The necessary written demands will be handed to proper authority before Billeting is commenced.

(5) Refilling point tomorrow; BEHO at 08.00.

(6) Blanket wagons will report to Lieut. Rayner at 08.30.

(7) Parade states will be rendered to Battalion H.Q. at 06.00.

(8) The Motor Lorry will report to 2/Lt. Johnson at ROGERY - BEHO road junction GERMANY 1/100,000, 7.C.55.82. at 09.00.

(9) Sick parade tomorrow will be at 07.00.

(10) ACKNOWLEDGE (Companies only).

                                            Shanks.
                                            Captain and Adjutant.
                                            1st Battalion Machine Gun Corps.

Issued at 22.00 16/12/18.

                Copies to (1) to (4) Companies
                          (5) Commanding officer
                          (6) Second in Command
                          (7) Transport officer
                          (8) Quartermaster
                          (9) H.Q. 2nd Infy. Bde.
                         (10) War Diary
                         (11) File

Abschrift.

Kriegsministerium. Berlin W, den 20.10.1917.
Nr. 5224/17. g.A.M.
Geheim!

Die nunmehr seit 6 Monaten stattfindende Pruefung der von Soldaten elsass-lothringischer Herkunft ausgehenden Briefsendungen hat zu Beanstandungen nur in geringem Umfange Anlass gegeben.

Deshalb werden die Bestimmungen ueber ihre Pruefung- Abschnitt II in der Verfuegung vom 20. 3. 1917 Nr. 1426/17.g.A. 1- aufgehoben.

Die Pruefung der Sendungen aus Elsass-Lothringen, die durch die Postueberwachungs- und Postueberwachungshilfsstellen erfolgt- Abschnitt I der angegebenen Verfuegung vom 20.3.17- bleibt dagegen bestehen.

Die Staerken der Postueberwachungshilfsstellen sind soweit zu verringern, als es ihre Aufgabe - Pruefung der vorbezeichneten Briefe und der Briefe aus besonderm Anlass(Verfg. des Chefs des Generalstabes des Feldheeres vom 29. 4. 1916 M.-J.Nr. 36061) - zulässt.

Jm Auftrage.
v. Wrisberg.

A. O. K. 6.
Nr. 62348/16706 P.

An alle Gruppen usw.

zur Kenntnis und weiteren Veranlassung;
Die angezogene Verfuegung vom 20.3. 17 Nr. 1426/19.g.A. 1 wurde mit A.O.K. Verfuegung vom 26.3. 17 Nr. 97809/12930 P bekanntgegeben.

V. s. d. O. K.
J. A.
gez. v. Ehrhardt.

Gruppe Souchez K.H.Qu., den 2.11.1917.
Ib Nr. 29 527.

Geheim!

An

17.J.D.   (35)   zur Verteilung bis zu Batln.,
1.G.R.D.   (40)   Abtlgn. und Staffeln.
207.J.D.   (40)

24. J.D. (125), Pi.Batl.31(1),Luftsch.A.68^b(2), Grufl.3(3), Flakgruko 2(1), Fs.Pk.Kp.1./Res.3(1),Pk.Kp.Ldw.Fs.47(1) Pi.Pk.Kp.19(1),Pi.Min.Kp.299(1),1./Arm.Btl.27(1),2./Arm.Btl.139(1), Wirtsch.Kp.27,175,182^b je 1, Str.B.Kp.35,Grukonach 706,Arendtgr.je 1, Fsp.Betr.Zug 1040^b,Gru.Funk.St.559^b,H.d.K. je 1, Staffelst.228(3),
Post(1),Gend.(1),K.H.Qu.(1),Erg.Kp.(1),Mun.Dep.Malf.(3)M.W.B.I(1)
zur Kenntnis.

Die von den Heeresangehörigen els.-lothr.Herkunft ausgehende Post ist kuenftig nicht mehr an die Postueberwachungshilfsstelle der Gruppe einzusenden, sondern unmittelbar zur Befoerderung aufzugeben.

V. s. d. Gr.
F. d. Ch. d. G.

Major.

Appendix II

1st BATTALION MACHINE GUN CORPS.
Order No. 80.
Reference Map Sheet GERMANY. I. E. 1/100,000

COPY No. 12

The Battalion will move to SCHONBERG and ANDLER tomorrow 18/12/18.

Order of March.	Starting point.	Head of column to pass starting point at:-	Route
H.Q.) "C" Coy) "D" ")	Junction of ALDRINGEN road with BEHO - RODINGEN rd.	07.00	ST. VITH - SCHONBERG
"A" ") "B" ")	SCHIRM cross roads	Join Battn. as it passes.	

The Battalion less "A" and "B" Coys. will parade on the ALDINGEN - BEHO road at 06.55, head of column at starting point.
"A" and "B" Coys. will assemble in above order on the ESPELER - SCHIRM road at 06.10, head of column at the cross roads SCHIRM, and will join the Battalion as it passes.

Billeting parties of Battalion H.Q., "C" and "D" Coys. will report to Battalion H.Q. at 06.00. Billeting parties of "A" and "B" Coys. will be at ESPELER Church at 06.15 where a representative of Battalion H.Q. will call for them. Billets will be taken over from 1/6th Welsh. Guides will meet Battalion on arrival at river crossing 1 km. W. of S. in SCHONBERG. Units are reminded that in enemy country they can demand accommodation, and all houses should be examined, and whatsoever rooms are required, without causing the inhabitants too great inconvenience, should be taken.

Refilling point tomorrow GRUEFLINGEN at 08.15.

The Motor Lorry will report to 2/Lt. Johnson at Junction of Railway with ST. VITH - SCHONBERG road at 09.00.

Blanket wagons of Battalion H.Q. "C" and "D" Coys. will report to Battn. H.Q. at 06.40. Blanket wagons of "A" and "B" Coys. will proceed with Coys. to SCHIRM crossroads where Lt. Raynor will arrange for them to join the remainder of 2nd line Transport.
O.C. "C" Coy. will detail 1 Officer and 20 men to report to Lt. Raynor at Battalion H.Q. at above time to accompany this party.

ACKNOWLEDGE (Companies only)

Captain and Adjutant,
1st Battalion Machine Gun Corps.

Issued at 22.00 hours 17/12/18

Normal distribution.

GUN CHART.

Army Form W.3768.

No.................Gun. ....Battery. Gun Commander...................................

Grid Bearing of Zero Line.. N.C.O. i/c..

Task	Clock Time		Zero Time		Angle of Deviation from Zero Line	Normal Q.E.	Corrected Q.E.	Traverse	Rate of Fire R.P.M.
	From	To	From	To					

CHART OF CONCENTRATION POINTS.

No. of Point	Angle of Deviation from Zero Line	Normal Q.E.	Corrected R.E.	Traverse	Remarks

PRINTED IN FRANCE BY ARMY PRINTING AND STATIONERY SERVICES. PRESS B. 1991. 50000. 4/18.

Signature..
Battery Commander.

1ST BATTALION, MACHINE GUN CORPS.

SECRET   ORDER NO.81.   Copy No.

Appendix 12

Reference Map Sheet Germany I.M. 1/100,000

(1) The Battalion, H.Q. "A" "B" and "C" Companies will move to KRONENBURG and "D" Company to BAASEM to-morrow, 19/12/18.

(2) Order of March   Starting point.   Head of Column   Route
                                           to pass starting

H.Q.   100 yds E. of   point at   AMDLER-
"I" Coy.   Cross roads in   MANDERFELD-
"A" Coy.   SCHONBERG.   08.50   HALLSCHLAG-
"B" Coy.   KRONENBURG.
                                                          (all wheeled
"C" Coy.   will join the   transport for
               Battn. as it   BAASEM to
               passes through   proceed via
               AMDLER AT 09.15   Road Jen.
                                                          1500 yds S. of
                                                          M. in BAASEM.

Battalion H.Q., "A" "B" and "D" Companies will parade on the SCHONBERG-AMDLER Road at 08.45 Head of column at starting point. "C" Company will parade outside billets at 09.10 and will join the Battalion as above.

(3) Billeting parties of Battalion H.Q. "A" "B" and "D" Companies will report to Battn.H.Q. at 08.45: Billeting party of "C" Coy. will be at AMDLER Cross will be on main road at 08.55 where Battalion representative will meet them. Guides will meet Battalion on arrival at 200 yards of the most westerly house of KRONENBURG.

(4) Baggage wagons will march in rear of the Battalion under Lieut.Rayner to whom wagons of Battalion H.Q. "A" "B" and "D" Companies will report to Battalion Headquarters at 08.30. Wagons of "C" Company will fall in in rear of the Battalion at AMDLER. O.C. "D" Company will detail 1 Officer and Section to march in rear to report to Lieut.Rayner at 08.45.

(5) The motor lorry will rendezvous at forked road 400 yards N. of the A. in AMDLER at 08.45 thence proceeding independently.

(6) Refilling point at MANDERFELD at 09.15 on 19/1 /18

(7) Sick parade will be at 07.00

(8) Acknowledge (Companies only)

                                           Captain and Adjutant,
                                           1st Battalion, Machine
                                           Gun Corps.

Issued at 22.30, 18/12/18

                          Distribution Normal

Appendix 8

SECRET.
1st BATTALION MACHINE GUN CORPS.
Order No. 77
COPY No. 11
Reference Map Sheet MARCHE, 1/100,000.

(1) The Battalion, H.Q., "A", "B", and "D" Companies, will move to REGNE and "C" Company to FRAITURE to-morrow, 15/12/18.

(2)
Order of March.	Starting point.	Head of column to pass starting point at:-	Route.
H.Q.	Road junction		ODEIGNE -
"B" Coy.	S. of OSTER LE		
"D" "	BAITY	09.40	REGNE.
"A" "	3H.89.18.		
"C" "			

The Battalion will parade ready to move off in the above order at 09.35; head of column at starting point facing East. "C" Coy. will march with Battalion to cross roads 3H.87.00 from which point they will proceed direct to FRAITURE.

(3) Billeting parties of 1 N.C.O. from Battalion H.Q. at 07.15 tomorrow and 1 Off. & 1 NCO from each Coy will report to Bn HQ at 15/12/18. Billeting parties will report to representative of 2nd Brigade H.Q. at 08.45 at REGNE CHURCH. Guides will meet the Battalion at 89 km. stone on REGNE - SAMREE Road. Guide for "C" Coy. as arranged by O.C. "C" Coy.

(4) Refilling point to-morrow will be at GRANDMENIL at 08.45 hours.

(5) Blanket wagons will report to Lieut. Rayner at Battalion H.Q. at 09.00. O.C. "D" Coy. will detail 1 Officer and 20 men to report to Lieut. Rayner at the above hour to march with these wagons.

(6) The Motor Lorry will report to Lieut. Johnson at 88 k.m. stone on MANHAY - HOUFFALZE road at 09.30 hours.

(7) Sick parade at 07.30.

ACKNOWLEDGE (Companies only).

Captain and Adjutant.
1st Battalion Machine Gun Corps.

Issued at 19.15, 14/12/18.

Copies issued to:- (1) to (4) Companies
(5) Commanding officer
(6) Second in command
(7) Quartermaster
(8) Transport officer
(9) H.Q. 2nd. Infy. Bde.
(10) War Diary
(11) File

Generalkommando
VI. Reservekorps.
IVa No. 5120.

K.H.Qu. Romagne, den 5.2.15.

Korpsbefehl I.

Während des Krieges ist Deutschland für die Ernährung des Heeres und des Volkes im wesentlichen auf die Vorräte angewiesen, die sich jetzt im Lande befinden, da auf eine Zufuhr aus dem Ausland in nennenswerten Mengen nicht zu rechnen ist. Namentlich muß daher mit dem Brote sparsam umgegangen werden, damit wir bis zur nächsten Ernte mit dem Getreide und Mehl auskommen. Es ist dringend notwendig, daß auch bei den Truppen die größte Sparsamkeit namentlich beim Brote obwaltet. Die Mannschaften sind darüber zu belehren, daß jede Verschwendung von Nahrungsmitteln in der jetzigen Zeit eine schwere Schädigung des Vaterlandes bedeutet. Diese Belehrung ist von Zeit zu Zeit zu wiederholen.

Um auch zur glücklichen Durchführung des wirtschaftlichen Kampfes beizutragen, bestimme ich daher, daß während des jetzigen Stellungskrieges die tägliche Brotration vom 7. d. Mts. an auf 500 g ohne Erhöhung der Fleischportion herabgesetzt wird. Wird von den zuständigen Mehl zum Selbstbacken des Brotes empfangen, so sind nur 360 g Mehl auszugeben. Die gegen die zuständige Brotportion von 750 g weniger empfangenen 250 g werden in Gelde vergütet.

v. Gfl[?]er

SECRET.

1st BATTALION MACHINE GUN CORPS.
Order No. 78
Reference Map Sheet MARCHE, 1/80,000

COPY No. 11

(1) The Battalion will move to-morrow to BOVIGNY 16/12/18

(2) Order of March

	Starting point.	Head of column to pass starting point at:-	Route
H.Q.	Road junction		SALMCHATEAU
"A" Coy.	E. of 21 km.	08.50	
"D" "	stone REGNE -		
"C" "	SALMCHATEAU		
"B" "	Road		

The Battalion, less "B" Coy. will parade ready to move off in the above named order on the REGNE - SALMCHATEAU Road at 08.45. Head of column at starting point facing East. "B" Company will parade on the SART - JOUBIEVAL Road, head of column on cross roads S.K.18.17 at 09.30 and will follow "C" Company as column passes.

(3) Billeting parties of 1 N.C.O. from Battalion H.Q. and 1 Officer and 1 N.C.O. from each Company will report to Battalion H.Q. at 06.45 tomorrow 16/12/18 ~~at 06.45~~. Billeting parties will take over from 1/6th W~~~~ H.Q. ~~Guides will meet the Battalion~~ at 08.30. Guides will meet the Battalion at 5 km. stone on SALM - CHATEAU - BOVIGNY Road.

(4) Refilling point tomorrow will be at SART at 09.00.

(5) Blanket wagons will report to Lieut. Rayner at Battalion H.Q. at 08.25. O.C. "A" Coy. will detail 1 Officer and 20 men to report to Lieut. Rayner at the above hour to march with these wagons.

(6) The motor lorry will report to 2/Lt. Johnson at 97 km. stone on REGNE - SALMCHATEAU Road at 09.00.

(7) Sick parade tomorrow will be at 07.00.

(8) ACKNOWLEDGE (Companies only)

Captain and Adjutant.
1st Battalion Machine Gun Corps.

Issued at 21.30 15/12/18.

Copies to (1) to (4) Companies
(5) Commanding officer
(6) Second in command
(7) Quartermaster
(8) Transport Officer
(9) H.Q. 2nd Inf. Bde.
(10) War Diary
(11) File

Appendix 13

SECRET.   1st BATTALION MACHINE GUN CORPS   COPY No. 13
Order No. 82
Reference Map Sheet GERMANY 1 K. 1/100,000

(1) The Battalion will move to BLANKENHEIMERDORF (H.Q., "A" and "D" Coys.); "B" and "C" Coys, to MULHEIM tomorrow, 21/12/18.

(2) Order of March.   Starting point.   Head of column to pass starting point at:-   Route
    H.Q.
    "B"   Road junction
    "C"   ¾ mile South of
    "A"   K in BAASEM.   09.40   DAALEN
    "D"

Headquarters, "B" and "C" Companies will parade on the KRONENBERG-STADTKYLL road at 09.35, head of column at starting point. "A" and "D" Companies will parade on BAASEM - STADTKYLL road at 09.35, head of column at starting point.
                                                                                                                                                                           -40

(3) Billeting parties of H.Q., "B" and "C" Companies will report to Battalion H.Q. at 06.45. Billeting parties of "A" and "D" Companies will be at starting point at 06.55 where a representative of Battalion H.Q. will meet them. Guides will meet Battalion on arrival at the road junction 1 km. south of the K in BLANKENHEIMER.

(4) Blanket wagons of H.Q. "B" and "C" will report to Lieut. Rayner on main road KRONENBERG at 09.25. Blanket wagons of "A" and "D" Coys. will follow in rear of those Companies to the starting point where Lieut. Rayner will collect them. O.C. "A" Company will detail a Section under an Officer as break down party (20 men) to report to Lieut. Rayner at the starting point at 09.35.

(5) Refilling point 21/12/18, KRONENBERG, at 08.30.

(6) The motor lorry will report to 2/Lt. S. Johnson at the fork roads 300 yds. South of the R in HALLSCHLOTTE, at 09.30.

(7) Sick parade tomorrow will be at 07.30.

(8) ACKNOWLEDGE (Companies only).

Issued at 22.00 20/12/18.
                                                                  Captain and Adjutant.
                                                                1st Battalion Machine Gun Corps

Normal distribution.

Appendix 14

SECRET. 1st BATTALION MACHINE GUN CORPS. COPY NO. 11
Order No. 83
Reference Map Sheet GERMANY, 1:M. & 1.L. 1/100,000

(1) The battalion will move to IVERSHEIM tomorrow, 22/12/18.

(2) Order of March.   Starting point.   Head of column   Route.
                                        to pass start-
                                        ing point at:-
    H.Q.)   Road junction,
    "D" Coy.)   S. of the M in   TONDORF -
    "A" "   )   BLANKENHEIMERDORF   09.05   HOLZMULHEIM -
                                                         NICHERSCHEID.

    "C" "   )   Road junction   Join column as
    "B" "   )   at MULHEIMER -   it passes.
                      HAUSCHEN

Battalion H.Q., "A" and "D" Coys, will parade on the BLANKENHEIM-
DORF - BLANKENHEIM road at 09.00 hours, head of column at starting
point.

"B" and "C" Coys, will parade on the MULHEIM - MULHEIMERHAUSCHEN road
at 09.50, head of column at starting point.

(3) Billeting parties of Battalion H.Q., "A" and "D" Coys, will
report to Battalion H.Q. at 07.00. Billeting parties of "B" and
"C" Coys, will be at MULHEIMERHAUSCHEN road junction at 07.15
where a representative of Battalion H.Q. will meet them. Billeting
parties to report to Burgomasters at IVERSHEIM at 09.00 hours.
Guides will meet Battalion on arrival on main road 500 yds. S. of
IVERSHEIM at 00.00 hours. Billeting officers must have with them
lists of accomodation required, ready to hand to the Burgomasters.

(4) 2nd Line Transport, H.Q., "A" and "D" Coys, will report to Lieut.
Raynor at 08.30 on main road opposite limber park. 2nd line Transport
of "B" and "C" Coys, will be at starting point of these Coys, at
10.10. O.C. "B" Coy, will detail 1 Section (20 men) under an
officer to report to Lieut. Raynor at 10.10 same place. This
transport will march brigaded under Brigade Transport Officer.

(5) Motor lorry will report to 2/Lt. Johnson at Road Junction 1,000 yds
N.W. of the first M in MULHEIM at 09.30.

(6) Refilling point for 22/12/18 at BLANKENHEIM at 08.30.

(7) Sick parade will be at 07.00.

(8) Sick parade for "B" and "C" Coys, at MULHEIM at 08.30.

(9) ACKNOWLEDGE (Companies only).

                                      Captain and Adjutant,
                                      1st Battalion Machine Gun Corps.

Issued at 21.00, 21/12/18

Normal distribution.

Appendix 15

SECRET.

1st BATTALION MACHINE GUN CORPS.
Order No. 54.
Reference Map Sheet 1 and 2 L, 1/100,000

COPY No. 3

1) The Battalion will move to FLAMERSHEIM tomorrow, 23/12/18.

2) The Battalion, less Transport, will parade on the road outside "A" Company's billets (Schoolhouse) at 10.00 hours. The Battalion will march in threes. The main IVERSHEIM - KIRSPENICH road must be kept clear until the Battalion moves off. Order of march A,B,C,D Coy.

3) 1st and 2nd line Transport of the Battalion will parade on the road outside "A" Coy's billets at 10.30 hours under Major Petrie-Hay, M.C. O.C. "C" Company will detail one Section (20 men) under an officer to report to Major Hay at 10.15 at same place.

4) Billeting parties of H.Q. and all Companies will report to Battalion H.Q. at 07.30. Billets will be taken over from Burgomaster FLAMERSHEIM at 08.30. Company and Transport guides will meet Battalion on arrival on the main road 300 yds. S.W. of FLAMERSHEIM.

5) Motor Lorry will report to 2/Lt. Johnson at 09.30 hours at cross roads 1,400 yds. S.W. of K in KIRSPENICH.

6) Refilling point for 23/12/18 at MUNSTEREIFEL at 08.15.

7) Sick parade will be at 08.00.

8) ACKNOWLEDGE (Companies only).

Captain and Adjutant,
1st Battalion Machine Gun Corps

Issued at 21.30 22/12/18.

Normal distribution.

Appendix 16

SECRET
1st BATTALION MACHINE GUN CORPS
Order No. 85
Map Reference GERMANY Sheet 2 L. 1/100,000
COPY No. 14

1) The Battalion will move to FLERZHEIM and LUFTELBERG tomorrow 24/12/18.

2)
Order of March	Starting point	Head of column to pass starting point at:-	Route
H.Q. "D" Coy. "B" " "C" " "A" "	FLAMERSHEIM - PALMERSHEIM road the most southerly house in PALMERSHEIM.	10.30	ESSIG - OBR - DREES - PEPPERHAVEN - RAMERSHOVEN - FLERZHEIM.

3) The Battalion will parade at 09.50 on the FLAMERSHEIM - PALMERSHEIM road head of column at starting point. Care must be taken to keep the road clear to allow No. 2 Field Ambulance to pass.

4) Billeting parties will report to Capt. Wilson, M.O. at FLERZHEIM Church at 90.00. Billeting Officers must have with them lists of accomodation required ready to hand to the Burgomaster.

5) 2nd line Transport will march in rear of the column under Lieut. J. Rayner.

6) Motor Lorry must pass cross roads 300 yds. W. of E in ESSIG at 09.30 and proceed independently.

7) Refilling point for the 24th inst. ODENDORF at 08.30.

8) Sick parade will be at 08.00.

9) ACKNOWLEDGE (Companies only).

Issued at 21.30 23/12/18

Lieut. & A/Adjutant,
1st Battalion Machine Gun Corps.

1919
WESTERN DIVISION
LATE
1ST DIVISION

1ST BN MACH. GUN CORPS

JAN - JLY 1919

1st Bn MGC Army Form C. 2118.

WAR DIARY
or
INTELLIGENCE SUMMARY.
(Erase heading not required.)

Place	Date	Hour	Summary of Events and Information	Remarks and references to Appendices
FLERZHEIM Germany 2L 1/100,000 9.C	1.1.19 to 31.1.19		Headquarters A & C Coys at FLERZHEIM B & D Coys at LUFTELBERG. 9.C. Battalion engaged during this period in training education & recreation. 8 Officers and 36 O.R. demobilized. Specimen of weeks training annexed.	Appendix A

J. Simpson Lieut
for Major Commanding
1st Bn. M.G.C.

TRAINING PROGRAMME for week ending
8th February 1919.

DATE	TIME	"A" Coy.	"B" Coy.	"C" Coy.	"D" Coy.
3/2/19	09.00	Educational Training.	Route March with Transport.	Range - Part I Table C & Revolver Practice.	P.T.
	10.00				Close Order Drill and Arms Drill.
	11.00			P.T.	Gun Drill T.O.E.T.
4/2/19	09.00	P.T.	Educational Training.	Route March with Transport.	Range - Part I Table C & Revolver Practice
	10.00	Arms & Close Order Drill.			
	11.00	Gun Drill - T.O.E.T.			P.T.
5/2/19	09.00 10.00 11.00	Company Tactical Scheme - introducing action from Limbers.	Do.	Do.	Do.
6/2/19	09.00	Range - Part I Table C and Revolver Practice.	P.T.	Educational Training.	Route March with Transport.
	10.00		Arm & Close Order Drill.		
	11.00	P.T.	Gun Drill T.O.E.T.		
7/2/19	09.00	Route March with Transport	Range - Part I Table C, & Revolver Practice	P.T.	Educational Training.
	10.00			Arms & Close Order Drill.	
	11.00		P.T.	Gun Drill T.O.E.T.	
8/2/19	09.00	Arms & Coy. Drill.	Do.	Do.	Do.
	10.00 11.00	Interior Economy.	Do.	Do.	Do.

O.C. Companies will arrange for at least 3 hours Limber Drill for all Company Transport.

P.T.O.

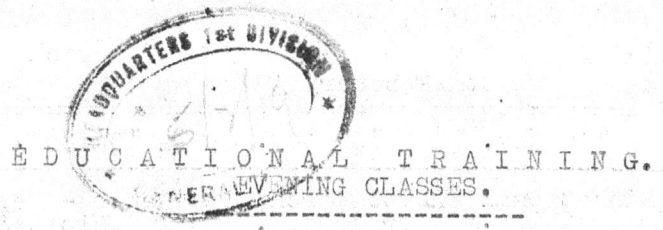

EDUCATIONAL TRAINING.
EVENING CLASSES.

	SUBJECT.	PLACE.	TIME.	LECTURER.
Monday 3/2/19.	German.	Flerzheim.	17.30.	Interpreter.
Tuesday 4/2/19.	Debate: Should drink be abolished.	Luftelberg.	"	Major Snowball M.C. Major Anson.
Thursday 6/2/19.	German.	Luftelberg.	"	Interpreter.
Friday 7/2/19.	French.	Flerzheim.	"	Capt. Shanks.

RECREATIONAL TRAINING.

PROGRAMME OF SPORTS - Week ending 8th February, 1919.

February 2. Football: "D" Coy. v. H.Q. at 14.30 hours.
" 3. Practice Football.
" 4. Battalion Football Team versus Engineers, at 14.30 hours.
" 5. Trial run.
" 6. Football: "B" Coy. v. H.Q. at 14.30 hours.
" 7. Practice Football.
"Spare Parts" Concert Party in Recreation Room, Flerzheim, at 18.30 hours.
" 8. Football: "A" v. "D" Coy., at 14.30 hours.

The Tug-of-War teams will be coached each day for 30 minutes by 2nd. Lieut. Green, "A" Coy., who will notify time and place.

Whist Drive will be held on Wednesday, 5th instant, at Recreation Room, Flerzheim.

Boxing every night at 17.30 hours, usual places.

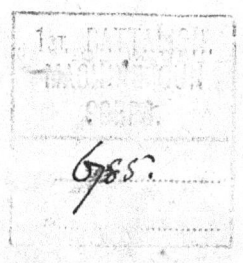

Army Form C. 2118.

WAR DIARY
or
INTELLIGENCE SUMMARY.
(Erase heading not required.)

Instructions regarding War Diaries and Intelligence Summaries are contained in F. S. Regs., Part II. and the Staff Manual respectively. Title pages will be prepared in manuscript.

Place	Date	Hour	Summary of Events and Information	Remarks and references to Appendices
FIERZHEIM	1/2/19		Battalion in billets in FIERZHEIM & LUFTELBERG. Battalion and company training carried out as per Afterdine A. Recreational training carried out in the afternoon and voluntary educational training in the evening	APPENDIX A
	2/2/19		Church services in the morning.	
	3/2/19		Training carried out in accordance with training programme (Appendix A). Recreational training (football, cross country run etc) taken (?) in the afternoon and voluntary educational training in the evening	-do-
	4/2/19		-do-	
	5/2/19		-do-	
	6/2/19		-do-	
	7/2/19		-do-	
	8/2/19		Church Services in FIERZHEIM and LUFTELBERG in the morning. Football match in the afternoon.	
	9/2/19			
	10/2/19 to 15/2/19		Training carried out in accordance with Battalion training programme (AppA). Recreation in the afternoon and voluntary educational training carried out in the evening	

Army Form C. 2118.

WAR DIARY
or
INTELLIGENCE SUMMARY.
(Erase heading not required.)

Instructions regarding War Diaries and Intelligence Summaries are contained in F. S. Regs., Part II. and the Staff Manual respectively. Title pages will be prepared in manuscript.

Place	Date	Hour	Summary of Events and Information	Remarks and references to Appendices
FRIEDRICHSFELD	16/4/19		Church services in the morning at FRIEDRICHSHEIM for the 11th Div. and at RUTTENBERG for other natives in the afternoon	(1) Appendix A
	17/2/19			(2) do.
	12/3/19		Evening lecture next Saving Programme (App. D) carried out in the week. Scout is training to be officers and voluntary subjects.	(3) B do
	23/3/19		Church Services in FRIEDRICHSHEIM, RUTTENBERG in the morning. Recreation Sports in the afternoon	(4) do
	24/3/19		Route to decentralise with the 35th Pioneers	
	6/4/19		Reinforcement drafts in the Glenryue received with (App A) overall strength of the Battalion though the later totalling officers 44, other ranks 807, 160 officers and approximately 150 other ranks (including sickness) Leave	(5) B do

N. Hazard? Col.

Officer Comdg. 11th Batn M.G.Corps.

TRAINING PROGRAMME
for week ending 8th February 1919.

Date.	Time.	"A" Coy..	"B" Coy..	"C" Coy..	"D" Coy..
3/2/19.	09.00.	Educational Training.	Route March with Transport.	Range - Part I Table C & Revolver Practice.	P.T.
	10.00.				Close Order Drill & Arms Drill.
	11.00.			P.T.	Gun Drill - T.O.E.T.
4/2/19.	09.00.	P.T.	Educational Training.	Route March with Transport.	Range - Part I Table C and Revolver Practice.
	10.00.	Arms Drill & Close Order Drill.			
	11.00.	Gun Drill - T.O.E.T.			P.T.
5/2/19.	09.00. 10.00. 11.00.	Company Tactical Scheme - introducing action from Limbers.			
6/2/19.	09.00.	Range - Part I Table C & Revolver Practice.	P.T.	Educational Training.	Route March with Transport.
	10.00.		Arms & Close Order Drill.		
	11.00.	P.T.	Gun Drill - T.O.E.T.		
7/2/19.	09.00.	Route March with Transport.	Range - Part I Table C, & Revolver Practice.	P.T.	Educational Training.
	10.00.			Arms & Close Order Drill.	
	11.00.		P.T.	Gun Drill - T.O.E.T.	
8/2/19.	09.00.	Arms & Coy. Drill.	do.	do.	do.
	10.00 11.00	Interior Economy.	do.	do.	do.

O.C. Companies will arrange for at least 3 hours Limber Drill for all Company Transport.

TRAINING PROGRAMME
for Week Ending, 15th. February 1919.

Date.	Time.	"A" Coy..	"B" Coy..	"C" Coy..	"D" Coy..
10/2/19.	09.00.	Educational Training.	Route March with Transport introducing Tactical Scheme.	Range - Part I Table C and Revolver Practice.	Coy. & Arms Drill.
	10.00.				P.T.
	11.00.			P.T.	Gun Drill & Direct Overhead Fire.
11/2/19.	09.00.	Coy. & Arms Drill.	Educational Training.	Route March with Transport introducing tactical scheme.	Range - Part I Table C & Revolver Practice.
	10.00.	P.T.			
	11.00.	Gun Drill & Direct Overhead Fire.			P.T.
12/2/19.	09.00. 11.00.	Company Tactical Scheme.	do.	do.	do.
13/2/19.	09.00.	Range - Part I Table C & Revolver Practice.	Company & Arms Drill.	Educational Training.	Route March with Transport introducing Tactical Scheme.
	10.00		P.T.		
	11.00.	P.T.	Gun Drill & Direct Overhead Fire.		
14/2/19.	09.00.	Route March with Transport, introducing Tactical Scheme.	Range - Part I Table C & Revolver Practice.	Company and Arms Drill.	Educational Training.
	10.00.			P.T.	
	11.00.		P.T.	Gun Drill & Direct Overhead Fire.	
15/2/19.	09.00.	Arms & Coy. Drill.	do.	do.	do.
	10.00. 11.00.	Interior Economy.	do.	do.	do.

TRAINING PROGRAMME
for week ending 22nd February 1919.

Date.	Time.	"A" Coy.	"B" Coy.	"C" Coy.	"D" Coy.
17/2/19.	09.00.	Educational Training.	Route March with Transport, introducing Tactical Scheme.	Range.	Arms Drill & Coy. Drill.
	10.00.				P.T.
	11.00.			P.T.	Tactical Section Drill.
18/2/19.	09.00.	Arms Drill & Coy. Drill.	Educational Training.	Route March with Transport.	Range.
	10.00.	P.T.			
	11.00.	Tactical Section Drill.			P.T.
19/2/19.	09.00.	Battalion Parade.			
20/2/19.	09.00.	Range.	Arms Drill & Company Drill.	Educational Training.	Route March with Transport, introducing Tactical Scheme.
	10.00.		P.T.		
	11.00.	P.T.	Tactical Section Drill.		
21/2/19.	09.00.	Route March with Transport, introducing Tactical Scheme.	Range.	Arms Drill & Coy. Drill.	Educational Training.
	10.00.				P.T.
	11.00.		P.T.	Tactical Section Drill.	
22/2/19.	09.00. to 10.00.	Company Training.			
	11.00.	Interior Economy.			

TRAINING PROGRAMME
for week ending 1st March 1919.

Date.	Time.	"A" Coy.	"B" Coy.	"C" Coy.	"D" Coy.
24/2/19.	09.00.	Arms Drill & Coy. Drill.	Educational Training.	Route March with Transport introducing tactical scheme.	Arms Drill & Coy. Drill.
	10.00.	Indication & Recognition of Targets.			Indication & Recognition of Targets.
	11.00.	P.T.			P.T.
25/2/19.	09.00.	Educational Training.	Range.	Range.	Route March with Transport introducing tactical scheme.
	10.00.				
	11.00.		P.T.	P.T.	
26/2/19.	09.00.	Two-Company Tactical Schemes. O.C. "B" and "C" Companies will notify to this Office the ground selected.			
27/2/19.	09.00.	Route March with Transport introducing Tactical Scheme.	Arms Drill & Coy. Drill.	Educational Training.	Range.
	10.00.	Indication & Recognition of Targets.			
	11.00.	P.T.			P.T.
28/2/19.	09.00.	Range.	Route March with Transport introducing Tactical Scheme.	Arms Drill & Company Drill.	Educational Training.
	10.00.			Indication & Recognition of Targets.	
	11.00.	P.T.		P.T.	
1/3/19.	09.00.	Interior Economy.			
	11.00.	Battalion Run - 3 Miles.			

1st M.G.C.

WAR DIARY
~~INTELLIGENCE SUMMARY~~

Army Form C. 2118.

WD 13

Place	Date	Hour	Summary of Events and Information	Remarks and references to Appendices
FLERZHEIM	1/3/19 to 31/3/19		The battalion in billets in FLERZHEIM & LUFTELBURG. Training was carried our daily from 9 until 12.30 in the morning in accordance with the training programme attached. Recreational training was carried out every afternoon in which Inter Company League matches were played, inter company tug-of-war carried out etc. and several tactical were played against other units of the Division. Educational training was continued each Company had one morning weekly of compulsory Educational training and voluntary classes in French, German, Bookkeeping, English, Arithmetic etc. Major Power filled M.R. (late D.S.O. KRRC) joined the battalion on the 27th and took over command from Capt M.Hay H.M. Ryland DSO who assumed duty. Second in Command. The strength of the battalion on 31/3/19 was 52 Officers and 931 other ranks. During the month 150 other ranks had proceeded to concentration Camp for demobilization. The battalion was reinforced by drafts of officers and other ranks from 58th & 94th Btns M.G. Corps during the month.	APPENDIX A

[Signed]
Comdr 1st Bn M.G. Corps

1st. BATTALION MACHINE GUN CORPS.

TRAINING PROGRAMME
for week ending 25th. March 1919.

Date.	Time	"A" Coy.	"B" Coy.	"C" Coy.	"D" Coy.
20/3/19,	09.00	Route March with Transport.	Range Musketry.	Arms Drill & Coy. Drill.	Arms Drill & Coy. Drill.
	10.00.			P.T.	Indication & Recognition. Rangefinder.
	11.00.			Indication & Recognition Rangefinder.	P.T.
21/3/19,	09.00.	Arms Drill & Coy Drill.	Route March with Transport.	Educational Training.	Range Musketry.
	10.00.	Indication & Recognition. Rangefinder.			
	11.00.	P.T.			
22/3/19,	09.00.	Range Musketry.	Arms Drill & Coy. Drill.	Route March with Transport.	Educational Training.
	10.00.		Indication & Recognition. Rangefinder.		
	11.00.		P.T.		
24/3/19,	09.00.	MASSED PHYSICAL TRAINING.			
	10.00.	INTERIOR ECONOMY.			
	11.00.	BATTALION RUN - 3 Miles.			

1st. BATTALION, MACHINE GUN CORPS.

TRAINING PROGRAMME
for week ending 15th March, 1919.

Date.	Time.	"A" Coy.	"B" Coy.	"C" Coy.	"D" Coy.
10/3/19.	09.00.	Educational Training.	Arms Drill & Coy. Drill.	Range – Rifle Grouping.	Route March with Transport introducing tactical scheme.
	10.00.		Direct Overhead Fire.		
	11.00.		P.T.	P.T.	
11/3/19.	09.00.	Route March with Transport introducing tactical scheme.	Educational Training.	Arms Drill & Coy. Drill.	Range – Rifle Grouping.
	10.00.			Direct Overhead Fire.	
	11.00.			P.T.	P.T.
12/3/19.	09.00.	BATTALION PARADE. (Full Marching Order, with Transport)			
13/3/19.	09.00.	Range – Rifle Grouping.	Route March with Transport, introducing Tactical Scheme.	Educational Training.	Arms Drill & Coy. Drill.
	10.00.				Direct Overhead Fire.
	11.00.				P.T.
14/3/19.	09.00.	Arms Drill & Coy. Drill.	Range – Rifle Grouping.	Route March with Transport, introducing Tactical Scheme.	Educational Training.
	10.00.	Direct Overhead Fire.			
	11.00.	P.T.			
15/3/19.	09.00.	Massed P.T.			
	10.00.	Interior Economy.			
	11.00.	Battalion Run – 3 Miles.			

NOTE:- The Programme of Educational Training will be the same in all respects as in the case of the two previous weeks.

RECREATIONAL TRAINING.

PROGRAMME OF SPORTS for week ending 15th March, 1919.

Sunday, 9th March.	at 14.15 hours.	Tug of War Pull Off. *
Monday, 10th "	" 14.15 "	Battalion Team v. Cameron Highlanders, on their Ground.
Tuesday, 11th "	" 14.30 "	Rugby pick up.
Wednesday, 12th "	" 14.30 "	Battalion Team v. 32nd M.G.C. Played at PLITZHEIM.
	" 18.30 "	Whist Drive, PLITZHEIM.
Thursday, 13th "	" 14.30 "	Football Match - Officers v. Sergeants.
Friday, 14th "	" 14.15 "	Knock-out Match - "C" Company v. "D" Company.
Saturday, 15th "	" 14.30 "	Battalion Team v. 2nd. Royal Sussex at Witterschlick.
	" 11.00 "	Cross-country Run.
	" 18.00 "	"Spare Parts" Concert Party, Recreation Room, LUFTELBERG.

* Tug of War.   S.K. Key, Captain - (Recreational Officer).
H.Q. 7. ,"A" Company, and "B" 7. "C" Company.

1st. BATTALION, MACHINE GUN CORPS.

TRAINING PROGRAMME
for week ending 8th. March 1919.

Date.	Time.	"A" Coy.	"B" Coy.	"C" Coy.	"D" Coy.
3/3/19.	09.00.	Educational Training.	Arms Drill & Coy. Drill.	Range.	Route March with Transport, introducing Tactical Scheme.
	10.00.	T.O.E.T.			
	11.00.	P.T.		P.T.	
4/3/19.	09.00.	Route March with Transport, introducing Tactical Scheme.	Educational Training.	Arms Drill & Coy. Drill.	Range.
	10.00.	T.O.E.T.			
	11.00.			P.T.	P.T.
5/3/19.	09.00.	BATTALION PARADE.			
6/3/19.	09.00.	Range.	Route March with Transport, introducing Tactical Scheme.	Educational Training.	Arms Drill & Coy. Drill.
	10.00.				T.O.E.T.
	11.00.	P.T.			P.T.
7/3/19.	09.00.	Arms Drill & Coy. Drill.	Range.	Route March with Transport, introducing Tactical Scheme.	Educational Training.
	10.00.	T.O.E.T.			
	11.00.	P.T.	P.T.		
8/3/19.	09.00.	P.T.	P.T.	P.T.	P.T.
	10.00.	Interior Economy.			
	11.00.	Battalion Run — 5 Miles.			

NOTE:— The Programme of Educational Training will be the same in all respects as that issued for last week.

WAR DIARY
1st. Battalion Machine Gun Corps.

Names of Officers reinforcing the Battalion in March.

Lieut.Col.J.F.R.Hope,D.S.O.	to Command.	27/3/19
Lieut. R. Henderson.		5/3/19
2/Lieut. A. Astbury.		do.
2/Lieut. J.R.Delmore.		do.
Captain J.H.Ashton		21/3/19
Captain T. Watkins.		do.
Lieut. O.P.Pratt.		do.
Lieut. E.E.Dowling.		do.
2/Lieut. E.F. Tidy.		do.
2/Lieut. A.W.Drennen.		do.
2/lieut. A.G.Pecket.		do.
2/Lieut. E.Thomas.		do.
2/Lieut. W.E.Garrett.		23/3/19
2/Lieut. C. Richardson.		31/3/19
Captain G.W.A.Wood.		do.
Captain W.A.Trent.		do.
Lieut. J.C.Knoth.		do.
Lieut. D.S.Laughland.		do.
Lieut. M.A.Cook.		do.
Lieut. H.E.Parsons,M.C.		do.
Lieut. E.C.Moryoseph.		do.
Lieut. G.W.Petrie, M.C.		do.
2/Lieut. A.Linley.M.M.		

Number of Other-Ranks reinforcing Battalion in March.1919

```
March 5th..............95
      21st.............100
      27th.............  1
      31st.............  7
                       ───
                       203
```

Names of Officers demobilized during month of March 1919.

Lieut. J. Bullpitt, M.C.

Numbers of O.R's. demobilized during month of March 1919.

42.

Names of Regular Officers to U.K. for duty during March 1919.

Major T.G.Anson.

Strength of Battalion on 31st. March 1919.

Officers.....61   O.R's......938.

Name of Officer Sick and evacuated during March 1919.

Lieut. C.O.Davies.

Army Form C. 2118.

No 1. M.G.C.

WAR DIARY
or
INTELLIGENCE SUMMARY.
(Erase heading not required.)

Instructions regarding War Diaries and Intelligence Summaries are contained in F.S. Regs., Part II. and the Staff Manual respectively. Title pages will be prepared in manuscript.

Place	Date	Hour	Summary of Events and Information	Remarks and references to Appendices
FIERZIHEIM	1/4/19 to 30/4/19		The Battalion is billeted in — FIERZIHEIM = One Company & Batt. H.Q. LUFTELBURG = Two Companies. MUTHMOSEN = One Company. **TRAINING** Parade hours 07.00 — 12.30. Machine Gunnery. Musketry & Physical Training was carried out daily. Route Marches were performed once a week. Gas Drill with a minimum of one hour per week continuous wearing of P.H. — **EDUCATIONAL** Each Company has one morning weekly of Company Educational Training. Files on loan daily. Evening Voluntary Classes were held in the following subjects. German. Book-keeping, English, Arithmetic &c — French. **AGRICULTURAL** Each Company has one acre of ground, and one hour daily is spent on this training. — **RECREATIONAL** Games out every afternoon. Inter Section Football match — Boat matches and other sports of the Division. The Strength of the Battalion on 30/4/19 was 65 Officers and 856 O.Rs. but of this number 12 Officers & 270 O.Rs have been ordered to Concentration Camps for demobilisation.	

Smith Lt. Col
Commanding 1 Batt M.G.C.

WAR DIARY.

1st Battalion Machine Gun Corps.

Names of Officers re-inforcing the Battalion in April

2/Lieut. W.F.Walpole.	3/4/19.
Lieut. P.Kimber.	5/4/19.
Lieut. H.Rodgers.	16/4/19.
2/Lieut. G.Westhead.	16/4/19.
2/Lieut. G.Ford.	16/4/19.
2/Lieut. J.F.Phillips.	16/4/19.
2/Lieut. F.S.Frith.	16/4/19.
2/Lieut. J.P.Gordon.	18/4/19.
2/Lieut. N.B.McLaine.	18/4/19.

Number of Other Ranks re-inforcing the Battalion in April.

1/4/19.	-	8
5/4/19.	-	1
7/4/19.	-	2
8/4/19.	-	2
10/4/19.	-	1
14/4/19.	-	1
15/4/19.	-	4
19/4/19.	-	1
21/4/19.	-	1
25/4/19.	-	1
26/4/19.	-	1
29/4/19.	-	2
30/4/19.	-	1
		26

Names of Officers demobilized during the month of April.

Major. J.S.Snowball, M.C.	15/4/19.
2/Lieut. W.McLean.	9/4/19.
Capt. A.Shanks.	10/4/19.
Lieut. J.E.Shead, M.C.	10/4/19.
Capt. J.S.Taylor. M.C.	10/4/19.

Numbers of Other Ranks demobilized during the month of April.

6/4/19.	-	2
7/4/19.	-	3
8/4/19.	-	33
9/4/19.	-	2
22/4/19.	-	6
15/4/19.	-	24
17/4/19.	-	4
		74

Lt Col.
Commanding 1st Batt.
M.G.C

WAR DIARY
or
INTELLIGENCE SUMMARY

Army Form C. 2118.

(Erase heading not required.)

Instructions regarding War Diaries and Intelligence Summaries are contained in F.S. Regs., Part II. and the Staff Manual respectively. Title pages will be prepared in manuscript.

Place	Date	Hour	Summary of Events and Information	Remarks and references to Appendices
FLERZHEIM	1/5/19 to 31/5/19		The Battalion was Billeted in:— FLERZHEIM. = One Company & Batt. H.Q. LUFTELBURG = Two Companies. AVTOMCHEN = One Company. **TRAINING** Parade hours 07 — 08 and 09.00 — 12.30. 1. Machine Gunnery, Musketry & Physical Training were carried out daily. 2. Part I Table C was fired on the 25" range by three Companies. 3. 100 Men attached from Cheshire Regiment were trained in accordance with programme rehearsed. 4. Gas Drill was carried out with a minimum of one hour per week. Continuous wearing of Box Respirators. **EDUCATIONAL** Each company had one morning weekly of Compulsory Educational Training. One hour weekly was also allotted for Education. A Lecture by 2nd/Lieut. LANDON PERKINS was delivered on "United States of America" **AGRICULTURAL** One acre of ground has been requisitioned for agricultural training for Coupland. **Recreational** Games and every afternoon. Inter Company v Battalion Bucket Matches. — from Cheshire Regiment. (9 R and 116) The Strength of the Batt. on 31/5/19 was 37 Officers & 707 O.R. & 100 Other O.R. [signature] Lt Col. Cmdg. No 1 Batt 19 [?]	

WAR DIARY.

1st Battalion Machine Gun Corps.

Names of Officers re-inforcing the Battalion in May.1919.

Major.	R.A.Helps.	10/5/19.
Lieut.	E.G.Palmer.	14/5/19.
"	F.W.E.L'Estrange Fawcett.	26/5/19.
"	C.McKerron.	26/5/19.
"	S.Bowker.	26/5/19.
2/Lt.	F.Lamb.	26/5/19.
"	E.G.Ball.	26/5/19.

Number of Other Ranks re-inforcing Battalion in May 1919.

```
        May 22nd. ........... 113.
Joined during month. ............  4.
                                 ----
                                 117.
```

Names of Officers demobilized during month of May 1919.

2/Lieut. G.Westhead.	Lieut. J.Rayner.
Capt. H.I.Strover.M.C.	" H.Rodgers.
Lieut.T.Watkins.	" G.W.Petrie.M.C.
Capt. W.A.Trent.	" J.E.Nicholls.
Lieut.W.Harriss.	

Number of Other Ranks demobilized during month of May 1919.

93.

1st. BATTALION MACHINE GUN CORPS.

COURSE FOR DRAFT OF THE CHESHIRE REGIMENT - WEEK ENDING 31st. MAY 1919. - SECOND WEEK.

TIME.	MONDAY.	TUESDAY.	WEDNESDAY.	THURSDAY.	FRIDAY.	SATURDAY.	REMARKS.
09.30 Hours to 10.30 Hours.	Single Shot Loading.	Stripping.	I.A.	Indication, and Recognition.	Indication and Recognition.	Fire Orders.	
10.30 Hours to 11.30 Hours.	Elementary Gun Drill.	Elementary Gun Drill. (including "action" & "out of action")	Elementary Gun Drill (including "action" & "out of action")	Gun Drill. (lowest position)	Gun Drill (lowest position)	Combined Drill.	
11.30 Hours to 12.30 Hours.	I.A.	Sight setting & Laying.	Stripping.	Traversing, & Searching.	I.A.	Points. B.D.A.	

All Companies to parade on the Cricket Ground.

Officers must watch their men's attention, and give short intervals of other work, games etc.; short talks on the use of Machine Guns in action are most useful also.

24/5/19.

Lieut. & A/Adj.,
1st. Battalion Machine Gun Corps.

COURSE FOR N.D.A.T - WEEK ENDING 24th MAY 1919.

TIME	MONDAY	TUESDAY	WEDNESDAY	THURSDAY	FRIDAY	SATURDAY	REMARKS.
09.00 Hours to 10.00 Hours	C.O's Inspection.	How to load Fire and Un-load.	Stripping.	Explanation of Gun.	Stripping.	Single Shot Loading.	
10.00 Hours to 11.00 Hours	Mounting and Dismount-ing Tripod.	Elementary Gun Drill.	Elementary Gun Drill.	Traversing Fire.	Searching Fire.	Elementary Gun Drill.	
11.00 Hours to 12.00 Hours	Explanation of Gun.	Explanation of Gun.	Aiming Instruction (including sight sett-ing,and Laying.)	Care and Clearing.	I.A.	I.A.	

P.S. Short lectures by O.C.Companies,or suitable Officer on personal experience showing enormous power of weapon and general principles of it's use.

18th. May 1919.

[signature]
Lieut. & A/Adj.
1st. Battalion Machine Gun Corps.

Army Form C. 2118.

WAR DIARY
or
INTELLIGENCE SUMMARY
(Erase heading not required.)

Instructions regarding War Diaries and Intelligence Summaries are contained in F. S. Regs., Part II. and the Staff Manual respectively. Title Pages will be prepared in manuscript.

Place	Date	Hour	Summary of Events and Information	Remarks and references to Appendices
FLERZHEIM	1/6/19		The Battalion in Billets as follows:—	
			FLERZHEIM — One Company + HQ	
			LÜFTELBURG — Two Companies	
			HOTTINGHOVEN — One Company	
			TRAINING	
			Parade Hours 0700 - 0800 hrs 0900 - 1230 hrs	
			1. Machine Gunnery, Musketry + Physical Training were carried out daily.	
			2. Part I (Instructional) M.T. Course was fixed by one Company + two men attached from the Cookers att. to the Battalion.	
			3. Route marches and Company Tactical Exercises with transport.	
			4. Gas drill	
			EDUCATIONAL	
			Each Company had one morning or 4 hours of Compulsory Education. The Facilities were also attached for Education.	
			AGRICULTURAL	
			One acre of ground per Company has been requisitioned for Agricultural Training.	
			RECREATIONAL	
			Inter-Company cricket matches have taken place during the season also Battalion matches with other Units in the Division.	
	20/6/19			
	21/6/19	do	During the period, A.B.+C. Companies were attached to the various Infantry Brigades of the Division ready for action if the Peace Treaty had not been signed:—	
			"A" Company was attached at BUISDORF —	
			"B" Company at BONN with one Section at SIEGBURG	
			"C" Company at WITTERSCHLICK — Battalion H.Q. and "D" Company were stationed at HERMERZHEIM.	
BATTALION, MACHINE GUN CORPS.	30/6/19	do	All equipment, ammunition & rifle Respectively issued to their former Billets. The Strength of the Battalion being 20 Officers + 707 other ranks apart from 3 Nurses & Other ranks from the [illegible]	

2449. Wt. W14957/M90 750,000 1/16 J.B.C. & A. Forms/C.2118/12.

WAR DIARY.

1st. BATTALION MACHINE GUN CORPS.

Names of Officers re-inforcing to Battalion in JUNE 1919:-

Major. W.T. Boughey. M.C.	3/6/19.
Major. R. Page.	do.
Capt. G.M.L.Pirkis.	do.
Lieut. A.H. Morrison.	do.
Lieut. F. Russell.	do.
Lieut. A.J.V.Rees.	do.
Lieut. P. Deehan.	do.
Lieut. R.L. Griffin.	do.
Lieut. F.I.B.Parry.	do.
Lieut. R.J. Wheeler.	do.
2/Lieut. J. Wilson.	do.
2/Lieut. F. Walker.	do.
2/Lieut. A.E. Francis.	do.
Lieut. J.S. Tanner.	do.
Lieut. W.T. Thornton.	do.
Lieut. L.L. DeSouza.	do.

Number of Other Ranks re-inforcing Battalion in JUNE 1919:-

```
June 3rd........................145.
Joined during Month............  8.
                                ----
                                153.
```

Names of Officers demobilized during month of JUNE 1919:-

Lieut. H.S. Sharpe.	Lieut. A. Cranford.
Capt. J.H. Ashton.	Capt. G.W.A.Wood.
2/Lieut. T. Green.	Lieut. J.S.Tanner.
Major. R.A. Helps. (To U.K. for duty).	

Number of Other Ranks demobilized during month of JUNE 1919:-

94.

Army Form C. 2118.

WAR DIARY
or
INTELLIGENCE SUMMARY.
(Erase heading not required.)

1st BATTALION, MACHINE GUN CORPS.
No. 4/04

Place	Date	Hour	Summary of Events and Information	Remarks and references to Appendices
FLERZHEIM	1.7.19		The Battalion in Billets as follows.	
			FLERZHEIM HQ & A Coy	
			LUFTELBERG B & D Coys	
			RAMERSHOVEN C Coy	
			Training Parade Hours	
			07.00 hrs – 08.00 hrs.	
			09.00 " – 12.30 –	
			1. Company training in musketry, arms drill, machine gun & physical training were carried out daily.	
			2. Part I (Instructional) M.G. Courses was fired by details	
			3. Route Marches & company tactical exercises with transport	
			4. Gas Drill	
			EDUCATIONAL TRAINING.	
			Each company HQ. has one morning each week compulsory Education. One hour every day was also spent in Educational training	
			AGRICULTURAL.	
	31.7.19		One acre of ground per company has been requisitioned for agricultural purposes.	

WAR DIARY or INTELLIGENCE SUMMARY

Army Form C. 2118.

Place	Date	Hour	Summary of Events and Information	Remarks and references to Appendices
FLIERZHEIM	14.7.19		General Holiday to commemorate the Signing of the Peace Terms.	
	5.7.19		The following amount was invested in War Savings Certificates for the week ending July 5th 1919. MKS. 42430.40.	
	8.7.19		The Battalion Sports were held at Flierzheim were a great success. The result for the Challenge Cup was, 1st D Company / 2nd A Company	
			The winners of the Championship Medals were 1st Silver Medal Sergt. McIntyre F Company 2nd Bronze " Sig. Scott D " 1st Batt. Machine Gun Corps won the Tent Pegging open to Lieut. C.H. Smythe, Officers of the Division	
	11.7.19		The G.O.C. IX Corps inspected the Battalion. After the inspection the Battalion marched past by Companies by P&E Comp.	
	12.7.19		The following amount was invested in War Savings Certificates for the week ending July 12th 1919. MARKS 21,037.50	
	17.7.19		The Battalion won the 2nd Round of the Divisional Cricket Cup, beating the 52nd Welsh Regt. 95 to 42.	
	19.7.19		The following amount was invested in War Savings Certificates for the week ending July 19th 1919. MARKS. 24986.90.	

Army Form C. 2118.

WAR DIARY
or
INTELLIGENCE SUMMARY.
(Erase heading not required.)

Instructions regarding War Diaries and Intelligence Summaries are contained in F. S. Regs., Part II. and the Staff Manual respectively. Title pages will be prepared in manuscript.

Place	Date	Hour	Summary of Events and Information	Remarks and references to Appendices
FLERZHEIM	24.7.19		A most successful Horse Show was held at Flerzheim. The result of the Competition for the Challenge Cup presented by the Commanding Officer Lieut Col. J.R. Hope D.S.O. was as follows:- 1st D Coy. 2nd B Coy.	
	26.7.19		Major H.V. Rees 1st Battalion Machine Gun Corps won the Open Jumping. The following amount was invested in War Savings Certificates for the week ending 26.7.19 MARKS 21,457.00	
	27.7.19		There was an Inter-Company Basket Ball Competition at Flerzheim starting at 14.00 hours. The winners were B Company.	
	29.7.19.		The catch weight tug of war Team & the Basket Ball Team were beaten by the 65th Brigade R.F.A.	
	31.7.19		The D.A. Group Aquatic Sports were held at Bonn. The Water Polo Team beat the 104th Brigade R.F.A. but lost to the 65th Brigade R.F.A.	
	1.7.19 to 31.7.19		STRENGTH The strength of the Battalion on 31.7.19 was:- 55 Officers 751 Other Ranks 93 " " attached from the Cheshire Regt. 1st Western Infantry Brigade.	

J. [signature]
Lieut Col.
Comdg. 3r Bn. M.G. Corps.

WAR DIARY.   JULY 1919.

Names of Officers Reinforcing Battalion in JULY 1919.

    Lieut. G.W.McCabe.   Posted from 65th. Bn. K.R.R.C.

Numbers of O.Rs Reinforcing Battalion in JULY 1919.

    From 46th Bn. M.G.C. 7/7/19   = 1.

Names of Officers struck off strength in JULY.

Lt. F.W.L.Estrange Fawcett.   Transferred to Military Governor's
                                Office. COLOGNE. 25/7/19.
Major. N.B.N. Good. M.C.   To Concentration Camp pending
                                transfer to U.K. for demobilization
                                and struck off strength 30/7/19.

Lt. E.E.Dowling.   )
Lt. W.T.Thornton.   )
Lt. R.J.Wheeler.   ) To U.K. for duty 5/7/19.
2/Lt. W.E.Garrett.   )
2/Lt. A.Chandler.   )

Numbers of O.Rs struck off strength in JULY 1919.

      Sick and Evacuated.   -   4.
      To Concentration Camp
      pending transfer to U.K.
      for demobilization and
      struck off strength;
        9/7/19.   -   4
        25/7/19   -   6
      Transfers to other Units. 3.

                            17.

1st BATTALION,
MACHINE GUN
CORPS.

Comdg 1st Bn. M.G.C.

www.ingramcontent.com/pod-product-compliance
Lightning Source LLC
Chambersburg PA
CBHW080915230426
43667CB00015B/2683